AF769202

Not the Perfect Victim

Nikita Hand is a former hairdresser and debut author whose book, *Not the Perfect Victim*, charts her journey through trauma, resilience and the pursuit of justice. She wrote it to challenge harmful myths around victimhood, believing that the stigma attached to the idea of the 'perfect victim' must change. She hopes her story shows that, no matter who someone is or where they come from, their voice and their experience matter.

Nikita is the mother of two girls and lives in Dublin.

Nikita Hand

Not the Perfect Victim

HACHETTE
BOOKS
IRELAND

First published in Ireland in 2026 by HACHETTE BOOKS IRELAND

1

Cataloguing in Publication Data is available from the British Library

ISBN 9781399755467

Typeset in Berling Antiqua by Bookends Publishing Services, Dublin
Printed and bound in Great Britain by Clays Ltd, Elcograf S.p.A.

Hachette Books Ireland policy is to use papers that are natural, renewable and recyclable products and made from wood grown in sustainable forests. The logging and manufacturing processes are expected to conform to the environmental regulations of the country of origin.

MIX
Paper | Supporting responsible forestry
FSC® C104740
FSC www.fsc.org

Hachette Books Ireland
8 Castlecourt Centre
Castleknock
Dublin 15, Ireland
(info@hbgi.ie)

Authorised representative in the EEA

A division of Hachette UK Ltd
Carmelite House, 50 Victoria Embankment, London EC4Y 0DZ

www.hachettebooksireland.ie

*This book is dedicated to my beautiful daughters,
Freya and Alba. I hope that you both grow up
in a world where you always feel empowered
to speak and where your voices are heard.
I love you both very much. Mammy xx*

*I also dedicate this book to victims and survivors.
Never stay silent. Silence only serves to protect
the people who hurt us, and our voices and
our truths are more powerful than we realise.
All my love, Nikita Hand xx*

This memoir contains accounts of sexual violence, physical assault, trauma and their lasting impact. It also explores themes of mental health challenges, including anxiety, depression, post-traumatic stress and the emotional toll of navigating the criminal and civil justice systems. Readers may find some descriptions and discussions distressing. While these experiences are recounted with honesty and purpose, discretion is advised, particularly for those affected by similar forms of violence or trauma.

If any aspect of this book raises difficult emotions, readers are encouraged to seek support from trusted friends, family members or professional services. A list of support organisations and resources is provided at the back of the book.

Contents

Prologue

Tuesday, 5 November 2024

The imposing granite walls of the Four Courts tower overhead. I tremble from head to toe walking the concrete ramp to the Chancery Place entrance. My solicitors lead the way, with my partner Gary and Clíona Woods from the Dublin Rape Crisis Centre supporting me on either side.

We enter through the grand panelled doors and submit to security scanning. As we pass through the glass doors into the corridor, I see someone I haven't seen in nearly six years: James Lawrence. My stomach drops; a lump of terror rises in my throat.

He is pacing the corridor – back and forth, back and forth – his movements sharp and agitated. He spots me seconds after I see him and freezes mid-pace. Even from a distance, I catch a shocked expression on his face, as if he's thinking: *Shit, she's actually shown up.*

Then another head swivels towards me. I tear my horrified gaze from him, twisting my body to face the opposite wall. I am gripped by panic so severe my body starts shaking. I cannot bear to look at him. Conor McGregor. The mere thought of his presence hits me like a sickening gut punch.

'I CANNOT DO THIS! I CANNOT DO THIS! I CAN'T!'

The words emerge like a screech. Everyone in the place must hear me.

Clíona reaches to calm me, but I bolt towards a flight of stairs. I don't know where they lead except away from the public corridor. Away from McGregor.

I race up the first few steps: one, two, three, four … but as I reach the landing, my legs become boneless. They fold under me on the next flight of stairs. My body is shutting down. I clamber on all fours, dragging, clawing, sobbing my way to the top.

The corridors echo with the sound of violent retching as my stomach convulses. Somehow, with Clíona's help, I stumble through a door upstairs: public toilets. I fall upon the sink, hyperventilating, retching. I splash cold water on my face, to cool my burning skin, and wait for the churning in my stomach to end.

It takes ten minutes before Clíona can steer me into a small vestibule outside the ladies'. It's progress. She props me against the wall.

'Breathe, Nikita, just breathe.'

Gary is here now too and takes my hand. I am sweating, my face red and hot. My chest is still heaving and I wheeze for breath. Is this what dying is? Someone, a stranger, stops abruptly, her expression aghast.

'My God, should I call an ambulance?'

'No, no,' Clíona says quickly. 'We'll calm her down. She'll be okay.'

Clíona grips both my hands.

'Can you feel them?' she asks urgently. 'Can you feel my fingers?'

'Yes, I can feel.'

'That's good. If you were completely numb, you wouldn't feel anything. You're still here.'

Susan Hannon, one of my barristers, runs up and down the stairs, checking on me while managing the delays below. Conversations are going on around me while I concentrate on breathing. Throughout it all, Clíona is by my side, soothing me, reassuring me.

Twenty minutes later, perhaps half an hour, I gather myself enough to leave the vestibule. As I do, I glance left. The public gallery is full – complete strangers queuing to observe the trial.

The sight of all these people makes everything worse. I lean on Gary, hoping he can keep me upright as I descend the stairs.

It isn't courage that moves me, step by step, towards the ground floor and along the corridor; it's necessity. I have no choice. I can't say, 'That's it. I've had enough. I'm going home,' even though there's nothing I want to do more.

This is *my* civil case. I have initiated this legal battle. I have wanted this moment in court, have fought six years to get here. While I've waited to tell my truth, my life has been in turmoil. I have suffered breakdowns and panic attacks; my mental health has failed; my reputation has been destroyed.

My home – my safe place – has been invaded and my partner stabbed; my child and entire family have suffered. I have lost my house, my job, my entire life as it was before. If I want any justice, I cannot give in now.

Trembling, tearful and nauseous, I enter Courtroom 24. I am braced for one of the worst ordeals of my life. Yet the version of me who steps through those doors that day still has no idea what's coming.

1.

The Christmas Party

Saturday, 8 December 2018

Festive lights flashed, and the salon's mirror-lined walls reflected around a dozen of us wriggling into our party outfits and blow-drying and tonging our hair.

The party officially started the minute the last client went out the salon door. Multiple bottles of Coors Light were lined up on the counters, surrounded by curlers, clips and make-up bags. It had been a hectic week, and we'd all been looking forward to our Christmas party.

I changed into a new red halterneck jumpsuit that I'd bought specially for the night from a high-street store online. It exposed bare skin on my neck, cleavage, shoulders and back. The hairdryer roared in my hand as I wound sections of hair around the brush, releasing strands in loose waves.

We were heading to a circus-themed festive dinner with

entertainment provided in the nearby Airfield Estate in Dundrum. My employer at Gerard Paul Hairdressing was among the many companies that bought tables in the huge marquee erected there. Before we left for the evening, I remembered to insert a tampon. It was a precaution, as I was due to have my period soon.

'Right,' said one of the girls, twisting an earring into her lobe. 'Who's ready to go?'

I pulled on my brown faux fur coat and left the salon in high heels and high spirits.

Around twenty staff from both our Goatstown and Naas salons attended the party, so the atmosphere was electric. I had a couple of drinks and then took some cocaine in the toilets. I liked the feeling of being more dialled up, energetic and radiant.

The first time I tried cocaine was in my early twenties. I'd always refused drugs before, but one night at a concert, a friend offered me a short line on her key in the ladies'.

'Just a bump,' she said. 'It feels great.'

And it did. After that, I took it on occasional nights out with the girls, or at the odd music festival when everyone else was doing it anyway. On big nights out, a few of the girls would chip in and we would share a bag between us. I loved dancing, and the rush from a line always meant the party went on and on.

While in Airfield, I posted a shot of me and a friend on my Instagram story. Around fifty people would have been able to see the photo in their feeds – one of them was Conor McGregor – a guy from my corner of the world who had made it big. I was startled when he responded.

Hey, where are you? his message said, something like that.

I felt flattered that a celebrity had acknowledged my picture. I pecked a reply on my phone, telling him I was at my Christmas party in Goatstown. Then I showed the other girls his message.

Conor McGregor had become an online acquaintance in recent months after I commented on a picture he posted. I can't remember the picture or my comment. 'Thank you, Nikita,' he'd replied with a heart emoji.

Soon after, McGregor posted a picture of his Proper No. Twelve Irish Whiskey. Like hundreds of others, I replied to his story.

'Ah, give us a bottle,' I wrote, adding laughing emojis.

'You can get whatever you want, Nikita,' he'd replied. I'd shown the girls at the salon then too, laughing at the absurdity of it. I'd even shown the message to my partner, Ste. I was gobsmacked that a celebrity had messaged me again.

Weeks later, I decorated my kitchen island with pumpkins, fake blood and fake severed fingers for a children's Halloween party. I posted a video of the scene on Instagram. McGregor was among those who could see it. He messaged me privately with some remark about the decor, I can't remember exactly what he said.

The gang left the Christmas party in Airfield around midnight and went back to the Goat Bar & Grill, a bar and restaurant directly across from our hair salon in Goatstown.

When the bar closed in the early hours, around ten of us ordered a drinks delivery to the salon and we continued the party there. People started heading home after that. By 8 a.m., only Danielle – a stylist from the Naas branch – and I were left in the salon.

Empty wine and beer bottles lay scattered around, but we still had plenty of vodka left to drink. We laughed a lot that morning. Everything seemed hilarious and not quite real. I was alert, hyper, not ready to end the night.

'What time is it now?' I asked Danielle.

'You asked that two minutes ago.'

'Well?'

'It's almost nine.'

'Christ, I'm not even tired.'

'Me neither.'

'Will we wait here until the Goat reopens?'

I looked out. The car park was empty, and the pub's windows reflected only darkness. It dawned on me that it could be hours before it reopened on Sunday morning.

Between long hours in the salon and caring for my seven-year-old daughter Freya, I hadn't been out in ages. In fact, the last time was for my mother's fiftieth birthday party in October, two months earlier. I didn't want to go home just yet.

Phone in hand, I had a lightbulb moment. My thumb hovered

over his Instagram page. The twenty-four-hour party man, who never seemed to go home, would know where the after-parties were. So close to Christmas, there were sure to be lots of fun events going on somewhere.

My fingers found the keypad. The letters swam.

Hey

Delete.

Hi

Delete.

I don't remember exactly what my message said, to be truthful. *Any parties going on now?* Something like that. I held my phone, showing Danielle the unsent words, still thinking this was a good idea.

I often think how different my life would have been if only I'd had the sense to put the phone down, go home, drink some water and go to bed. Much as I wish I could rewrite that night, I can't. That morning, the party felt infinite and tomorrow didn't exist.

I pressed send on an Instagram DM to Conor McGregor.

The whoosh sound made my heart thump. There was no going back now. I watched the screen, waiting for the typing dots. Danielle was convinced nothing would happen, but there they were. I can't recall the exact sequence of messages, and I have no record of them because I deleted them in a panic later.

I was suspicious that whoever was messaging me was an

imposter, so I asked for his phone number. As soon as he sent it, I rang.

'You're not Conor McGregor!' I said accusingly.

'It is me. It's Conor. Where are you?'

'I'm in a salon in Goatstown. We're looking to go to a party. There's just my friend Danielle and me left.'

'All right,' he said. 'I'll come and collect you.'

I beamed as I told Danielle that Conor McGregor was coming to pick us up and take us to a party. She looked sceptical.

'No, he is!' I insisted.

By this stage the sun was up. I looked at myself in the mirror in a red halterneck jumpsuit. It was evening wear and flaunted too much cleavage for the daytime. I rummaged in the staff room and borrowed a black jumpsuit belonging to one of the other girls – a spare work outfit she had stored in the salon. We often borrowed each other's clothes.

The jumpsuit was sleeveless but otherwise covered me from my neck to my ankles. It was neutral, black, safe. Danielle changed out of her party clothes and put on a dress we had at the salon.

I texted Ste. He was at home minding Freya. I asked whether it would be okay if I stayed out longer. I pretended I was still with all the girls, so he told me to enjoy myself. I never said who we were meeting. I knew Ste wouldn't think going to a party with Conor McGregor was a laugh. He'd worry and advise me to come home.

Time passed. I looked at my phone again. 'I don't think he's coming,' I said. I rang back a few times to check.

'Just tell us if you're not coming because we're going home,' I said. But McGregor insisted he was on his way. He and I messed around on the phone, laughing and joking. Around 10 a.m., McGregor said he was near the garage across the road. I locked up the salon.

I saw the car – black, sleek, windows tinted dark so that you couldn't see inside. I'm not good with cars but later learnt it was a BMW 740 sedan.

I remember walking over to the car in the black jumpsuit with Danielle, shoes in hand, excitement rising. The party was kicking off again. Only this time we were with a celebrity! As we reached the car, I felt only a sense of thrill. I had no reason to be cautious. After all, I had grown up around him and his friends. I never thought for a moment that this would be the worst decision of my life.

2.

Our Little Family

I can't pinpoint when I first crossed paths with Conor McGregor. He was just there, a Crumlin boy, part of the fabric of Dublin 12's pub and nightclub scene when I was in my mid to late teens.

Both of us would have known the same faces. My friends and I met in the Black Forge Inn or the Plaza in Tallaght on weekend nights from our late teens on. Everyone our age from Crumlin and Drimnagh hung out in the same places, and some people I knew from Drimnagh, where I was from, had friends in the Crumlin circle McGregor hung out with. We might sometimes have spotted them in the clubs in town and exchanged a wave, a quick greeting in passing. One of my cousins was a close friend of his, but over the years of early adulthood McGregor and I never connected or even had a proper chat. A nod here, a brief hello there. 'Hi, Nikita', 'Hi, Conor'. That was the extent of it. Nothing more. I never paid much attention to him.

Around 2007, McGregor's name started coming up more frequently in conversations. Something to do with sports. It wasn't boxing, I gathered; it was fighting with bare hands, though I couldn't have told you more than that. I was a girly-girl with no interest in sports.

I was eighteen that year, and absorbed in my own life. After completing the Leaving Cert, I went straight through the doors of Gerard Paul Hairdressing in Goatstown as their new apprentice. Four or five years stretched ahead of me and I couldn't have been happier, because hairdressing was all I had ever wanted to do.

Surrounded by a dozen staff members and under the supervision of directors John and Gerard, I soon claimed my corner in the salon. Hair colour and its creativity captured my imagination. I wanted to be a colourist, learning everything from highlights to lowlights, balayage, dimension, depth and the whole alchemy of mixing.

I loved everything in that salon: the sharp smell of developer, the satisfaction of a perfect blend of colour, the quiet pride that came with seeing a client's hair transformed. I loved my colleagues, my bosses and the clientele. I was good at it too. I skipped into work every morning, looking forward to the day ahead.

When I bought my first car – a silver Clio – at age nineteen, I felt like a proper adult. I drove it the twenty-five minutes each way to work and back, relishing my newfound independence.

At age twenty, after a year of being single, I met Stephen at a nightclub in town. I didn't realise it that night, but that meeting marked the beginning of a significant new phase in my life.

Ste is one of several people whose lives have intersected with mine, but whose stories are ultimately not mine to share. When I write about experiences involving him, I'm only telling my own story.

More than a year after we met, I was overjoyed to be expecting a baby. I'd always wanted a house full of children – probably because I grew up as an only child. We decided I'd complete my final year in training, then leave to be a stay-at-home mother during our child's early years.

I was still living with Mam when the contractions started, and Ste drove me at dawn through the quiet city streets to the Coombe Hospital. When our daughter entered the world at 3.00 a.m. on 29 July 2011, it was the best moment of my twenty-two years. Even now, thinking of it, I feel the tears welling up again. She was utterly beautiful – all eight pounds, nine ounces of her. Her huge eyes opened and looked up at me from beneath a head of thick, straight, platinum-coloured hair. She was flawless. She had tiny rosebud lips that formed perfect bubbles. I couldn't stop gazing at her.

Throughout the pregnancy, I'd pored over a book of baby names, dog-earing pages and making lists. Ayla had been at the top of that shortlist for months. But the moment I saw my baby, I realised she wasn't an Ayla at all. She was Freya – the Norse goddess of love and beauty. We called her Freya Lily.

From the start, Freya's personality blazed. Even as a baby, she was dramatic and hilarious. Raising Freya almost felt easy. By the time she was ten months old, I found a place of our own – a rented house on Stannaway Road in Crumlin – and we settled into our little home.

When Freya turned four, I went back to work in a busy salon in town. Soon Gerard Paul in Goatstown rang to ask if I'd return to work for them, and I didn't hesitate. Every morning, I dropped Freya off at school, keeping her small hand in mine until she ran through the gates. Then either Mam or Ste's mam would collect her until Ste or I finished for the evening and could bring her home again. In my mid-twenties, I loved my job and my little family. I felt very fortunate.

We had been saving like mad to put a deposit on a house, but when Ste's thirtieth birthday came around in 2015, I wanted to mark the occasion. Thirty deserved something memorable, so I surprised him with flights to Las Vegas that summer.

The timing was good. One of Ste's closest friends was going to Vegas that summer to see Conor McGregor's first big bout in America. Ste's friend was the brother of Dee Devlin, who was Conor McGregor's girlfriend.

Ste and I went to Las Vegas with several members of the Devlin family in July 2015, arriving in desert temperatures of 40 degrees Celsius. The vast MGM Grand on the Strip soon sprawled before us. A giant cage, a replica of the octagon, dominated the hotel's marble-floored lobby. This was where the McGregor vs Chad Mendes featherweight fight would take place. The Ultimate Fighting Championship (UFC) fight was clearly the main event in the hotel that week.

Ste and I had not gone to Vegas to see the fight. Tickets cost around $800 apiece, and we had better things to spend our money on. I wasn't interested in mixed martial arts, or MMA, anyway. Instead, we wandered the Strip and saw the Bellagio fountains dance to opera music. We watched a holographic version of Michael Jackson moonwalking across the stage at the Mandalay Bay and saw Calvin Harris command the DJ booth at a pool-party-type event.

Ste was offered a free ticket to the weigh-in the day before the fight, so he was among 11,000 fans who watched the fighters face off. I can't remember where we were the day of the fight, but we soon heard that McGregor had won by a knockout, taking home a prize fund of around €500,000. The Irish contingent was in celebration mode.

'Fair play to him,' I said. 'It's something, isn't it? A guy from our area making his mark in Las Vegas.'

We knew that the after-fight party was at Foxtail Nightclub inside the SLS Las Vegas Hotel, a taxi ride away from the MGM. When we turned up, the club was pulsing with lights and music, and drinks were flowing freely. Across the room, I briefly glimpsed McGregor holding court among well-wishers and hangers-on.

Ste and I found a few familiar faces, clinked glasses and made small talk over music that was too loud. I was relieved when Ste agreed to leave the club after an hour. The celebrations continued at the same resort the next day, but Ste and I were already far away, somewhere else in the Nevada sun.

Because of Ste's connection to Dee Devlin's brother, we attended a couple of events held by her family back in Dublin. I met Dee at a Devlin family First Communion party. She was carrying her and McGregor's recently born first son, Conor Jr, in her arms.

'Oh, he's lovely,' I remarked, admiring her baby as all mothers do. She beamed with pride, and we exchanged brief recollections about our experiences at the Coombe Hospital. That was it. I don't remember McGregor at any of the Devlin family occasions I attended, but he could have been there.

When Freya was five, Ste and I made a successful offer on a three-bedroom terraced house on Errigal Road in Drimnagh. The house was in terrible condition, but Ste was handy and could tackle much of the work. We knocked down a wall to create a large sitting room and extended the kitchen. I loved my enormous kitchen, with its off-white cabinets and big white granite worktop. I was twenty-seven and couldn't believe that we had bought our own home.

Other friends and family members were making different choices: some were travelling around the world, others were focusing on their careers. I'd stayed in Drimnagh to work, save for a house and raise a child. I had a partner and a wonderful little girl – a united family under our own roof. I could never have dreamt that it could all fall apart in a single night.

3.

The Penthouse

Sunday morning, 9 December 2018

I peered into the car as the rear door swung open. Conor McGregor was sitting on the far left side of the back seat. I slid in first, settling into the middle seat, bag, shoes and vodka bottle in hand. Danielle climbed in after me, taking the seat to my right. A driver sat silently up front. As he pulled away from the kerb, we had no idea where we were going.

We passed the vodka bottle around and everything in the car seemed breezy and fun. Every joke landed – it was like we were old friends on an exciting adventure. I was drunk enough to find McGregor more charming and hilarious than I'd ever imagined. I didn't think to ask him where he'd come from before collecting us.

At some point, McGregor stuck his wrist between Danielle and showed off his designer watch.

'Look at this,' he said, tapping its face with a flourish. 'Cost me more than this car!' He kept at it – price, brand, stuff about his other watches. Danielle listened for a while, then laughed, telling him to stop showing off.

The effect was immediate – like glass smashing on tiles. The mood snapped, and my laughter faded as McGregor's grin disappeared. He began screaming.

'PULL OVER! PULL OVER!' he roared at the driver. 'Get her out of the fucking car! Get her out! Throw her out on the fucking side of the road!'

The speed of his explosion shocked me. I was in the middle of them as they screamed at each other – him telling her to get out, her telling him to shut up. My hands were flapping, panicked, trying to defuse the situation. I wanted everything to be perfect, for everyone to get along. We were out for a fun time after all.

'Hey, no need for this!' I cried. 'We're going out! Danielle was only having a laugh!'

The car stopped and just as I prepared to exit with Danielle, McGregor switched again. He was back to normal, full of jokes and banter as if nothing had happened. Both of them began laughing again.

'Oh, you like me now again, do you?' I remember him saying to Danielle.

We drove through residential streets that I sometimes

recognised. The drive and the minutes stretched on and on. My drunken euphoria began to thin, giving way to a creeping confusion. Where were we going?

The driver pulled up outside a house, and Conor told him to sound the horn. He beeped several times and we waited. Nothing. More beeping. Another house. More beeping. A window flew open, and someone shouted down that whoever Conor wanted wasn't there.

My face burned. 'Please stop, Conor.' I slid down into my seat, not wishing to be seen. It was a Sunday morning on quiet streets where families were sleeping. Danielle and I felt embarrassed as he wound down the window at one point. The last thing we wanted was anyone seeing us in that condition, still drunk from the night before. This wasn't the party I'd imagined. McGregor ignored us.

We reached a house in Drimnagh and, this time, he got out and went inside. The minutes stretched on and on, and after twenty or twenty-five minutes, Danielle and I were fed up waiting. I asked the driver why he was taking so long and what he was doing in there.

'Conor takes as long as Conor wants,' the driver responded in accented English, putting us in our place. Danielle and I glanced at each other, rolling our eyes.

Eventually, McGregor returned with another man. I didn't know him, but I knew of him through a cousin. His name was

James Lawrence, and he lived in his family home in Drimnagh, near where Ste and I had bought our house.

Lawrence got into the passenger seat beside the driver. McGregor got back in, carrying a plastic bag filled with what I assumed was cocaine. I took a pinch of the powder on a coin, and Danielle did the same. I realised afterwards that I never actually saw McGregor or Lawrence take it. I assumed they had but, when asked, I had to admit I hadn't actually seen them take anything from the bag. Then the drugs disappeared, and that was the last I saw of the bag.

We continued driving around for quite a while. McGregor started displaying the Louis Vuitton runners he was wearing under his jeans, and I dragged them off his feet and wore them in the car. Then, before I realised it, we had descended into an underground car park. We didn't know where we were, but we sat in the car, chatting, laughing, waiting for some cue from McGregor's security that we could go inside.

After a wait, we left the car and entered a lift that opened into a standard hotel corridor. Someone opened a room door for us, and I noticed the silence inside. No one else was there. There was no party. I asked where we were and was told we were 'in the middle of nowhere' and wouldn't be getting home anytime soon. I don't remember who said this, but it wasn't said in an intimidating way, and it didn't upset me. But I interpreted it to mean that we were stuck there until McGregor told the driver to bring us home.

It was okay, though. Everyone was getting on, and the atmosphere was happy and light-hearted. We were giddy and drunk in a huge hotel suite. I was happy to have a few drinks and keep the party going.

A freestanding slipper bathtub stood in front of a large window in the bedroom. I slid into the tub fully dressed, messing around. When McGregor threatened to turn the taps on, I leapt out again, laughing. I walked into the room next door and around the suite, admiring the place, commenting on how nice it was.

We all settled in the large living and dining area with its giant daybed. I sat on the daybed with Danielle, and McGregor lay on it near James. I remember a lot of joking around and laughter. McGregor told us to order whatever drinks we wanted from room service. There soon arrived an array of bottles and mixers, including a bottle of Bacardi for me – we could help ourselves. McGregor's bouncers or bodyguards came in and out of the suite, three of them, I think, including the driver who brought us there. I don't remember any more drugs after those taken in the car.

In my confusion, I assumed we were in The Morgan Hotel in Dublin's Temple Bar. I'd stayed there with Ste for his twenty-fifth birthday, and the bedroom with the freestanding bathtub, along with the padded lift we had taken from the car park, were very similar. I would learn much later that we were in a sister hotel to The Morgan.

If I'd looked out past the translucent voile curtains on the window, no doubt I would have seen the largely industrial landscape, the motorway and mountain views in the distance. But I was drunk and disoriented and ignored my surroundings. Neither do I remember the conversation.

Other things, though, I do remember clearly – moments that stuck in my mind because of how uncomfortable they made me feel. The first had been McGregor getting aggressive with Danielle in the car; the surge of rage that came out of nowhere.

Another thing that unsettled me was when I was walking through the suite, admiring the interior. I walked through to the bedroom area. There, through the door to the en suite, I recall accidentally seeing McGregor use the toilet. 'Suck on that!' he said, thrusting his hips towards me in the outside room. I blanked him, trying to pretend I hadn't seen or heard him, and rejoined Danielle outside.

At another point, I remember being back in the bedroom. McGregor was there, and I saw one of his security guys at the window. Another security guy was at the door between the two rooms. That instant in the bedroom burnt itself into my memory because I felt a real unease. *I'm the only girl in this room, and there are three men here,* I thought. I moved to leave the room to rejoin Danielle and McGregor's friend in the sitting room.

I've tried, but I don't remember how or why I ended up alone with McGregor in the bedroom later. Danielle and Lawrence were in the dining–living-room area on the other side of the door. I went to leave, but McGregor called me over. That's when the attack began.

4.

The Fog

Sunday, 9 December 2018, continued

I woke up and rose from the bed in a dark haze, my mind groping against a dense barrier between the present and the past. My heart was hammering, but I didn't know why. I was confused, befuddled. I was fully dressed. Conor McGregor was next to me, lying to my left. I don't remember to this day if he was dressed or not.

Nothing made sense. I'd always found it difficult to sleep after taking cocaine. This had never happened to me before. I tried to piece together the previous hours, but the memories lay beyond reach. The recent past was like a word on the tip of my tongue. Had I been sleeping for minutes or hours? I had no idea. I felt dislocated.

Pieces of my previous life surfaced, and I remembered Ste. 'Oh my God, what time is it?' I needed to contact Ste to let him know I was okay, that I was coming home soon. My Michael Kors watch wasn't working; I only wore it as jewellery.

'What time is it?' I indicated the watch on McGregor's arm, the one he had been bragging about earlier.

'This? Doesn't work.' He sniggered as he stretched on the bed. 'You won't get the time off this.'

The world was spinning. In the fog, shapes moved, and I saw half-formed images that might be real or might be my mind trying to fill the gaps with its worst guesses. I had a sense that I had been crying. I found my bag under a table with my phone. I realised Ste had texted me. *Are you okay? Are you having a good time?*

I was all over the place, confused, disoriented and increasingly anxious. I later understood that I texted back Ste when we returned to the car park, telling him *I'm fine. I'm so drunk.* I lied in that message, saying that I was in the Goat Bar with the girls. I couldn't have told him where I was, even if I wanted to. I knew he'd be furious with me if he learnt that Danielle and I had spent hours drinking in the hotel suite with two men.

Now, McGregor got up to leave. He was in a hurry. Danielle seemed panicked. She had been sleeping too and was confused about the time. She lived with one of her parents in Naas and knew they would be worried about her. I was hyper and felt flares of dread rising inside me.

'No, stay, everyone. What's the rush? Would everyone relax

for a minute? Let's sit down and have a drink!' I felt frantic, confused. Nothing felt okay. 'Why is everyone going?'

I couldn't understand it, but McGregor was leaving, and Danielle was going with him.

She had asked McGregor to drop her off on the way. She knew he lived somewhere in Straffan, near her home in Naas. I learnt later that McGregor had initially refused but then changed his mind. He said James and I should take another car together as we were both going to Drimnagh, and told us he'd sort it.

We went down in the lift to the car park. I would later learn from CCTV footage that I was barefoot; so was James Lawrence. I remember seeing Conor and Danielle leave in the back of his black BMW, but everything felt strange and disjointed.

My next memory is of Lawrence and me returning to the hotel suite. As soon as I walked through the door, memories – not memories exactly, just shards of them – began resurfacing. I felt a tenderness across my throat. Each swallow sent a raw ache down my windpipe. I looked at bruises that were appearing down my arms, exposed by my sleeveless jumpsuit. It wasn't a bad dream.

Fleeting images and feelings were surfacing in my drunk-waking state. McGregor's red face, his weight expelling the air from my lungs. There and gone. Choking. Gasping. An elbow around my neck, then nothing. The bed board. Bare flesh on flesh, struggling. I saw shapes and outlines I could not yet hold. Tangled limbs … fighting. Nothing was in order.

I stared at my bare arms, turning them, gazing at thumbprint marks, shaking my head. Lost hours written in blue. An image flashed into my mind, McGregor on top me, forcing himself inside me. My stomach lurched and tears brimmed. For the first time, I voiced what my mind already knew but didn't want to face. I turned to James Lawrence. 'Do you all put a blind eye to what Conor does to women?'

'What do you mean?' he replied.

I showed him my arms, tears now rolling down my face as images and memories continued to flash unbidden into my mind.

'Are you saying that Conor did this to you?'

I recall him sitting at a window, putting a hand to his head.

'I can't believe I was in the other room while this was happening to you.'

I couldn't catch my breath. I started shaking, and the tears came faster, blurring my vision.

Lawrence urged me to sit and relax. 'Have another drink,' he said. My head was spinning as I raised the glass to my lips. Everything continued to feel like a strange dream. Each time it felt like I had pulled myself together, I broke down again.

One of the security men was coming in and out of the room as we talked. I think he was the one who ordered food for the three of us, and we all sat down and ate a room-service delivery of burgers.

At one stage, I started saying something about the assault, but Lawrence stopped me. 'Give us a minute, will you?' he said to the bodyguard, and the man went outside.

I know I was near hysterical at times, but I was also in and out of consciousness, as if lost in a fog that would lift for a moment, then fall again. That's the only way I can describe it. I know I felt safe with James, though. He was listening to me, looking out for me. I thought he was being kind, a sympathetic ear, a friend.

My next memory is of a taxi driver leaning into the back seat from outside, demanding to know if I had any money. It was dark outside, and his tone was angry and accusatory as I scrambled to find my credit card. I found a fifty euro note that I didn't know I had.

'Yes, I have money!' I cried, pushing the cash at him.

I was still disoriented. I wanted the taxi driver to bring me to my partner's sister Jen but she wasn't replying to my texts. I texted another friend, who had been out with Jen the night before. *Where is she? Where is Jen?* I felt desperate that I couldn't reach her. I needed to talk to her.

Then I remembered a text from my manager, Eimer, saying she needed the salon keys. I'd taken them that morning to lock up, and she needed them to open the place the next day. I rang her but broke down during the call. The fog was lifting with terrifying speed. The images that had come in flashes back in the hotel room, when I'd asked James Lawrence if he knew what McGregor did to women, flooded in with renewed force. I texted her to say I was on my way and told her about McGregor. *He raped me, Eimer, I am black and blue, I am battered, I am broken.*

The taxi dropped me off at Eimer's front door in Walkinstown. Later, I'd learn it was around 11.30 p.m. on Sunday night, and that McGregor and Danielle had left the hotel around 6 p.m. Yet I had little memory of the over five hours that had passed since.

Eimer was the first person I confided in about the assault. I broke down as I told her what had happened to me, alternatively numb and in shock, then reeling in distress and tears. She noticed the bruising on my bare arms and asked to see the rest of me. She helped me peel off the jumpsuit, and I saw her mouth open as she did.

'Oh my God, Nikita!' she gasped. I cried even more when I realised the bruising was as bad as I feared. I agreed to let her take a half dozen or so photos of my body.

'Don't shower or change,' she urged. 'You need to go to the Rape Crisis Centre tomorrow.' I nodded in agreement, but I was already certain I would not be involving the guards.

While there, I must have sobered up a bit, because I began to feel increasing pain and discomfort. Then I remembered the tampon. My period had started, but the tampon was buried deep inside me. I panicked even more when Eimer reminded me of the risks of toxic shock syndrome. 'You need medical help, Nikita,' she said.

First, though, I had to go home. I dreaded telling Ste what had happened. I had lied to him about where I'd been, and I felt different: tainted. How could I expect him not to feel the same way about me?

When I finally returned, in the early hours of Monday, 10 December, I was a completely different person to the one who had left bright-eyed and cheery for work on Saturday morning.

I didn't have a key, so Ste opened the door. I can still remember his eyes widening when he saw me, my hair in disarray, eyes bloodshot, bare arms black and blue. I was reeling and disoriented.

He stood staring, shocked, as I slumped on the sofa. I dropped my head in my hands, crying, trying to relate what had happened to me. I told him straight away I'd been raped. He got my pyjamas and tried to help me get ready for bed.

'Let me close that for you,' he said, helping me with the buttons. 'Let me do it.'

I lied to him, desperately trying to protect my relationship. I told him other girls from the salon were there. I didn't want to admit to my partner that it was just Danielle and me in the hotel with two men, including the man who sexually assaulted me.

Understandably, he wanted to know who had done this to me and where it happened. I couldn't cope. I grew angrier and more distraught. 'Ah, fuck off, Ste. Fuck off, I'm after being raped, and all you care about is who it is who did this to me.'

My anger was mainly with myself, though. If I hadn't lied to Ste, if I hadn't done these reckless things – drank too much, took coke, got into a car with men that I barely knew – none of this would have happened.

I realise now it was traumatising for him to see me in this state and to learn what had happened. We both needed different things at that one time. Naturally, he wanted this guy caught for doing this to his partner and grew increasingly frustrated when I wouldn't call the guards. I wanted him to care for me, to tell me everything would be okay.

I felt as if a grimy film clung to my body. I imagined Ste could see that and saw me as dirty – contaminated. He didn't do or say anything wrong, but I imagined he was blaming me for my behaviour, for getting drunk, for 'asking for it'. I remember saying to him, over and over: 'You're not going to look at me in the same way again.'

I told Ste lies to stop that from happening. Even in my trauma, I realised everything had changed. Even though I was in a vast amount of pain, I knew from that night that things would never be the same again between us. I was heartbroken. My world had imploded, and I didn't know what to do.

I remained adamant that I would never tell Ste who had done this to me. I was filled with terror. I didn't want repercussions. How would McGregor react if I told people what he'd done? I just wanted to see a doctor, fix my body and move on from this. I wanted to forget it had ever happened.

As soon as I went upstairs to lie down, Ste got into the car and drove up to my manager Eimer's house. I had no idea of the time, but it must have been after 2 a.m. Ste quickly learnt the man who sexually assaulted me was Conor McGregor.

At home, I lay in bed but couldn't sleep, absorbed in my own world of pain and terror. The pain that had started as dull aches in Eimer's house now wrapped itself around me and tightened its grip. Every part of me hurt so much that it felt like I had been hit by a car. Something felt terribly wrong with me.

I was overwhelmed with fear: fear that McGregor would hear that I'd been telling people about what he had done; fear that Ste would report the assault to the police; fear that people would find out what had happened to me; fear of closing my eyes and feeling McGregor choking me again.

As I lay trembling in my bed in the early hours of that morning, I didn't realise that this fear response would continue to follow me everywhere from then on. I couldn't have known then that I would no longer be able to stay in the house on my own, or that I would cower at every knock on the door.

Though fragments of what I had just survived had yet to reveal themselves – and God knows they would in the days and weeks to follow – there was one detail already registered in my body with chill precision. My neck in a chokehold, my body frozen. The cold, hard awareness that if I didn't survive, I would never again see my daughter. The sense of life draining from me. Survival meant one thing and one thing only: total surrender.

My personal conviction that McGregor could have killed me, that loss of control, that feeling that I was powerless to stop the man, didn't end just because the assault did. The assault had ended, but its effects were only just beginning.

5.

Mam

Monday morning, 10 December 2018

Darkness pressed against the windows when I got into my car and drove. I was a twenty-nine-year-old running to my mother. It sounds childish but, in that moment, I needed her more than I needed anyone.

I had lain awake on my bed waiting for the clock hands to move until morning. Freya was still asleep when I left her with Ste. I couldn't be a mother to my seven-year-old that morning. I needed to be held and minded by my own mam.

My hands shook as I sent Mam a text from outside her house, which was a short drive from mine. No reply. It wasn't even 8 a.m., so I knew she was probably asleep. I emerged from the car in my pyjamas. Every shadow was a threat, every sound a footstep following me. Panicked, my fist struck the door once, twice, harder.

'Mam, Mam, let me in!'

I heard her footsteps on the stairs inside. Her voice carried through the door, irritation in every syllable.

'What are you doing banging down my door at this hour of the morning?'

The door swung open. Whatever complaint had been forming on Mam's lips died there. Her expression changed as soon as she saw me. I went straight through her house to her couch. The words came out flat, tears pouring down my face. I'd been raped, and I needed her to bring me to A&E.

Her hands shot to her mouth. The poor woman looked grey in the electric light of her sitting room as she scanned my face in disbelief. Her eyes moved over me, taking inventory of damage she couldn't yet see – searching for blood, for marks, for proof this wasn't happening.

'Jesus Christ, Nikita.'

I told her who had done it, warning her that no one could know because I feared he would kill me, but the perpetrator barely registered with her. She was still scanning for visible damage to her only child.

My body felt as though someone had hit me repeatedly with a lump hammer. Or like a car had hit me and rolled over me on the road. Every movement of my limbs brought searing agony, and each breath brought pain. I thought I might be dying, that perhaps it was too late to go to A&E anyway.

Nausea rose and fell in waves, but at least I was with my

mam. That brought relief. I was back in the same hands that had bathed my scraped knees and cuddled me through every heartbreak before this one. I was home and safe.

Since the day my mam, Debbie Hand, gave birth to me in the Coombe Hospital in February 1989, it had been just her and me. She christened me Nikita after the much-loved Elton John song of the same name that was released four years before I was born. And from the time I was a newborn until I was twelve years old, we lived in a two-bedroom flat in P Block of Dublin's Fatima Mansions, in Rialto.

The flat had no hot water or central heating, so my breath came out like dragon's smoke on mid-winter mornings. I remember being able to draw pictures with my fingers on the ice inside our windows. Mam moved a double bed into the sitting room one terrible winter so we could share the warmth from the small open fireplace there.

The accommodation was basic, but a tight-knit community of hardworking, decent families lived in beautifully kept flats surrounding us. The blocks had an active community centre, a creche for toddlers and a football club for kids.

In the nineties, Dublin's drugs epidemic exploded and transformed Fatima Mansions into a nightmare for ordinary residents. The maze of alleys, exits and stairwells around the fourteen-block complex became a mecca for dealers. People with addiction from across the city descended on the place every day in search of heroin. My mam would often play a hide-

and-seek game, her hands covering my face in the stairwells. Years later, I realised she had been shielding me from the sight of sick people openly shooting up.

It was a tough place to raise children. Mothers swept the walkways each morning, scanning for the glint of metal and discarded, bloodied syringes that their children could fall on or pick up. Screaming rows over drug deals raged throughout the night, along with the sounds of joyriders screeching through the place. As more and more residents moved out, the flats left behind were boarded up.

But I grew up blissfully ignorant of the social problems and the visible presence of drugs and crime around us. My childhood memories are happy ones.

'Watch me, Mammy! Watch!' I'd call as I grabbed the rope dangling from the washing-line pole and ran, lifting my feet off the ground so momentum carried me round and round. Often, I'd call for my best friend, Jessica, clutching my Baby Born doll. We'd arrange our dolls on the wall, pour invisible tea into plastic cups and dive into make-believe worlds.

Thursday was Mam's payday, my favourite day of the week because she bought me a Lucky Bag. I loved peeling it open, a lollipop rolling out, a rubber ball, maybe a colouring book with a princess on the cover. It was like opening a treasure chest every week.

I never noticed Mam's eyes sweeping the complex, following the guys in tracksuits with hoods pulled high. I never understood why her hand tightened around mine when we passed another burnt-out car smouldering in the yard.

It's only now, raising daughters of my own, that I realise how stressful it must have been. I had lovely coats and dresses, and my long, dark hair was carefully brushed and glossy. I was loved and safe, and I had no idea how much work that took.

Mam was a hard worker. She was a cleaner and, later, a carer for elderly and disabled people. Every morning, she still managed to bring me to Loreto Primary School in Crumlin, dressed in my red-crested jumper, my white shirt and pressed grey skirt. And at half past one, when the bell rang and we spilt out the doors, Mam was there – scanning the sea of grey skirts and red jumpers until she found mine.

I never knew my dad; he was never in my life and died when I was eight. Mam was my protector, provider and emotional support growing up. It was always Mam and me.

'You'll never guess, Nikita,' she said one day, her eyes shining.

'What, Mam?'

'We're moving to a house!'

'Our own house?'

I was twelve when we moved to a two-bedroom terraced home in Drimnagh, Dublin 12. I was just starting at Presentation Secondary School in Terenure. I remember the thrill of carrying a box of my things up the stairs to my new bedroom. A real house with our own stairs! I could touch a button and have central heating and hot water on tap for the first time in my life.

However, the social problems Mam thought we'd escaped soon caught up with us. One winter evening, a couple of girlfriends and I sat perched on a nearby garden wall, legs kicking. It must have been a weekend night as I wasn't allowed out on school nights. The rows of identical houses around us had their curtains drawn against the cold, and the streetlights threw a dim white glow. We were fourteen or so, probably chatting about boys, Westlife or *Pop Idol.* We all lived close to each other.

We didn't pay much attention as a figure approached on the opposite side of the road. He wore all black – his hood, jacket, gloves, a scarf wrapped around his face, obscuring everything. He stopped almost directly across from us, scanned us and turned to face a house on his side of the road. His hand went inside his jacket. When it came out again, he was aiming a gun. I froze, not quite believing what I was seeing. I'd only ever seen anything like this on the telly before. One of the girls started screaming.

BANG!

The first shot split the night open.

Then another bang. And another. Three, maybe four times. The sound cracked through the quiet residential road, echoing off the rows of houses and concrete pavements. I'd never heard gunfire before that moment, but there was no mistaking it for a car backfiring or fireworks. This was real and terrifying.

We were already running, crouched low, tears flowing, stumbling and scrambling towards my friend's front door. We stayed low to the ground, hammering the door with our fists, begging to be let in. It could only have been seconds before the door opened – but it felt endless. Time seemed suspended before my friend's mam tore open the front door and we tumbled to safety inside. Everyone frantic, hysterical.

The irony was that Mam had been so anxious to escape the drug-infested environment of Fatima Mansions for the quieter area of Drimnagh, but as soon as we moved in, the Crumlin–Drimnagh gangland war kicked off. Sixteen people were murdered and scores more were beaten, stabbed and shot before it ended more than a decade later.

The shooting I witnessed was probably one of the early incidents in that feud. Still, it was my only close encounter with crime in all my years in Drimnagh. After that, the drug wars existed somewhere vague, far away from my world.

I went from a happy child to a happy teenager. My weekdays were filled with school and classes at Thunder Dance Academy on Whitefriar Street. Weekends meant competitions, bright lights and dancing. Weekend nights were filled with girly sleepovers, and sometimes the Kilnamanagh disco in Tallaght for teenagers. Despite the world around me, I had a protected childhood – maybe overly protected.

So, that December morning as I lay sobbing on her couch, Mam continued to shake her head in disbelief. She couldn't imagine how this could have happened to her child. But purpose soon overrode her shock.

'Nikita, I'm not bringing you to A&E,' she said. 'I'm calling 999 and an ambulance.'

'No!' I screamed. 'You'll bring the guards down on me, and he'll kill me.'

But Mam's decision was firm. She was quiet and calm in her response.

'You need proper care, and no way is anyone getting away with doing this to you, Nikita.'

Though I begged her not to, she called an ambulance. I was red in the face with tears, fear and fury. I couldn't understand why my own mother would put my life in danger – such was my level of raw terror in that moment. In time, I would be so grateful that she made that decision for me, but then it felt like a betrayal.

When the ambulance crew arrived, I sobbed my heart out. The female paramedic checked me over in Mam's room with quiet and gentle efficiency, but the last thing I wanted was for the authorities to be informed.

I'm not sure if emergency services or the ambulance crew

alerted the guards, but they arrived as well. While Mam dealt with the guards in the hall, she kept one promise to me and did not name my assailant. She told the guards that I was too scared to say who assaulted me.

When gardaí appeared at Mam's bedroom door, I was frantic.

'Leave me alone! I'm not telling you who did this. Just leave me alone!'

One paramedic ushered the guards away and brought me downstairs, still in my pyjamas, and led me through the open doors of the ambulance. Mam followed, still in her dressing gown. I lay on their trolley, as sitting was too painful.

The doors slammed shut, the engine rumbled to life and my stomach twisted and rose into my throat. I retched into a sick bag, but I had nothing inside me to vomit.

The male paramedic reached out to steady me, voice low and calm, but the words didn't land. Nothing landed. The journey seemed to stretch endlessly ahead. I felt each second trapped in that metal box. I needed to be anywhere but moving toward a hospital where I would have to tell medics what happened and let them see the evidence.

'Why is this taking so long?' I asked. St James's Hospital was only five minutes up the road. It felt like I'd been trapped in the ambulance forever now.

'We're bringing you to the Rotunda, Nikita.'

I cried more. Why were they bringing me to a maternity hospital on the far side of the city?

The paramedic explained they were bringing me to the Sexual Assault Treatment Unit (SATU) in the hospital, a place which provided medical care and gathered forensic evidence after an assault.

'No!' I cried. 'Leave me alone. I want to be checked in A&E. I want this tampon removed and to go home.' By now, I was terrified of Toxic Shock Syndrome.

My mam sat there with tears in her eyes. I saw her, years later, on CCTV recorded from inside the ambulance, shown to me in my solicitor's office. On that footage, I saw myself curled in the foetal position on the stretcher, agitated and distressed. Despite the pain, I moved to a chair at one point, bent over, clearly crying and being comforted by the paramedic.

Mam sat there, gazing at me, then staring into the middle distance. It was hard to watch because she looked so dazed and heartbroken. Her world was turned upside down that day, too.

Meanwhile, I just wanted everything to stop. I wanted to turn back the clock to Saturday night, when my life was happy and normal, before a man I barely knew destroyed it.

6.

The Sexual Assault Unit

A wheelchair was waiting when the ambulance pulled up outside the Rotunda Hospital. The paramedic tried to wrap a blanket around me in the chair, but I pulled it over my head instead; a makeshift shield against the fluorescent lights and the faces turning towards me in the corridor.

If no one could see me, maybe I could pretend this wasn't happening. Perhaps I could hide the acute sense of shame that filled me.

I was wheeled down corridors to a private room. Mam followed and sat on a chair in the corner.

'Relax, Nikita,' she said quietly. 'You're doing the right thing. You're in good hands here.'

But the walls of the room pressed close, and the silence between us grew. My anxiety was almost choking me. I had to double over to catch my breath. I heard the screams of women in labour reverberating through the maternity hospital. Tortured sounds. They were screaming in the way I wished I had.

I kept replaying it, the same disturbing loop in my mind. The part of me that blamed myself for what had happened was subjecting me to a relentless cross-examination. I tried to make sense of my actions. The truth was that I never screamed. I knew I didn't. There were many things I didn't remember, but I did remember staying quiet. Why didn't I open my mouth and tear my throat raw?

I always thought I would. I always imagined that if any attacker cornered me, I would rise, sharp and furious, kicking, clawing, howling. And I did fight – at first. I fought hard. But when his elbow closed around my neck, when his arm flexed, all of that resistance disappeared. There was only the pounding of blood behind my eyes and that silent, terrified need to breathe again. My body made a decision to stop fighting and survive. Now my mind wouldn't forgive that decision.

Sickening memories rolled around my head. I wondered what I should have done – what I could have done – to stop it. I berated myself. I tried to reason with him, but he did not listen to reason or to my pleading. Did I give up too soon? As soon as he choked me, I went quiet and small and distant. I had a daughter at home, and all I could see was her face when I thought he was killing me. I decided to live.

I could already hear the doubt in imaginary voices. *Why didn't you call out? You didn't run? Why didn't you do something?* As though survival wasn't something. As though having breath in my lungs wasn't something.

Who would believe me? I was a mess who had made a catalogue of bad decisions. I was drunk. I took drugs. I had left a good partner and a cherished daughter at home. I had gone drunk to a hotel room with a man I barely knew. And I hadn't screamed. If I was picking apart every choice I made, how could I expect anyone else not to do the same? If I blamed myself, everyone else would, too.

A caterer entered the room, offering a hospital tray of warm food. The smell hit my throat and I gagged. I'd been retching since the day before. I couldn't hold anything down. The wait to see a doctor or nurse stretched on and on. I wanted to go home, but Mam remained obstinate.

My phone buzzed. It was a message from my partner's sister, Jen. She asked me who had done this to me. Ste must not have told her everything.

I'm not saying, and I'm not pressing charges, I replied. *It's too traumatic, and he will probably get away with it anyway.*

He was famous, rich, powerful and vicious. I had experienced his violence at close quarters, and I was terrified.

I sent a text message to Danielle, who had been with me in the hotel. She was shocked when I told her I was in the Rotunda. She had been in the next room in the hotel suite and hadn't suspected anything. I had no witnesses. No one would believe my word against his, even if I were brave enough to speak out. And I wasn't. I was resolved that I would say nothing, and this would go away.

But gardaí had followed the ambulance and were hovering outside the room. One female garda kept coming in and trying to question me. She wanted me to name my assailant. My mam had to leave anytime she entered. I knew Mam wanted me to give a statement, but I wouldn't.

'Leave me alone,' I pleaded. 'I'm not going to tell you his name.'

I silently glowered at Mam every time she returned to the room. I blamed her for making me go to the Rotunda, for alerting the authorities. This was not what I wanted. I had been trembling for twenty-four hours at this stage. I didn't know if I would ever stop shaking.

I continued messaging with Ste's sister, Jen, looking for her reassurance.

I'm not pressing charges, 100%, I wrote. *Police can't do anything to him without me saying it, can they?*

I was waiting an hour, maybe more. All the time, my stomach rolled with anxiety and self-disgust. A soft knock on the door, and a nurse led Mam and me to another building where the Sexual Assault Trauma Unit (SATU) was located.

Mam remained in the waiting room while the nurse brought me to another room where a male detective waited for me. A doctor sat in, too.

'I'm not pressing charges, so I don't want this,' I said.

Exhausted and in pain, I slumped on the desk in front of me, head down on my arms.

The detective told me it was important, that it was for my protection, that it was the right thing. He repeated my mam's words. My hair stuck to my face, damp with tears that I couldn't seem to wipe away. He assured me I didn't need to decide whether to press charges yet.

'Can you tell us what happened in your own words?' he pressed me.

I forced the information out, haltingly and broken with half-breaths and half-sobs. I didn't tell them who had done this to me. I answered the detective's questions as best as I could. I was embarrassed telling him about the drink and the drugs and the blackouts.

Afterwards, medics administered emergency contraception and meds for potential infection. When they brought me to the forensic examination room, I braced myself for the worst. It was like any hospital room, everything white and chrome, clinical and austere, with an examination table stretching before me like a threat of things to come. Everything felt too bright, too close.

The staff – the same doctor and two nurses – spoke quietly, as if they were trying not to startle me. Their words came as murmurs; their voices practised in gentleness. Someone explained what would happen. They told me that the guards would only receive the test results if I allowed it; the SATU could preserve the evidence for a year, allowing me to decide months later.

'We need to know what happened so we can assess your injuries.'

Then came the examination. I shook and cried as I peeled off my clothes and stood under the lights in nothing but my bare skin. One nurse and the doctor worked around me, combing through my hair, swabbing beneath fingernails. Their gloved hands were tender, yet felt invasive. They measured each bruise with a ruler, catalogued every cut and scratch. They swabbed and prodded me. I followed their instructions mechanically. *Turn this way, please. Lift your arm for me now. Tilt your head slightly, please.*

I heard the doctor dictate the coordinates of damage as he moved around my body: 'Face: abrasion noted on the right side of the mandibular jawline, 0.5 cm long. Bleeding noted. Neck: purple bruise noted on the right side of the neck, 3 cm by 1 cm. Abrasion noted on posterior aspect of neck, 4 cm by 1 cm …'

My legs felt as if they would give way beneath me when they asked me to lie on the examination table. I grabbed the edge of the table, gripping it as if it might anchor me.

'Please, I just want to go home,' I said.

'We're nearly there,' they said.

My breath was too thin and fast. The paper sheet under me crackled. *Can you lie this way, please? Can you turn to me now?* I stared at the ceiling, willing this all to end, for me to end.

'You're in control,' they assured me. They patiently explained each step, asked permission and apologised for each intrusion. My body had become a crime scene, and they were as gentle, kind and humane as they could be in a horrendous, dehumanising process.

Clinical detachment may have replaced the raging violence, but echoes of the assault remained. A hand touched my thigh, and I jerked away with a sob. Sometimes, a scream tore out before I could stop it. I felt completely raw.

I cried 'stop!' when I feared I'd vomit or pass out. They waited, watching me with that careful, professional kindness. I wished they knew that only days ago I was a normal girl, not the hysterical, overwrought figure in front of them. But I couldn't speak, and I feared they would not believe me if I did. I knew I couldn't stop the process for long. The longer I delayed, the longer it would take for the ordeal to end.

'I'm sorry,' I heard myself saying time and again. 'I'm sorry.' The words fell from my mouth.

'You've nothing to be sorry for,' they said.

But I couldn't stop.

Another indignity loomed – the removal of the tampon, forced deep inside me for almost twenty-four hours. It became apparent that the extraction would not be easy.

'We can give you an anaesthetic to take this out,' the doctor said. I shook my head emphatically.

'Just get it out, please get it out,' I cried.

He used a forceps to extract it, shocking me with the level of pain inflicted. I screamed as loudly as the women I heard earlier in the labour ward. I felt split open, exposed; every nerve jangled. The room was far too bright for the darkness that drowned me.

When it was finally over, I was spent. They gave me a small bundle of clean clothes – leggings and a top – and led me to a shower. I looked at the sterile shower cubicle and exhaled. I was alone at last to wash away the pain and humiliation.

In the steaming water, I waited for a sense of relief; instead, I felt lost and alone. The water pooled around my feet, circling the drain as I sobbed. The impact of the water spray hurt every square inch of my sore body, but it was nothing compared to the pain and anguish inside me.

I lost a part of myself forever in that violent assault, but I felt like the victim of another ordeal in the SATU. I cried a lifetime in that shower.

The guards drove Mam and me back to her home afterwards. I sat in the back of the car, staring out the window into the grey December gloom. I couldn't find the words to respond to my mam asking if I was okay. I was not okay. I feared I would never feel okay again. I was a broken woman.

7.

Headline News

Tuesday, 11 December 2018

The newspaper headline stopped me mid-swipe – *Gardaí Investigate Claim Famous Sportsman Sexually Assaulted Woman in Hotel.* I could hardly breathe with shock. Back home, the morning after I attended the trauma unit in the Rotunda, I'd woken to discover that the worst thing that had ever happened to me was now headline news.

I wanted to cry, scream, breathe, but I couldn't manage any of them properly. The most degrading experience of my life was now public property – breakfast reading for neighbours, commuters and strangers. I felt like I was trapped in a nightmare I couldn't wake up from.

Gardaí are investigating an allegation that a well-known sportsman sexually assaulted a young woman in a Dublin city centre hotel in the early hours of yesterday morning. The man has not yet been arrested, but sources have revealed the allegation made by the woman in her 20s is being considered 'extremely credible' ...

My hand trembled so much, it took me several attempts to call my mam.

'My God, how do they know this?' I cried. 'Who told them?'

I hadn't even begun to process what had happened, and now national newspapers had splashed my trauma across their pages. Sick with anxiety, I remained determined to stay silent. I felt sure that, with time, I could compartmentalise the trauma and move on. But the media reports left me feeling exposed; I didn't know what would happen next. My phone buzzed. A text from a friend who'd heard: *Have you seen this?!!* I put my head in my hands and cried again.

A garda had called Ste in the early hours of that morning. He advised me to deactivate my Instagram account, saying people had been accessing my account and could copy my photos. My heart raced. *Who is accessing my account? Why? Who knows?*

I had already blocked McGregor on my Instagram account soon after the assault. But as soon as the guards rang Ste, I deleted my entire account.

The prospect of people posting my photo on WhatsApp groups terrified me. I went through my phone and deleted every message McGregor and I had exchanged and the messages that I'd sent to Eimer and Jen after the attack. I asked Eimer, Jen and

Danielle to do the same. Eimer also cleaned the photos from her phone at my request.

Danielle hadn't observed anything or heard anything, and McGregor had dropped her off at her home address. She didn't want to be dragged into anything, and I understood, but her reaction made my stomach churn with even more anxiety. Trouble was not only at my door; I felt I was dragging innocent people into my troubles.

Now journalists were writing about that night. Any minute now, I feared McGregor or his mates would start banging on my door. I pulled the venetian blinds shut, sat in the dark and scrolled on my phone. People on social media were openly speculating that McGregor was the unidentified 'sportsman' in the news reports.

By late that afternoon, people were remarking that the woman in the story was 'Nikita from Drimnagh'. Drimnagh is a small place and, as far as I knew, I was the only Nikita there.

I couldn't go out now even if I wanted to. I felt like everyone knew. Friends screenshotted messages from WhatsApp groups and sent them to me. My private life had been laid open to the world, and strangers were already expressing their opinions about the story, batting my humiliation around public forums.

I felt under siege. I knew James Lawrence and Conor McGregor could be reading the same things.

Woman reportedly filed complaint before being taken to

sexual assault unit, appeared in another report that day. I hadn't filed a complaint, but they already knew I'd been to the SATU. I was in complete hell. 'Who's giving them this information?'

Ste had told the gardaí the identity of my attacker despite my begging him not to. While I had been in the Rotunda the day before, the guards had escorted him home from work to collect my jumpsuit and coat as evidence. But I remained adamant that I didn't want their involvement. I was relieved to know there was little they could do unless I made a complaint. I just wanted it all to go away.

McGregor was at the pinnacle of his career, widely admired, especially around my area – his area. What was the point of filing a complaint? No one would believe me. It would be my word against his, and I was a nobody. I knew people would question my motives and believe I was seeking attention, his money or both. And my character would end up on trial rather than his actions. I had gone with him to a hotel room while my partner was at home with my child. How was that going to look? I could already anticipate the sideways glances, the knowing looks and the rolling eyes.

You had how much to drink? And you took cocaine? And you went with him to a hotel room? Are you sure you didn't lead him on? Sure, you can't even remember half of what went on.

And if I reported him, even more people would discover my identity. I would be hounded from my home if it became public. No, I wouldn't even consider taking a statement to the police.

Still, the gardaí persisted. They called to Mam's house again that day, where I'd gone to, still trying to persuade me to make a statement.

'I'm looking at your hands now, and I can see the bruises,' a garda said. 'That's not okay. The longer you leave this, the more chance you will let this person get away with it.'

I was furious that Mam even let them in the door.

The guards told her they were anxious to get a photographic record of my injuries.

'It doesn't mean you have to name him or press charges,' Mam said. 'But have photographs taken of what he did to you in case you ever change your mind.'

I begged my mam to leave me alone, but she persisted.

'Please, just do it for me,' she said.

She didn't give me time to change my mind. A female garda from the Scenes of Crime Unit arrived at the house soon after to photograph me.

I stripped off in my old bedroom at the back of the house, and she mapped the discolourations and abrasions across my entire body, holding up a ruler to measure each cut and bruise. The trembling in my body that hadn't stopped since Sunday intensified, and I shook like a leaf throughout.

I went home when Ste returned from work that Tuesday and I went straight to our bedroom. My eyes avoided my reflection in the bathroom mirror and the blooms of blue and purple that covered my entire body. I closed the bedroom blinds, pulled the bedcovers over my head and sobbed.

The mattress might as well have been packed with stones because every inch of my body still ached. The tears wouldn't stop, even though every sob hurt my windpipe. Nine days later, when I still felt pain with every swallow and cough, I went to my doctor, fearing my throat was permanently damaged from his arm.

That night, I spent hours staring at the ceiling trying to remember what had happened. How had I ended up in the room alone with Conor McGregor? I remembered being careful and leaving the bedroom earlier when his security was there. And why did I fall asleep? That had never happened to me before, no matter how wild the night. How did I end up in a taxi on my own? Hadn't there been a car waiting for James and me in the underground car park of the hotel? So many details I couldn't remember. I had lost hours of my life. Everything remained a blank.

Other parts were hard to forget. Flashbacks of McGregor in that hotel room kept coming into my mind. I remembered things he said and did, and it took considerable effort not to vomit.

Sleep evaded me. That night I went on my phone and Googled 'What is rape and date rape?' I never thought for a minute that I was in danger when I got into that car with

McGregor on Sunday morning. Was I naive to go with him to a hotel room? I'd known of him all my life – I never imagined I was taking a risk.

He was the boy-next-door, the guy down the road. Everyone around me in Drimnagh knew him or of him. I Googled many things, looking for answers, trying to make sense of what had happened. I could not understand how someone I knew, or I thought I knew, could do this.

I didn't know then that the majority of sexual assaults are committed by someone the victim knows. Or that knowing your attacker, or thinking you knew him, adds even more layers of confusion to the aftermath.

I questioned again and again why I didn't keep fighting back, why the fight went out of me. I went on Google and opened an article called *She didn't fight back: 5 misguided reasons people doubt sexual misconduct victims*. I know this because the guards looked through my searches afterwards.

So many questions rolled around in my head that night, and in the weeks and months that followed: questions about what I could have done differently, about what I should do now. But underneath all of the concerns that filled my sleepless hours were two questions I couldn't silence: Would I ever feel whole or normal again? And would this feeling of terror ever go away?

8.

Nanny

Late December 2018

The cemetery paths were frosty ribbons of white. Freya walked between my mam and me, our breaths rising as clouds in the December air. Freya gripped a Christmas wreath of pine and red holly berries, tied with red ribbon, while Mam carried some pots of winter pansies.

We found Nanny's grave, the date of her death in 2010 clearly etched on her headstone. It was hard to believe that she had been gone for nearly nine years. I missed her more than ever. *Nanny, please give me the strength to get through this,* I begged. I'd been praying to her, asking her for help and intercession since the attack.

Mam crouched down as she cleaned the grave and arranged the plants. Nanny loved her flowers. She made her living from them all her life. As a child, I'd spent many days with Nanny on her stall on Dublin's Meath Street in the Liberties.

'Two pound the bunch of daffodils!' I'd call, mimicking my nanny's cry, my arm stretched high in the air, waving the golden trumpets. A woman pulled her purse from her shopping trolley.

'I'll give you one fifty.'

I couldn't stand for that. 'Two pounds! You won't get fresher in the whole of Dublin. Me nanny collected them from the market herself at the crack of dawn.'

'Well, there's no haggling with you, is there?'

She delved into her purse for two one-pound notes, which I proudly handed to Nanny.

'That's me girl!' Nanny said with her hoarse, throaty laugh. 'We'll make a street trader out of you yet, won't we, Nikita?'

It was always just Mam and me at home, but once we stepped outside our four walls, Nanny was the one who helped shape my world.

She was born Mary Farrell in 1940. When she was seventeen, she and her boyfriend, Paddy Hand, went to Dublin's North Wall and fled on a boat to England. In 1950s Ireland, pregnant girls like her disappeared behind the locked doors of mother-and-baby homes. She avoided that fate. Paddy and Mary were married in London, but she never settled in that sprawling city. Instead, some years later, now a mother of three, she returned with her family to Dublin and moved into a flat in Fatima Mansions.

Granddad Paddy was a handsome man and a character who made us laugh until our sides hurt. He was the life and soul of every party, but he never stayed for long. He'd arrive back in Dublin for a few weeks, then he was gone again, back to England for work, or just gone – too fond of the Guinness to ever be dependable.

Nanny lived as a single mother for most of their married life as Paddy came and went. In time, she was the sole provider to eleven children, of whom ten survived. Her large family eventually moved from Fatima Mansions to a three-bedroom terrace on Rutland Grove in Crumlin. She had five boys squeezed into one room; five girls into another.

Nanny was an incredibly hard worker whose hands always had to do the work of two. Like her mother before her, she was a street trader and her pram wheels rattled across Smithfield Market's cobbles before dawn every morning. Flower selling was Nanny's financial lifeline and the way she supported her large family. She hauled crates and pushed her loaded pram in all weathers, six days a week.

Some afternoons, Mam would work with Nanny on Meath Street, both of them perched on upturned crates beside a blaze of dahlias, carnations, chrysanthemums and roses. I'd watch them work, their hands in constant motion, wrapping the bouquets, rummaging through the leather pouches at their waists or rearranging the carnival of colour on the stall.

I'd often head to my classes at Thunder Dance Academy on nearby Whitefriar Street and join them afterwards behind the stall. Nanny would press a few coins into my palm and nod towards Fusco's, one of the original Dublin chippers. I'd dart down the street, returning with a brown paper bag, greasy with oil and vinegar. I'd eat the chips behind the stall while Mam cleaned up and Nanny counted the day's takings, the city revolving around us.

Despite the grind and daily graft, Nanny refused to let the harsh work dim her glamour and shine. She kept a standing appointment with a hairdresser who came to the house every week to set her shock of fair hair in perfect curls. For evenings out, she'd button herself into one of those long wool coats, the kind with deep fur collars that framed her face. And when she smiled, as she often did, her whole face lit up.

Less than two kilometres separated my childhood home in Drimnagh from Nanny's terraced home on Rutland Grove. Most days, we drove the few minutes to her house, and on Saturday nights I slept over. We'd climb the stairs to her bedroom together and watch whatever was on – a quiz show, the news, some old film – until we both drifted off.

Christmas, Easter, birthdays – every occasion, the family came to her place. The house swelled with uncles, aunts and cousins crowding around the table. She'd often have been cooking since early morning: a hearty stew thick with carrots and pearl barley, or a Sunday roast with potatoes crisped in beef fat. Sometimes she'd go to the market and come home with fresh fish wrapped in paper, and fry us golden fish and chips. The noise, the chaos and all those relatives meant a lot to me as an only child. Hectic family gatherings were among the highlights of my childhood.

When Nanny was diagnosed with lung cancer, I refused to believe the disease could touch her. Not our nanny. She'd survived so much and always fought so hard. She threw away her cigarettes at last, and I waited for the treatment to work, convinced she would bounce back to full health.

We only had seven months with her. Two weeks before the end, she looked at me and said, 'I wish God would just take me.' The words landed like arrows in my chest. That was the first time I knew – really knew – she would not beat the cancer.

We gathered around her bed on 15 February 2010 to be with her as she passed, just as we'd done for Granddad five years earlier. She had remained in her home in Rutland Grove, the way she wanted, until the end.

Every single heart in that house broke that day. Our matriarch was gone. She was the woman who'd held us all together, who'd been the living heart of our sprawling family. To this day, we have a close bond, but our gatherings are no longer the same. We're like a huge choir missing its lead vocalist.

Standing at her grave days before Christmas, I knew what she'd have said to me if she were alive. Nanny wouldn't have hesitated. I could hear her: *Get down to that bloody garda station now, Nikita Hand. You're not letting him get away with this!*

By now, I had already tried and failed to make a statement. The first week after the assault, everyone's advice bounced off the wall of fear that surrounded me. Then one morning, I woke up, and the terror had shifted. The bruises were fading in patches – yellow, then green – but I knew the mental anguish was here to stay.

The fear would never go, but something else was elbowing its way to the forefront: anger. How dare that man think he had the right to do that to me or any woman? In a rare moment of bravery, I decided I wanted to make a statement after all. Ste made an appointment at Crumlin Garda Station, and soon after we walked through its big wood-panelled doors, wearing peaked caps pulled down low. The guards had advised us to conceal ourselves in case someone was watching the station.

The interview room was smaller than I had imagined, and a table and chairs. I'll never forget the bright lights. They hummed above me, fluorescent white, flooding every corner with a glare that left nowhere to hide. I could see the fading bruises on my hands as I stuffed my cap into my bag and set it on the floor. Ste sat beside me.

My throat, still aching, narrowed to a pinhole. Saliva filled my mouth, and nausea rose in my constricted throat. Two detectives sat opposite me, looking at me expectantly as they introduced themselves. The walls were shrinking, the lights getting brighter, and I couldn't breathe.

'I'm sorry,' I cried, grabbing my bag. I scrambled to my feet and bolted through the door and back down the corridor and out into the night air. My head was spinning, and I needed to throw up. I couldn't go back there. Ste was soon by my side.

'I'm sorry, Ste, I can't – I'm sorry.'

The statement would have to wait. Everything would have to wait until I could form the words without feeling like I was going to die. I asked the gardaí to let me get through Christmas. I wanted to keep the occasion as normal as possible for Freya. It sounds unlikely, but I thought of McGregor's partner, Dee, and her children, too. They didn't deserve to have their Christmas upended because of what he did. I needed to put everything behind me and think about it again after it was over.

But as I watched Freya tend to Nanny's grave with my mam that day, the thought arrived cold and clear: *What if some man ever does the same to her?* I shuddered.

All around us, families were arriving with flowers and wreaths for their loved ones. Christmas was just days away, and the world continued as if nothing had changed, and maybe that was the problem. These vicious assaults would keep happening while women like me stayed silent. I felt fragile and sick, but looking at Freya, I knew I had to find the strength to stand up to McGregor somewhere.

We buried Nanny beside Granddad, but the headstone bears her maiden name, Mary Farrell. She'd been separated from

Paddy Hand for years, so using the name she'd been born with was a mark of her independence and strength. She was the strongest woman I'd ever known, and I always liked to think she'd passed some of that onto me.

Now I knew I couldn't take the easy way out. I would not try to forget, move on and pretend it hadn't happened. I would not be demeaned by a man who had raped me, who had treated me as a worthless object.

'I know you, Nikita,' Mam had said. 'This will eat you up if you don't do something. You'll never recover if you try to bury this.'

She was right. A bad thing had happened, and my life felt shattered. I was still scared. Still sick. But I owed it to myself – and to Freya – to face him.

I decided I would reach deep for whatever piece of Nanny still existed inside me, find some of her iron will and that same refusal to break. I was determined to make my statement to the gardaí in the New Year.

9.

Statements

Saturday, 5 January 2019

The automatic doors opened into the atrium and Freya pulled free, running three steps ahead into the shopping centre before stopping to stare up at the glass ceiling. Rain spotted the panels overhead and grey winter light filtered through the centre.

'Stay close, like a good girl,' I said.

We drifted past House of Fraser, where mannequins posed in pastel colours that nobody would wear for months. Tinsel stars still hung from the ceiling. Freya tugged on my sleeve outside the children's accessory store, Claire's. 'Can we go in?'

I glanced at Ste. 'You can go in with your dad in a bit.'

We looked like any other family in Dundrum Shopping Centre that Saturday morning. We could have been exchanging unwanted gifts, looking for bargains in the sales or spending our Christmas vouchers like everyone else. But we weren't.

I heard the ping of the incoming message on Ste's phone.

'They're here,' he said, squinting at his screen in the light. He said they were waiting outside one of the restaurants near the main entrance to the shopping centre.

We strolled out and instantly spotted one of them in his smart coat. I crouched down, putting myself at Freya's eye level. 'Why don't you check out Claire's with Daddy while Mammy has a chat with this man?'

Freya's eyes moved between us. 'Why are you chatting with him?'

'Oh, it's just boring grown-up stuff,' I said.

Heart pounding and tears brimming, I said goodbye to her and Ste and watched them disappear back into the crowd. I wanted to run after them, but I followed the detective to Winters Bar, where he and his colleague had parked their car. I got into the back seat.

The police investigation into the sexual assault had continued throughout December. The gardaí soon discovered I had been in the penthouse of The Beacon Hotel, rather than its sister hotel The Morgan. Dundrum Garda Station took over the investigation, which Pearse Street Station had previously handled.

The detectives in Dundrum had left me alone over Christmas as I'd requested. I still hadn't returned to work since the assault. I couldn't face it. I hadn't been in my right mind in the weeks since. But during those weeks, the positive forces that surrounded me finally helped push me through the fear. Family, friends and my prayers to God and Nanny all helped me pull my head together and accept that the worst had happened, and that I needed to deal with it. I kept reminding myself of how I'd feel if he did this to another woman. And how would I feel if, someday, another man thought he could do this to Freya?

The helpline number for the Rape Crisis Centre had glowed on my phone screen several times before Christmas, my finger hovering over the green call button, before I finally pressed dial.

One ring. Two rings. 'Hello—'

My lips had moved like a fish out of water. The words would not come. I jabbed the red button and dropped the phone as if it had burnt me. My hands were shaking, and my breath came too fast. I did it again later and held on a second longer this time.

'Hello, you've reached—'

Again, I hung up.

Someone finally made an appointment for me at the centre on Leeson Street, but the therapy session felt like another trauma. I didn't want to communicate. How could I form the words to express what really happened to me that night without stirring up more revulsion, nausea, anxiety and pain? I couldn't talk about it.

Much as I'd tried, for Freya's sake, to keep things as normal as possible over Christmas, the turkey dinner had sat untouched on my plate. I smiled through the days but stared at the ceiling every night in bed, as. 3 a.m turned into 4 a.m. By the time my phone displayed 5 a.m., I prayed Ste or Freya would soon wake, so I could get up.

It was the worst Christmas of my life. By St Stephen's Day, a dress that had fit perfectly a fortnight earlier hung loosely. I had lost so much weight that in just a couple of weeks I had dropped a dress size to a size eight, the thinnest I had been in years. I was a million miles away, dwelling on this moment when I would have to make a statement.

And now the time had arrived. The detectives drove me to the Sandyford interview suite, a dedicated facility in South Dublin designed for interviewing vulnerable witnesses. The place is meant to be more relaxed than a regular garda station interview room, but the spartan, office-like room did little to calm my nerves that day.

I sat in one chair, and Detective Sergeant Peter Woods sat facing me, close enough to hear me clearly but far enough to give me space and let me breathe. There must have been a small table because I remember a box of tissues sitting near me.

Peter explained he would conduct the interview while Detective Ger White and Detective Garda Lorraine Mulvin would record and monitor everything in the next room. They did their best to make me feel comfortable and safe, assuring me I could take a break whenever I needed.

And so I began telling them every detail I could remember about that night: going to Airfield Estate, posting my photo on Instagram, McGregor responding, Danielle and me in the salon, how I direct-messaged him and how we thought we were going to a party.

I feared that I'd see doubt in the detective's expression or body language, but that didn't happen. Straight away, I had a sense that he believed me. Or maybe he was trained to make me feel that way, to make the whole ordeal easier.

He scribbled a few notes as I talked, rarely interrupting. When I stopped, stuck on a word I couldn't reach, he waited – no rushing or prompting – just listening and nodding.

He was apologetic and considerate when he needed more information. He prefaced all the worst questions with statements like: 'I'm sorry that we have to go into such detail, I know it's very hard for you, but I have to ask this ...' Especially when we reached the part where the sexual assault took place.

'I don't know how I ended up in the room, but I remember standing there, and he was trying to kiss me ... and I remember saying to him, I don't feel comfortable, Conor. No, I don't feel comfortable. I don't want to ...'

The sobbing started, my shoulders shook, and soon I couldn't stop crying. My whole body convulsed when I had to speak about what had happened, about what McGregor had done to me. It took a long time to tell.

'I kept saying, I'm sorry, I'm not going to tell anybody … I thought if he choked me one more time that he was going to kill me. He was really angry, like he was really rough, and it was like … I can't, I'm sorry …'

Making the statement was the first time I had to vocalise exactly what had happened and rethink every step of the assault. Of course, I had talked about it with Jen, Ste and Mam, but not in depth or detail. I could barely talk about it at all.

That day, I felt raw, like an open wound. Having to describe the scene, what he'd done, where I was and how I was positioned was excruciating. It brought me right back there and was one of the hardest things I've ever had to do in my life. I couldn't imagine anything worse – until I had to do it again years later in open court in front of a courtroom full of strangers.

I remembered the detective gently asking whether there was any way McGregor would have believed I consented to have sex with him.

'How could he have thought that? I fought and fought him,' I argued. 'He'd have never choked me if I hadn't fought. What man would think a girl would give consent after choking her? For him to attack me like that, choke me like that, it's because I fought and I hurt him. He knew I didn't want to go near him!'

The statement took hours to complete, and I was reeling from the process. I think the guards brought me home afterwards, but I can't say for sure. I only remember arriving home and going straight to bed, head pounding, emotionally wrung out by the experience.

That night, I knew I had done the right thing. I wanted Freya to know that women had a voice and men were accountable for what they did. I had stepped forward, steady but scared, reminding myself I would be a role model for my daughter. One day, when she was older, she would know her mother fought back. I didn't know then that the fight would continue for six more years.

Even though I knew I had done the right thing, I felt no sense of relief, no invisible weight lifted from my shoulders. People talk about 'truth setting you free' moments, but it didn't happen that way for me. If anything, the nights got worse. I'd lie in bed, eyes open in the dark, while my mind replayed everything on an endless loop. Sleep became something other people enjoyed.

Soon, wine was a nightly occurrence. The first glass blurred the edges. The second glass quieted the noise. By the third, I could almost convince myself I was normal again and could make it through another night. Before long, I needed more and more to reach that same numb place where nothing hurt quite so much.

From that day on, everything started to go downhill.

10.

A Second Time

Monday, 4 February 2019

The fluorescent lights glared white overhead, and I sat with my hands clasped in my lap, fingers worrying at each other. It was mid-afternoon, and I was back in the Sandyford Suite, facing Detective Peter Woods again and not quite sure why I was there.

I guessed they wanted to go over specific points of my statement. Maybe they wanted me to clarify details that McGregor had brought up during his arrest and questioning two weeks after I had made my statement.

I had learnt that, on 17 January, they planned to bring McGregor in for questioning at Dundrum Garda Station. The following day, the media reported the arrest without identifying him.

A man has been questioned by gardaí in connection with an alleged sexual assault at a Dublin hotel last month. The man was arrested yesterday …

McGregor had presented himself with his solicitor, from Michael Staines Solicitors, at Dundrum Garda Station. Several years later, I learnt that McGregor only read a prepared statement at the interview and then exercised his right to silence. He offered no comment on any extracts from my statement that the detectives put to him.

The day of McGregor's arrest, the investigating team attempted to take a witness statement from James Lawrence. However, he said he first needed to attend his solicitor's office in Dublin, also at Michael Staines Solicitors. He arranged to meet detectives at Blackrock Garda Station the following day instead. But I knew nothing about the contents of his statement at that point either.

I had to wait a few minutes in the Sandyford Suite while they adjusted their recording equipment, and then the questioning started.

'If you could tell us,' Detective Peter Woods began, 'what you remember happening between approximately six and half-past ten when you left the hotel that evening.'

My heart beat a little faster. I wished I could, but most of those hours were a blank.

'I can't.'

'Can you tell me why that is?'

'Because of what happened before in the room. I was traumatised and hurt.'

'Do you have any memory of what happened after Conor McGregor left?'

'I just remember walking with James and Danielle down to the car park. Then I remember going back to the room with James and …'

I wondered why they were asking me this again. I'd already gone through it with them, but I repeated everything about showing the bruises on my arm to Lawrence and asking if he and his friends turned a blind eye to what McGregor did to women.

I spoke about food coming, plates of burgers and chips; I told how one of McGregor's security was there. Everything else about that time was vague.

'I remember bits, in and out, on and off.'

The detective leaned forward slightly. 'We have CCTV footage from the car park area. Have you any memory of being there?'

'When we arrived, yes. And when I walked Conor and Danielle down.'

'Do you know how long you were in the car park?'

I shook my head.

'Were you on your phone?'

'I don't remember being on my phone.'

It went on like this. Then the detective paused and looked at me closely.

'At about a quarter past seven, you leave the hotel in a BMW with James and the driver. Do you recall this?'

My heart sank.

What's he talking about?

I had no recollection of leaving the hotel then.

'No.' The word was barely audible. I recalled going back up to the room after Danielle left with McGregor and believed I had remained there until I became conscious in a taxi late that night.

The detective consulted his notes.

'We have been told that you spilt a drink over the driver and that you were kissing James in the vehicle. Can you recall anything about this?'

'No.' I started sobbing, shaking my head in disbelief. *How can I not remember any of this?*

'We've been told you mentioned the Marble Arch pub. Do you recall this?'

The Marble Arch was what I regarded as an old lads' pub in Drimnagh.

'No.'

'You know the Marble Arch pub?'

'Yes, but I never go there.'

'We've been told you agreed to return to the hotel room with James.'

I left the hotel and returned?

'No!' I was louder now, through the crying. 'I don't remember agreeing to anything like that. No!'

'Can you tell me about your level of intoxication at that time?'

'There was alcohol. And I don't know – I was asleep … I can't—' I pressed my palms against my eyes. 'I don't remember.'

The detective waited a moment.

'James said he went back to the room with you when you returned to the hotel.'

'I don't remember any of that.'

I was in tears now. *What is wrong with me? How can I have no memory of leaving and returning to the hotel?* My shoulders shook.

'I'm sorry. That doesn't even sound like me. I don't understand why I'd go back to a room with James on my own. That's why it's very upsetting for me—'

I couldn't finish, I was crying so hard. The detective paused again. I knew he wasn't accusing or judging; he was just quietly presenting new information.

'James said he had sexual intercourse with you in the room. '

My hands dropped from my face. I stared at the detective as if he'd struck me.

'I don't remember – I wouldn't have done that! I didn't go there to do anything!'

I felt broken in pieces. *My God, have I gone mad? I can't remember leaving the hotel, and now they are saying—*

'Do you remember your clothes being off at any stage when you were with James?'

'No! Not at all!'

'James states he used a condom. Have you any memory of that?'

I wanted to scream that this was bullshit, but all I managed to say was, 'No!'

'He says you talked for a while, and the food was ordered after you'd had sex.'

I gripped my seat to hold on to some sense of reality. What could I say?

'I don't remember. I can't comment on what I don't remember. When I woke up at half six, I only remember bits. I wasn't right.'

'He said that he asked the security man to give you both a while, and he had sex with you again after he left.'

This sounded crazy. I remembered crying with James. Bawling, in fact. I had felt traumatised. I would never have agreed to sex.

'I don't remember any of that. I remember crying and James saying, "Give us a few minutes", because I was upset after what happened to me in the room.' The words came fast now, urgent. 'I was raped by Conor, and I was hurt …'

My head was spinning.

'If James had sexual intercourse with you, was it consent?'

'No, I would not consent to it. Like, why? Because I have a boyfriend. I did not want it. I was after being raped and hurt. I was confused. I wouldn't have had sex with James.'

'Were you attracted to him in any way?'

'Not at all!'

'Could James have believed he had consent to have sexual intercourse with you?'

'No, because I was crying.' My voice began to rise. 'He could see I was hurt. He could see the bruises. I wasn't right, and he knew I wasn't.'

The detective began asking about the taxi home.

'Do you remember James being in the taxi?'

I told them, as I had earlier, that I only remembered the taxi driver coming around and looking to see if I had money.

'Do you remember dropping him off?'

'No.'

James had been in the taxi, and he left me drunk and crying. I wondered if any of this could be true. I had thought James was kind, helpful and caring. But he left me in that car in that condition.

The detective reached for a file and passed it to me. 'I'd like to show you some photos.'

I saw a stack of grainy CCTV stills with time stamps in the corners.

'Who is that?' the detective asked.

'One of the bouncers.'

He flipped over another image. 'Who is that?'

'Conor McGregor.'

'And this?'

He continued flipping over images, and I named the figures in each one.

'Me, Danielle and Conor.'

'I don't know who he is, but looks like one of Conor's bodyguards. They were all dressed in black.'

'That looks like me.'

My jumpsuit in that image was hanging open, ripped from the back.

'Do you want to comment on the jumpsuit?'

'It doesn't look like it's right. You can see my skin there.'

They showed CCTV images of me walking around the car park. Even the photos were hard to look at. In them, I was barely able to stay upright. I remembered nothing of what I saw.

'I look like I have my hand on my head.'

'Can you comment on what's happening?'

James was pulling me in through a door back into the hotel.

'I'm trying to leave. He's pulling me back.'

The images continued. I was walking barefoot in the car park, phone to my ear. Detective Woods said we seemed to be having difficulty getting back into the hotel.

James was standing with me, also barefoot. He left his house in Drimnagh barefoot and got into the car like that.

Then I saw images of us in reception, apparently getting a new key card.

Then, half an hour later, the detective showed CCTV images of us in the lift with a security guard. We were leaving the penthouse on the seventh floor. I was gripping a Bacardi bottle.

'Seven ten p.m. The BMW leaving.'

Lawrence and I are leaving in that car?

'I don't remember that.'

He showed me another with James and me back in the car park, time-stamped 7.29 p.m. *We left the hotel for nineteen minutes?*

'I've no shoes on my feet,' I said. 'I don't even see them in my hands.'

'Can you comment on where James's arm is?'

'Yes, it looks like it's around me, high up around my shoulder.'

'Is there a reason why you don't have a memory between 6.10 p.m. and when you got to Eimer's house?'

My voice was small. 'Probably a lot of drinking; drugs in my system, and after what I went through with Conor in the room. I don't know why I was not looked after. I remember breaking down crying. I would have been vulnerable.'

'Do you want to say anything about what James said happened between you both in the room?'

'I don't remember any of that. I can't comment on it. I feel sick after what he had to say.'

'In the light of what you know about what James said, do you want to say anything further?'

Instinctively, I didn't believe what Lawrence had told the guards. It didn't make sense. I knew myself that I would never have consented to sex with Lawrence. I remembered clearly crying about being mauled and beaten by McGregor. But how could I deny having sex with James Lawrence when I couldn't remember? I wiped my eyes again.

When I spoke, my voice was steady for the first time since the interview began. I thought of the detective's words: *In light of what you know about what James said, do you want to say anything further?*

'It just makes me feel like I was raped a second time. That's all.'

11.

Self-Hatred

The house was quiet in that unnerving way of a home in the early hours. Ste was out, and I sat at the kitchen counter, drinking wine, one elbow leaning on the kitchen island. I eyed my plastic container of antidepressants standing upright at one end of the counter. At the other end, my eye rested on the steel knife that lay on the chopping board from earlier.

My mind felt strangely calm, as if the fog had faded and left only two doors, both waiting for me to choose.

I wondered how many pills it might take to do the job. Could I Google it? I didn't need to test the knife blade. It cut through gristle and meat with ruthless efficiency. I imagined the neatness of it. No drama. No calling for attention. Just an ending.

The thought should have frightened me, but instead it settled over me like a blanket. Comforting. How easy it felt to imagine slipping out of my own life. But the thought didn't rest for long. My mind conjured another image: my daughter Freya. I saw her standing in the doorway, small and blinking, searching for me. Not finding me.

And then came another face – my mam's. Mam, who had dedicated her life to rearing me, didn't deserve that kind of pain or betrayal.

But my mental health hung by a thread in the weeks and months after making my statement to police. I moved through the days because I had to, because I had no alternative. Or because the alternative was not an option.

I didn't tell Ste about Lawrence's claims of consensual sex with me. Things were already strained between us, and I remembered very little about those few hours when Lawrence, the security guard and I were together. Yet, I didn't believe Lawrence's claims. The more I thought about it, the more outlandish it seemed. I was sick and upset after being assaulted by McGregor and would never have consented to sex. I felt sure that it was a story concocted between him and McGregor to undermine me and my accusation of rape against McGregor.

And yet terrible thoughts, suicidal ones, still came in waves. Sometimes, without even realising it, my mind travelled along dark roads, mapping out methods so all this pain could be resolved.

It wasn't every day. Some days I'd feel grand, almost normal again. Then, like a flick of a switch, a deep, dark state of fear and anxiety rose out of nowhere. Often, I didn't know what triggered this switch. It was like these thoughts lived just beneath the surface, breaking the waves occasionally and threatening to drown me.

I wasn't the same person anymore, and I didn't love who I had become. My spirit was weighed down, and soon, my body was too.

My relationship with my body was already strained with the pain, shame and anger over the assault. Now, extra weight was accumulating as I swung from eating very little to comfort eating. I looked bloated from drinking too much, and shadows grew under my eyes from the stress and sleepless nights. The extra weight added more layers of shame I couldn't shed.

I hated what I saw in the mirror. I no longer recognised myself. The girl staring back at me was broken and ugly. She was disgusting to me. I'd stand there getting angry at my own reflection, cataloguing my failures.

Anxiety and depression weren't entirely new to me. The months before the assault had been difficult. Everything had seemed to pile on top of me at once. I had gone looking for my father's grave the year before the attack. I was at a stage in my life where I was seeking closure around my father's death when I was just eight years old, and I wanted to find his grave and place a plant on it. I remember standing before his headstone, my eyes tracing the letters of his name, hoping, maybe, to find some small measure of peace. Yet, I found none. Around the same time, Ste and I were in the middle of renovating our first house.

It should have felt like a new beginning, but the excitement came wrapped in a lot of stress. Builders and tradesmen were tearing the place apart while the three of us were squeezed into my mother's small home nearby. I worked full days and had a child demanding my attention. Our borrowed space pressed in on me.

Grief, exhaustion and a sense of displacement seemed to hit me all at once. My GP, Dr Frank Clarke of Walkinstown Medical Centre, was and is amazing and never pushed medication where there was a better alternative. I had never wanted medication either. For the first time, however, he prescribed a low dose of sertraline, an antidepressant, to steady me through the upheaval.

After the rape, I experienced a whole different level of depression and anxiety. I'd never felt such a weight before. It crippled me to the extent I didn't want to get out of bed most days. The doctor increased my dose of sertraline. I hated that the dosage had to go up so that I could function, so that I could even just get out of bed; but I was unravelling, mentally, physically, every which way. I didn't have a choice.

The new dosage worked in its own way. The shattering anxiety and fear flatlined, but a tiredness crept in that dragged at me. My spark disappeared, and I felt aimless. Everything dulled to nothing. The tablets smoothed the edges but also contributed to my weight gain.

I was also weighed down with guilt. Guilt over the gaps in my memory and the parts of that awful day and night that I couldn't piece together; guilt that I couldn't be a better mother, and that my mam had to pick up the slack; guilt that I wasn't working and had left all the financial pressures to pile onto Ste.

Endless guilt.

My mind became my enemy, circling constantly, trying to force recollection where there was only darkness. I was lost.

In mid-February, Ste came clean and told me he had secretly recorded me on the morning of Monday, 10 December, when I returned battered and bruised. He explained he wanted to remember what I had said because he was afraid I would forget.

He was apologetic. Listening back, he said he had been horrible to me and wished he had done things differently and called an ambulance. But Ste was too hard on himself. He wasn't horrible. He had been quiet-spoken and caring and responded to the crisis in the only way he knew. He did his best that night to do the right thing, to call the police, to help me help myself, but I was too frightened and too traumatised to think straight.

He said he hadn't told me about the recording because he was afraid I'd be angry. But when the gardaí had asked for his phone as part of the investigation, he knew they and I would discover the recording. I had already given them my phone so they could retrieve the texts I'd deleted.

I never got angry with Ste. He was only doing what he thought was right. But I couldn't bear to listen to the recording.

I never wanted to hear the soundtrack of one of the worst nights of my life.

In the months after the attack, Ste and I had no great showdown. Our relationship disintegrated bit by bit. I had withdrawn from my partner and from life in general – I no longer cared about him or myself. I couldn't handle sexual intimacy now either.

Looking back, I don't believe Ste and I were meant to stay together. We would have split up eventually, but the stress and trauma of what happened to me caused the inevitable to happen sooner. In that sense, our relationship was another casualty of what happened on 9 December 2018.

Freya was seven years old when Ste moved out in May 2019. I was relieved he was gone. I was a broken-hearted shell of a person, unable to cope with my own feelings, never mind anyone else's. But after he left, my life became considerably worse.

On the days Freya went to stay with her dad, I drank consistently and heavily. On the days I had Freya, I did my best to perform, wearing my happy mask. I became an expert at pretending, frighteningly good at it. I'd move through the house, keeping everything clean, putting dinner on the table.

But I was no longer the mother I had been to Freya, my vivacious, energetic little girl, despite trying my best to paper over the cracks. I have a photo on my phone, taken a week after Ste left, and I'm in my pyjamas, cuddling Freya. I have a beaming smile. It's hard to reconcile that photo – my happy mask – with the pain I was in. I functioned for a few days a week for Freya. My mam waded in to help when the facade cracked and I simply couldn't manage. When Freya was gone, the bed and alcohol claimed me.

Many nights I lay in the dark with Daisy, my little Yorkshire terrier, curled against the curve of my neck, licking the tears from my face. Daisy was a stray that Mam took in back in 2012 and she became our family dog. After Mam had asked me to mind her months earlier, Daisy had refused to go home. It was as if she knew she couldn't leave me, as if she had a mission to care for me. She was my tiny best friend during some of the loneliest nights of my life.

I found other outlets for my pain. When my anxiety peaked, my fingers would wrap around a strand of hair at my crown and tug. I wasn't entirely conscious of the action – it simply happened, a reflex born of self-hatred and stress. Over weeks and months, that spot on my crown became damaged, the hair growing back short and patchy. I've since learnt that hair-pulling is a disorder and even has a name: trichotillomania, another form of self-harm, just less obvious than drinking. This inward anger was a difficult habit to break.

My eating habits also continued to swing between extremes – periods where I'd feel like eating nothing, followed by frantic consumption for comfort. My relationship with food became as fractured as everything else.

Before that day in The Beacon Hotel, I'd always been naturally slim, energetic and comfortable in my skin. I loved to cook and eat well, and all the running around at the salon and chasing after Freya kept me trim. Back then, I'd sometimes catch my reflection and feel good about what I saw. After the rape, that all vanished. The mirror showed only the wreckage of the girl I used to be. I was a girl abusing my body with alcohol, pulling out my own hair and eating to fill a void that couldn't be filled. I was someone new: a Nikita who I couldn't love or accept. I lived within this self-destructive cycle of behaviours, observing myself with disgust but unable to bridge the gap between the woman I'd been and the woman trauma had turned me into.

12.

The Salon

The packet came unstuck as I tried to wrap it around a section of the client's hair. I pulled another one from the trolley. I could see the client eyeing me in the mirror.

'Sorry!' I said.

Her reflection smiled up at me. 'Take your time, love,' she said.

I knew she must be wondering what had happened to her usual chatterbox colourist. These days, I couldn't summon the energy for cheery banter.

My hands moved mechanically through the familiar choreography. Section the hair. Weave the mesh. Paint the lightener. Open the packet. I'd done this ten thousand times and could do it in my sleep. I used to do it in my sleep, back in the days when I did sleep and when my dreams were more pleasant.

The salon bustled around me, filled with the roar of hairdryers, laughter erupting between the stylists and clients and the sound of tinny pop music from the radio. This place should have felt like home. It always had before. But since I'd returned to work after an extended leave of absence, everything felt different.

I had always loved my job. From the day as a little girl when I'd unwrapped Santy's present and found a doll's head and hair styling kit, I knew what I wanted to do. The doll's wavy, blonde synthetic hair mesmerised me as a seven- and eight-year-old. Mam would find me on the floor, comb in hand, parting, smoothing, sectioning and twisting her blonde hair into ponytails, pigtails, curls and French braids. I washed and blow-dried her hair, then added all the accessories – ribbons, slides, headscarves, clips and pins. I was obsessed.

At fourteen, I was a part-time waitress, serving full Irish breakfasts on Saturday mornings at a popular café in Kimmage. But Mam already knew my dream was to work in a hair salon when I left school.

'I know someone who works in Roches Salon in Crumlin,' she said one day. 'She might get you sweeping the floors on Saturdays.'

My eyes popped.

'Ask her!' I grabbed Mam's arm. 'Please, Mam. I'll sweep, I'll scrub the sinks, I'll do anything they want me to do.'

That first Saturday in Roches, I pushed the broom across the tiles and breathed in the scent of apple shampoo. I eyed stylists' scissors snipping – watching how they'd step back, assess and move in again. I saw them angle the blow dryers and roll the hair around their brushes in one fluid motion. I watched them flip through colour charts and envied their skills as they mixed and matched hair colours. I wanted to be one of them.

My long, dark hair was soon lobbed off. I began experimenting with colour at fifteen – my hair was copper brown one week and highlighted the next. I was hooked by the time I started applying colours in the salon.

School was something I had to endure between shifts in the salon. Mam insisted I stay in school until my Leaving Cert, but working in a salon was my dream. It was hair and nothing else.

In February 2019, two months after the assault, I summoned up the strength to return to work. Everyone insisted it would be good for me, but no one knew how deeply my fear and anxiety were embedded by then. I found it exhausting to present the old, cheerful version of myself. Gerard Paul had always been my favourite place to work, but my focus was gone. Persistent intrusive thoughts affected my ability to concentrate.

A client was reading her newspaper one morning, the broadsheet rustling in front of her as I applied her mesh highlights. As she turned the page, the headline of an article blazed before my eyes: another story about the investigation into the 'Irish sportsman' and an anonymous woman alleging rape.

My hand froze. I couldn't move. Only my bosses and manager

knew about the case and the criminal investigation. Still, sometimes it felt like everyone was watching and talking about me. Maintaining the 'secret' felt overwhelming and isolating.

Heart-pounding panic attacks could hit me anywhere now. Nowhere was safe. Only a day earlier, I'd been in Tesco, my hand reaching for a can on a shelf, when an image came into my mind of his twisted face; his fingers clawing at me. A flashback. It lasted two seconds, maybe three. But in that fragment of time, I'd been transported to terror. My chest heaved for breath as another shopper pushed her trolley past me, staring.

Panic lay waiting around every corner: At work, in the queue at the post office or walking down the road, it could seize me. The triggers were random, merciless. One moment, I was present, functioning, normal. The next, I was back in that room, feeling his hands, seeing his rage.

In the salon, I sometimes had to excuse myself, find a quiet space and force myself to breathe deep. Then I'd return to my client and pretend that the ground beneath me hadn't just opened up. The flashbacks never asked for permission. They arrived in split-second ambushes, inserting terror and violence into the mundane. His angry face was in my weekly shop. Memories of his chokehold seized me as I walked down the street.

When the Rape Crisis Centre referred me to a group session for the first time, I dreaded the thought of it. I arrived on my first night to find all the women already sitting in a circle.

'You can sit anywhere,' the facilitator said. I chose a chair nearest the door because I didn't know if I would stay. Then I heard a woman describe how difficult it was to leave the house. Another spoke about how she was drinking too much. Others were talking about excessive eating, or comfort eating. I felt something in my chest open in that first group therapy session. Not relief, exactly. It was more like recognition, like finally hearing someone speak a language I thought only I knew. I found myself nodding, sometimes crying, as I listened to the others.

My manager's voice came from far away. 'Everything all right, Nikita?'

I blinked. A glob of colouring cream was threatening to fall from the brush suspended over my client and her newspaper. My manager had been keeping an eye on me. I had mixed the wrong colour for another client that week – someone else caught it in time, but more evidence that my head wasn't in the game anymore.

'Yes. Sorry. Just …' I set the brush down on the trolley, took a deep breath and picked it up again. My manager caught my eye in the mirror.

'Are you okay?' she mouthed.

I nodded, tried to smile and turned back to my client's hair. Stared at it. Ash blonde, I'd written on the colour card.

This woman had sat in my chair once a month for two years now. She trusted me completely, and I couldn't remember why

I'd chosen this placement pattern for the packets. I couldn't remember what I'd been trying to achieve.

The client folded the newspaper and set it aside, oblivious. 'Any holidays planned this year?'

'Nothing,' I said. 'I'm a bit broke after buying my first house …'

Talk, just talk. Talk about anything, I admonished myself as I forced myself to reach for another packet.

The salon carried on around me with the laughter, the radio, the familiar smell of ammonia. And I stood there, looking at my client's half-finished head, understanding with absolute clarity that I couldn't do this anymore. Not today. Not tomorrow. Maybe never again. Shortly afterwards, I handed in my notice and left a job I had treasured for years. I never went back.

13.

Allegations

My phone buzzed: *Did you see this?* I clicked the attached link, and my hands began to tremble as I scanned the news article.

An Irish sports star, already under investigation for rape, is facing another sexual abuse allegation …

That Monday morning in October, ten months after being sexually assaulted, the story was everywhere. Reports claimed that the alleged incident had occurred in a car outside a Dublin pub the previous Friday night.

Car seized as gardaí investigate claim of sexual assault against sports star …

My throat closed, but my fingers kept flicking through a compulsive loop, from Google to Reddit to various news sites. By now, I had deleted all my social media apps, but friends and family still forwarded screenshots.

I couldn't stop scrolling. Each news report carefully avoided any identification that might trigger libel laws, but on social media people were using less restraint. The incident was said to have taken place outside a pub in Drimnagh.

Days later, *The New York Times* confirmed McGregor as the sports star being investigated over a sexual assault allegation. His publicist said McGregor 'emphatically' denied 'any report accusing him of sexual assault'.

I cried as I read and reread the reports. The fresh allegations brought everything rushing back, and remembering made me want to crawl out of my own skin.

Since I'd made my first statement in January 2019, I'd heard nothing back from the Director of Public Prosecutions (DPP) about advancing a case against Conor McGregor. I tried not to bother the detectives. I figured they had enough to do and would let me know if they had news. But the wait was painful. I had cooperated while gardaí investigated and verified details, and then – silence. The detectives had said it would take 'a few months'. Every week, Mam and I said, 'We'll probably hear at the end of this week' or 'We'll hear by the end of this month.' But still the months rolled by, and we heard nothing.

McGregor continued to walk free, living his life, attending parties and posting strutting selfies, while my life felt on hold, waiting for someone to decide if what had happened to me even mattered.

And now, there were allegations that another woman was

involved in a different investigation. I paced the kitchen, my phone buzzing in my hand with more messages and alerts.

The reports that morning were only one of many controversies surrounding McGregor that year. It seemed every time I'd idly scroll through Google News or pass a newspaper stand in a newsagent, I'd see his face, that jolt of recognition a sharp blow to my gut.

In March 2019, police had arrested McGregor in Miami Beach, USA, for allegedly smacking the phone out of a fan's hand, stomping on it and then grabbing it before leaving the scene. However, charges of criminal mischief and strong-armed robbery were later dropped after a reported settlement.

Shortly afterwards, I watched the viral video of McGregor sucker-punching a much older man in the Marble Arch pub in Drimnagh. One minute, McGregor was full of geniality, sharing shots of his whiskey with patrons at the bar; the next, out of nowhere, he punched the man with a left hook, before being dragged away by his entourage. McGregor attacked the man because he had twice refused a complimentary shot of his Proper No. Twelve Whiskey. For me, the footage revealed how quickly the showbiz facade could vanish and the monster emerge. Even diehard McGregor fans were appalled this time.

McGregor pleaded guilty to the assault in Dublin District Court that year and received a fine of €1,000 – loose change for him. The court heard that he had already compensated the victim an undisclosed sum.

But the thought that another woman may have endured what I did while the DPP sat on my statement upset me more than anything I'd read before. It triggered every emotion from fear to anxiety and anger. I gripped my phone, scrolling, refreshing pages for new comments, reading the same stories over and over.

Friday night's allegations are completely separate to a rape allegation the sportsman is facing, in which gardaí have sent a file to the DPP. The DPP has yet to make a decision on whether he should be charged with the offence.

The anger inside me became a wave of heat. My fingers found the number for Detective Ger White, and I called. It rang twice.

'Hi Nikita.'

A pause.

'I was going to call you,' he said.

'Were you?'

I was pacing again, my free hand clenched.

'Because I've been waiting ten months for the DPP to make a decision. And now I'm reading reports that gardaí are investigating another alleged assault while my case sits fucking shelved somewhere.'

'I understand you're frustrated—'

'Frustrated?' My voice sounded too loud, even in my head. 'He attacked me. I gave you everything. I've given you all the evidence of that attack, but he's still out there and free to do whatever he wants.'

'Unfortunately, I'm just a detective – this is in the hands of those higher up the food chain than me ...'

I was near boiling point. It was pointless listening to the same excuses I'd heard many months ago.

'How is she? Can you tell me that?'

He was silent again. I understood he couldn't speak about another investigation, but the thought of another allegation, possibly another woman ...

'When are they going to do something? What else do they need?'

I was crying now, tears of anger and distress. I knew I was taking my frustration out on a detective who had always done his best to help me. He had the decency to answer my call and now he had to bear the brunt of my frustration with the legal system.

I felt furious with the Office of the DPP. They had no idea what it was like to watch everyone debate my truth. People were accusing me of lying, slut-shaming me and defending McGregor online while my statement sat on someone's desk.

While those in the Office of the DPP could go home every evening and get on with their lives, I'd lost the life I'd been living. I never got to forget. My work was gone; my mental health was destroyed; my once large circle of friends had dwindled to a handful. My life had been turned upside down.

I experienced the added hell of watching McGregor out there, living a life he should have lost the right to when he violently raped me ten months earlier.

When I put down the phone to the detective, my heart was beating wildly, and my stomach was in a knot. I pulled the fridge door open and welcomed its cold draught. The wine sat waiting, condensation glistening on the glass. My hand closed around the neck of the bottle, its weight familiar and comforting. I filled my glass and lifted it to my lips. The Sauvignon Blanc hit my palate and throat, cold at first then spreading through my chest with that familiar thin warmth that promised more. I took another drink. I knew once I finished a couple of glasses, the edges of the afternoon would blur.

After a few glasses, I felt better able to cope. I would return to the fridge, knowing the rest of the bottle was waiting. Or, sometimes, I'd take the bottle and glass and slide into the couch, legs folded beneath me. The bottle rested on the windowsill next to me as I raised my glass and tilted my head back again. Better. My night was already better, and another bottle waited in the fridge when I finished this one.

Only then could I exhale and perhaps sleep. But any sound outside had me frozen with fear, unable to breathe, terrified that someone was trying to break in.

Every story I read about McGregor left me crying for days. I grew more and more frustrated. *When will they charge this man?* I asked myself repeatedly. And then I reached for yet another numbing glass of wine. And in this way the months passed.

14.

The DPP

I was sitting bolt upright on the couch before the second ring. The detective's name was flashing up on my phone. *Could this be it, at last?* It was June 2020. I had been waiting eighteen months for this call.

I took a breath before answering, cautioning myself not to get my hopes up. How many times had I feverishly responded to his calls before, only to be disappointed? Ger was a kind man, and we had developed a good relationship. However, his previous calls had only been to check in, asking how I was doing, or to share what little news he had on the case. Even kindness could bring disappointment, as my hopes were again dashed.

On each occasion, his patient voice had explained that these things took time, that they had built a thorough case and that the DPP took its own sweet time.

Now, I swallowed, answered the phone and for a minute we exchanged social niceties. But then I heard a pause, and my body stiffened.

'Look, I don't have good news for you, Nikita.'

My head began to spin.

This cannot be happening.

'The DPP is refusing to take on your case …'

His words were soft, but that somehow made the blow worse.

'They don't believe they have a reasonable prospect of obtaining a conviction … don't have enough evidence to proceed … these cases are always complex. I'm sorry but …'

I hung up, cutting him off mid-conversation. The phone lay on the couch where I dropped it. My fingers were still curled, as if holding the ghost of it. The shriek that rose in my throat emerged as a half-strangled wail. There was a tremble in my entire body that I couldn't control.

Nearly eighteen months since I made my statement. A year and a half of an agonising wait for this call, my anxiety rising with each passing week. Eighteen months of telling myself that justice was worth waiting for, that the system worked slowly, but it worked.

Eighteen months of drinking far too much, trying to quell the anxiety that left me staring at the ceiling every night. Of checking locks. Of jumping at any knock at the door or footsteps behind me.

Eighteen months during which I had lost my job, my car, my life as I'd known it.

The waiting game had been agonising – and it had all been for nothing.

The phone buzzed again, flashing up Ger's name. 'Fuck off,' I muttered, but the cheery ringtone continued. 'FUCK OFF!' This time, I roared at the ringing phone, and the words reverberated through the entire house.

My mind was spinning backwards through all those months of naively believing I would have justice, that as soon as the DPP read everything – when they understood everything – they would swing into action. I had done everything I could: given the guards every detail; answered every humiliating question; handed over my underwear, my clothes and my phone. I endured the traumatising forensic hospital examination, standing naked under bright fluorescent lights and posed for intrusive gardaí photographs. I made the statement, then a second statement.

During all this time, my mental health had been on a knife-edge. Each media report and online comment sent me into a spiral of anxiety. I endured terrible nightmares, and the group therapy I found so valuable had come to a crashing halt with the first Covid-19 lockdown in March 2020. I had already increased the dose of my antidepressants. And now this news.

The law had weighed both McGregor's and my statements and evidence and found mine wanting. As far as I was concerned, their refusal to prosecute him implied he was truthful and innocent, and I was a liar.

I paced the sitting room, my heart racing. I pulled the blinds and locked the doors. *Not enough evidence?* I was the evidence. My body was the evidence. The DPP had a woman saying something happened, and a man saying it didn't. But I knew, and he knew. And now he knew something else: that he could get away with it, and he had, and no one would stop him.

I thought back to my interactions with the guards. They had assured me that the DPP would proceed with a prosecution because the evidence was so strong. The detective told me he had even met with the Office of the DPP and urged them to watch the video of my statement, not merely read it.

'If you look at the video recording we took, you can see the emotion and the shock, and you'll know she's telling the truth,' the investigating detective said he told them. 'You will see that a jury will believe her.' But did they look at the video recordings? I will never know.

I felt rage at myself and the world. I felt stupid because I had believed them – all of them. When they took my statement and told me that he would be held accountable, I believed them. I believed the gardaí, my family, my therapist, my friends, everyone. I rearranged my life around this belief, held myself together with it. Told myself the nightmares would stop once he was held accountable and was behind bars. Told myself I could heal and move on when I had justice. What a naive view of the world I had – that I would have justice.

The jolly ringtone on my phone started up again, and the detective's name flashed for a third time. I ignored it. It buzzed after he hung up. A message: *Calling to your house. Will be there in 10*. He could call all he wanted. I wouldn't answer the door. I didn't want to talk to him or anyone.

Everyone knew the DPP's decision was overdue. Everyone had been waiting, checking in, asking if I'd heard anything. Everyone had been asking why it had been taking so long. Now I had to tell them. I had to say the words out loud, and say it over and over, and I would hear the things they wouldn't say: *Maybe if you hadn't sent that photo; maybe if you'd reported it right away; maybe if you hadn't drunk so much; maybe if you hadn't taken drugs; maybe if you hadn't lied to your partner; maybe if you hadn't gone into a hotel room with him.*

Maybe, maybe, maybe. Maybe if I'd been the perfect victim, I'd get justice. But I wasn't. I was just a girl on a night out who naively trusted someone she thought she could.

Bright afternoon light beamed through a gap in the closed blinds. It was a beautiful June day, and I could hear the kids' shrieks as they played outside. The world hadn't stopped because of that phone call. It didn't stop that night, and it wouldn't stop now, even though it felt like the end of the world.

I used the backs of my hands to dry my face and try to calm myself. My head was heavy and aching. I wondered how I was supposed to keep living in a body that no one believed. How was I going to rebuild my life when my trust in people, the legal system and my own judgment was so low? Most of all, I wondered how I would form the words to tell my mam – my family, everyone – that the DPP said my battered body was insufficient evidence; that Conor McGregor would not be prosecuted.

I sat in the silence of my empty home. Eighteen months ago, I thought the worst thing that could happen to me had already come. I was wrong.

15.

Pursued

The streetlight ahead flickers, but I keep walking, my front-door key threaded between my index and middle fingers, my chin tucked into my collar against the cold. The terraced houses on either side stand unlit and lifeless, curtains pulled tight. I can't quite remember how I ended up on my own in Drimnagh after dark, and I silently berate myself.

Then I hear the shoe scuff behind me and my heart beats harder. I quicken my pace. The turn to my road is 200 metres away. My house is just around the corner, offering safety.

I lengthen my stride, but the footsteps behind seem to match my speed. My breath comes shallow and quick as I pick up the pace again. The footsteps behind me are clearer now despite my heartbeat thrumming in my ears.

My runners slap faster against the pavement, and my keys bite harder into my palm and fingers. But behind me, the footsteps accelerate. I can hear them echo on the road – heavier, closer. A streetlamp throws my shadow long and thin across the sidewalk. My heart leaps as I see a second shadow loom behind it, and I glance over my shoulder.

He's only metres away. His hoodie obscures most of his face, but the streetlight catches the darkness of his eye sockets and the angle of his jawline, and I know it's him: jaw determined and predatory eyes fixed on me. I gasp and run, my footsteps pounding past darkened houses, past closed gates, towards lights or people, towards safety.

My lungs pull air in ragged gasps, but his feet hammer the ground behind me, louder than my own. I run and run, finding a speed I didn't think I possessed, but the corner isn't getting any closer.

His breath is in my ears, almost on my neck. I feel rather than see his hands reaching out for me, and I lurch forward. The pavement rushes up to meet my face, and I scream the high-pitched cry of a cornered animal.

That's when my eyes snap open. In the darkness of the bedroom my heart is still running and I am still screaming. The nightmare is always the same. He is pursuing me, trying to kill me. I'm on a street, sometimes it's in Drimnagh, sometimes it's in the city centre. Sometimes, I don't recognise where I am, but I always hear the footsteps behind me. The chase begins, and I'm running for my life. I wake up, my body sweating, the sheets soaked and my throat raw.

After the DPP turned down my case, all the trauma of the

assault rose to the surface again with a vengeance, bringing more flashbacks and nightmares. Especially the nightmares. The same one, over and over.

I had called the detective who broke the news of the DPP's decision the following day. My hopes soared when he said I could question the decision or ask for a review.

I sent a letter questioning the decision days later, on 17 June 2020. They replied with an acknowledgement of receipt and said the request would take longer than usual because of the pandemic. Nothing more.

On 7 August 2020, a brown envelope arrived. I opened it standing in the hallway, hands shaking. The director of the DPP had personally considered all the available evidence, it said. The decision stood. There was not sufficient evidence to prosecute.

The letter explained what I already knew – criminal cases required proof beyond a reasonable doubt. If the evidence wasn't strong enough, there could be no prosecution. I had twenty-eight days to request an official review.

I couldn't understand it. I felt the medical evidence alone should have been enough. Rightly or wrongly, I believed that my attacker's fame may have resulted in the DPP's caution and reluctance to prosecute. I read their letter twice and then spoke to my counsellor in the Dublin Rape Crisis Centre.

'I'm not letting this go,' I said. 'I want to make them realise that I'm serious about getting a prosecution.'

My counsellor and I drafted the letter together; each sentence deliberate, each word carefully chosen. On 11 August, I signed it and sent it off.

Dear [A senior prosecutor in the DPP's Victims Liaison Unit],
I received your letter dated 7 August 2020 regarding my request for an explanation as to the reasons why the DPP have decided not to prosecute in relation to my complaints of rape. I am very disappointed and upset with the content of this letter.

You have outlined the criminal offences that were considered, given an account of what the DPP received in the file from the gardaí, referred to the guidelines for prosecution, and outlined the high burden of proof required in a criminal trial. However, at no time have you given me any real reasons as to why the DPP are not prosecuting.

Over twenty months have passed since the assault. The gardaí have been incredibly supportive throughout the process. But the coverage in the newspapers and on social media has been very difficult for myself and my family. I always felt that I was doing the right thing by reporting and that there was more than enough evidence for a trial.

We were shocked and very disappointed when we were told that the case would not be prosecuted. I am very unhappy with this decision and feel that I am being treated differently to other victims because one of the suspects is a famous person. I believe that this is the reason why the DPP have decided not to prosecute.

I would like to ask for a review of this decision. I would also like to know the reasons as to why the DPP are not prosecuting and to know why it took from May 2019, when the file went to your office, to June 2020 before your office made a decision.

I look forward to hearing from you.

In my mind, someone in the DPP's office would read my letter, realise their mistake, change their mind and say, *Yes, we will prosecute McGregor.* I waited, trusting. Friends said I was too naive, but I believed my letter would magically change the DPP's decision.

A couple of months later, another letter arrived. The review was still under consideration, and they would inform me as soon as they completed it. I was hopeful. They were looking into it. I was sure my letter made all the difference.

Meanwhile, another news report about McGregor landed. This time, he had been detained and questioned by authorities on the French island of Corsica for alleged indecent exposure and sexual assault in a bar. He had spent two days in custody following the incident.

His representative quickly responded: 'Conor McGregor vigorously denies any accusations of misconduct.' Eight months later, police would declare a lack of sufficient evidence to justify a criminal prosecution.

Every time he made the news, the feelings of fear and hypervigilance soared. I checked and double-checked the doors and windows. Any noise outside at night made me jump.

Although I no longer felt comfortable in my own home, I was in no position to move. Ste continued paying the mortgage, while I was supporting Freya and paying the bills. I couldn't work, so I couldn't afford to go anywhere else.

I felt trapped. Everyone said I needed to get back out there and begin living a normal life again. My therapist spoke about 'moving forward'. A social life and dating was part of that, but I had been with Freya's dad for most of my adult life, and going on a dating site felt scary. Meeting any man seemed fraught with danger. I'd already made the worst mistake of my life arranging to meet a man I thought I knew of well enough to trust. How could I trust my judgment when meeting a complete stranger?

I had summoned my courage and downloaded the Bumble app – then deleted it – several times. Now, on a summer evening in 2020, I tried again. I tapped it and watched the screen load, but my heart started beating too hard. *Maybe not.*

I placed my phone face down on the couch beside me. I wasn't ready for this. I picked up my glass of wine and took a sip as the TV droned in the background. Would I ever be ready?

But I was tired of being alone and afraid. I've always been an affectionate and demonstrative person and longed to feel the promise of a connection with someone special. My hand found the phone again, and this time, I got as far as the profiles: a man in hiking gear on a mountain. I swiped left without reading his bio. A guy flaunting his abs on a beach. Swift left.

Left, left, left. My finger moved on autopilot until a guy with kind eyes made me pause. I'd matched with him before, and we'd exchanged a couple of messages, but then I'd taken fright and deleted the app. My eyes lingered on his face, and I looked through his profile photos again. I was still drawn to him. I took a deep breath and swiped right. I didn't know that swipe would be a life-changing moment.

The phone lit up in my lap soon after – a notification from Bumble. 'You have a new match!'

It wasn't a new match. It was the man with kind eyes again. At that time, Bumble required the woman to message first in heterosexual matches. Now the cursor blinked in the message box, waiting for me to respond. I typed something like, 'Hi again, how's your week going?' and he replied.

We messaged for a few days, and then he asked me out on a date. I took another deep breath and sent him my number before deleting the app. We texted each other for a week or two, getting to know each other a little. On Sunday, 19 July 2020, I found myself walking towards Café en Seine, on Dawson Street in Dublin's city centre, to meet Gary for the first time.

At this stage, I was still in legal limbo, anxiously awaiting the DPP's review of my case. Now, meeting this relative stranger only added to my anxiety.

As I got closer to the bar, I regretted ever agreeing to this date. What if he wasn't anything like the person he presented as or the person I'd built up in my head? What if he rejected me once he realised I was the anonymous woman who had been all over the news, the one who alleged she'd been beaten and raped by a well-known sports star?

He stood outside the café bar, taller than his photos had suggested, his fair hair catching the light, blue eyes scanning the street. When he spotted me, his face opened into a smile that gave me butterflies.

I'm tall myself – five feet seven and a half without heels – and he cleared six feet easily. Six foot four, I'd learn later. But it was his smile that caught me; the way it lit his entire face and reached his eyes. I fell in love with him right there on the pavement on Dawson Street.

Inside, the restaurant buzzed with the energy of Dublin emerging from lockdown. Covid restrictions still dictated everything: 'substantial' meals were required, and one-hour-forty-five-minute bookings were the maximum permitted. I ordered a starter I didn't want – my stomach was too tight with nerves to consider food. But soon after I sat across from him, the nerves dissolved.

We had none of the usual first-date awkwardness. I talked

freely, the words coming easily. And then, before I could second-guess it, I told him about the case.

I watched his face as I spoke, measuring each reaction, waiting for the moment his expression would close and he'd check his phone, make an excuse and reach for his jacket. Then recognition dawned. His eyes widened slightly and his face hardened, but not at me – at my story.

'I can't believe you're the woman I read about. I never expected . . .' He shook his head. 'I'm so sorry you went through that.'

But more than his words, I saw his belief. I had laid everything bare, and he was still sitting across from me, and he believed me.

Gary, in turn, was honest with me. He told me about his gambling addiction and his recovery in Gamblers Anonymous. He told me about the troubled years after his mother died. That made me fall even harder for him. We both carried trauma from the past. Mine was playing out in the full glare of the media; his was more private. Neither of us was perfect, nor were we expecting perfection. We were real people who struggled, stumbled and experienced pain, but we had survived and were healing.

Our first night out was soon followed by a second date in an Italian restaurant. 'Wet' pubs were still closed due to Covid, and dining still had time limits. On our fourth date, he suggested that he cook at my place instead. He arrived that evening with a shopping bag after travelling across the city. He moved around the kitchen with the confidence of someone who knew his way around a hob. We chopped together and laughed together, discovering a mutual love for cooking and each other.

In the background, however, the DDP's review dragged on. I became more disheartened. The decision, when the envelope arrived in November, felt light and thin. In my heart, I already knew what it said before I opened it: 'After careful consideration,' they believed their initial decision not to prosecute was correct.

Their reasons included Lawrence's claim that he had consensual sex with me after I was raped, the amount of drugs and alcohol involved and CCTV evidence from The Beacon Hotel showing my actions after the attack. This was footage I had never seen.

They said there was no reasonable prospect of conviction. They also said that the suspects' identities had no bearing on the decision or the outcome of the case. I set the letter down on the kitchen counter.

The first refusal had ripped something open inside me. It felt like the DPP didn't believe me, like they had judged me and found me wanting. This letter confirmed what I'd been trying not to believe – that hoping had been a mistake. I felt despair. And rage. I imagined McGregor laughing at me, rubbing his hands with glee. I pictured him celebrating in the pub, toasting his success with Lawrence and all his crew.

I had achieved nothing. Instead, I had wasted months of my life and my mental health had declined further. After nearly two years, I'd reached a dead end. There was nothing left to appeal in terms of a criminal conviction.

The guards confirmed my only alternative now was a civil claim. I dismissed that option immediately. Why would any solicitor believe me when the DPP hadn't? I didn't know if I had the energy to go on, anyway, and I wasn't sure what a civil case entailed or how I would go about it.

But a painful realisation was slowly dawning: McGregor was about to get away with this. Everyone would say I'd lied. I had to do something. I didn't know where to start. But I couldn't go on like this – a living mess, by day overwhelmed by fear and anxiety and by night lost in nightmares, fleeing from my attacker down dark, empty streets.

16.

Legal Action

After a while, the phone calls blurred together. I would dial the number, wait until the automated greeting ended, then repeat the same rehearsed words to yet another receptionist. *My name is Nikita. I'm a victim of sexual assault. I'm looking to take up a civil case …*

The response was always the same. The voices on the other end would shift, suddenly alert when I mentioned the assailant was a sports star.

Who is this sports star?

I'd feel myself stiffen. 'I'd rather discuss that in person. Could I make an appointment to speak with someone?'

But the people at the end of the phone persisted. They wanted the name first, wanted to know who it was before deciding whether to help me. I'd ended each call the same way: 'I'll get back to you.'

After the DPP's second refusal to prosecute McGregor, when a civil case became the only option, I was still doubtful. Why would a solicitor agree to take on the case when the DPP hadn't? My mam encouraged me down this path because she recognised what I couldn't see in myself.

'It's going to be impossible for you to just put this behind you, Nikita,' she said. 'You're going to see this man on TV. You're going to see him in the papers. You live in the Dublin 12 area, so he's going to be in your face for the rest of your life. You're the type of person who fights for what's right. Even if you try to forget, this will eat you up inside.'

Her words resonated deeply. She was right. How would I ever put this behind me? Every time I thought about McGregor getting away with it, I felt more anger than fear. The thought that he'd never be held accountable was unbearable.

I decided there was no harm in looking into it, talking to a solicitor and seeing what a civil case entailed. I opened my phone and typed into Google: 'solicitors', 'sexual assault victims', 'civil cases'. I rang several solicitors, but no one would see me without explaining all the details over the phone. I needed to feel trust. I needed to know that they believed me. I couldn't do that over the phone.

Coleman Legal LLP appeared among the search results. I clicked through to the website. *Multi-party, personal injury, medical negligence* … and there it was: *sexual abuse.*

Reading their website, they appeared to have had years of experience helping people like me. I dialled the number. The woman who answered had a soft and welcoming voice that made me feel at ease. I delivered my rehearsed speech once more, bracing myself for the inevitable question about the identity of my assailant.

Instead, the woman said, 'Yeah, no problem at all. I'll book you in with our managing partner, Dave Coleman. It'll be in Dave's private office – very safe, very quiet and you both can have a chat.'

I felt a small light of hope ignite inside me. *Maybe this will be okay. These people seem different.*

The woman – who I'd later learn was Clodagh – scheduled an appointment for a few days later, near the end of 2020.

When the day arrived, my mam drove me into town and parked around the corner while I went in alone. Coleman Legal LLP was on Talbot Street in the heart of the city, within sight of The Spire on O'Connell Street. As I climbed the stairs to Dave Coleman's office, my heart thumped from fear rather than exertion.

The office occupied a penthouse-level space, with windows overlooking city rooftops. A silver-haired man with a kind presence, Dave greeted me with his easy smile when I entered. His handshake seemed firm, steady and warm. I saw family photos sitting in frames on his desk. Everything about the place told me I was safe there.

He gestured to a chair, and an assistant sat nearby, pen and pad poised to take notes. His voice was measured and professional.

'Go ahead and tell us your story,' he said. 'You don't have to tell us who it is yet. Just tell us what happened, and we'll let you know if we can help.'

The last time I had told this story had been nearly two years earlier, in the Sandyford interview suite, with Detectives Ger White and Peter Woods from Dundrum Garda Station.

The words came slowly at first. Soon after starting, the tears started and wouldn't stop. I had wanted to keep it professional and maintain my composure, but I couldn't. This man in a suit actually listened. He asked a few questions but mostly encouraged me to talk. When I finished, he was resolved.

'We can help you,' he said.

Four words, but the relief was overwhelming. I suddenly realised that I'd been carrying this weight alone for a long time. Someone in authority, in law, was going to help me at last. Only then did Dave ask who it was who assaulted me. I had no hesitation telling him. I knew my story wouldn't leave this space except through proper legal channels.

The cost of this legal action hadn't even entered my mind. I wanted justice, to make McGregor accountable. Gardaí had told me a civil action was possible, and I'd acted on that information without considering the cost. But Dave explained the arrangement: no-win, no-fee, and they would work with me to win this case.

The conversation lasted about an hour. He asked a few more questions – had McGregor tried to contact me? Were there any attempts at communication?

I mentioned a registered letter I'd missed. I'd received an An Post notification about it. I had been feeling unwell at the time and found it hard to summon the courage even to leave the house. By the time I got to the post office in Crumlin Village, they said it had already been returned to the sender.

I had no idea who would have sent me a registered letter. It was only later that I wondered if it had been a legal letter from McGregor's solicitors. But the registered letter will now remain a mystery.

When the meeting concluded, he walked me out of the building and insisted on escorting me back to Mam's car, where he shook her hand and introduced himself. That simple gesture impressed me even more. For the first time in months, I felt real hope that something might come of this; that I would have a day in court and make that man accountable.

Dave set the legal process in motion, and it was established that the case would need to go to the High Court. As soon as my legal team officially registered the case, the media seized on it. Almost immediately, the headlines appeared. My name and his remained protected, but the story of a civil action taken against a sports star and allegations of sexual assault made the news.

I felt a familiar weight descend. Every mention in the

newspaper or on social media left me feeling exposed all over again.

As news of the civil case broke, friends and family applauded me. 'Well done for staying strong and not letting him get away with it,' they said. 'You're amazing to take him on, so brave.'

The most frequent adjectives people used were 'brave' and 'strong' to describe my actions. I often blinked in surprise, hearing them. The words I would have used were 'sick', 'fragile', 'broken' and 'hanging onto my sanity by my fingernails'. My sense of self was still shattered.

I never felt strong, even while doing things that required strength. I now know that finding the right legal team, walking into that office to initiate a case and speaking to Dave required strength. But, at the time, I wasn't yet able to acknowledge my own strength. I felt nothing but fear and vulnerability.

17.

Lockdown

On nights Gary stayed over, he watched my drinking increasing and it troubled him. 'This isn't the answer,' he'd say, sitting acoss from me, searching my face for some flicker of recognition. 'This won't make you feel better. Can't you see that?'

Even love couldn't get between me and my devoted companion, wine. What made it worse was that 2021 began with the most severe and extended lockdown. Schools closed. Businesses shuttered. The city emptied. The courts closed, and my civil case stalled along with everything else as the entire world seemed to stand still.

I already felt isolated, and the pandemic lockdown deepened my loneliness. Everything was closed outside, and the world had sealed itself shut. My world seemed claustrophobic and small, just Gary, Mam and me – and Freya for part of the week, when she wasn't with her dad.

Hi Ciara. Long time, no see. Call me for a catch-up!

The catch-ups never happened. The circle of friends I had before the attack had dwindled as my dependence on alcohol soared. When the first lockdown came, friends gathered at my place with their drinks. But those nights soon stopped. I knew the reason: I had changed. I became messy. I shed too many tears. Anger surfaced without warning. My edges sharpened, and my mood hardened, making me difficult to be around. Friends couldn't handle it. They couldn't handle me. The mixture of alcohol and trauma was not a good combination. It brought me to dark places.

If the situation had been reversed, and this had happened to one of them, I would have stayed. That's what I told myself, at least – that I would have stood by any friend who was drowning. But I know that I couldn't have been easy to handle – and in the end, maybe it was for the best.

By the second year of the Covid-19 pandemic, my circle was a small, tight-knit group of people I trusted completely, and they remain with me today. I wouldn't change that for anything.

By early 2021, Mam was struggling too. She wasn't sleeping well, didn't call as much and often didn't pick up my calls. With schools closed, Freya was at home some weekdays, too. There were mornings when I could barely muster the energy to shower, let alone homeschool my daughter.

I had hoped Mam would help, but she hadn't been up to it, especially since Christmas. Yet when she ended up in St James's Hospital due to stress at the end of January 2021, it took me by surprise. I hadn't recognised the decline in her mental health. I had been drowning for a long time and had let my mother dive in to rescue me far too often. The water had been rising over both our heads, and I couldn't see it.

For the first four or five months of our relationship, Gary and I existed in the spaces during Freya's visits to her father. Our worlds remained separate. By the end of 2020, that needed to change. We gathered his two sisters, my mother and Freya in my living room one evening. My hands shook slightly as I poured the wine, feeling the tension of families meeting for the first time.

Freya, nine years old and wary, watched Gary from across the room for half an hour. Then she crossed the room and sat beside him. She fell in love with Gary as quickly as I did.

I loved being with Gary – the ease of it, the laughter, even the shared silences were cosy. But I also craved the security his presence brought. The assault had left something permanent, a fear that never faded. When he was there, the house felt safer. I felt safer.

Gary did his best to nudge me away from the bottle of wine chilling in the fridge at night and, some days, his frustration broke through. I'd make promises in the bright hours of morning, declarations that today would be different, that this was the day I'd turn over a new leaf. Then evening would arrive, and with it, he'd see my hand reaching for the comforting bottle.

'You said you wouldn't tonight.'

His disappointment cut me deeper than anger ever could. I'd

sigh and tell him I'd be awake all night if I didn't have even a couple of glasses. I told myself that alcohol was the only thing that made me relax and let me fall asleep. Yet, I happily gave up the evening glasses of wine whe we decided to try for a baby. Soon after, I discovered I was pregnant. Gary and I were ecstatic. He called his family immediately. I told my mother. We never anticipated a problem, but five weeks later I miscarried. It was devastating.

We tried again. And lost again. The second time, we had braced ourselves and tried to prepare. It broke our hearts anyway. The doctors assured us we were healthy and talked about chronic stress, about how emotional trauma and post-traumatic stress disorder (PTSD) affect the body.

We kept trying, still hoping to have a much-wanted baby in our arms. My life felt so steeped in stress and anxiety that I wondered if a child would ever happen.

Then came the news that McGregor was buying my local pub.

The Black Forge Inn had been my corner of the world as a young adult. I'd been going there since my late teens – before Freya was born, before I met Ste, before any of this. The bar was around the corner from my house.

I'd long stopped going. I couldn't bear the weight of eyes on me when I entered the place. *There's that one, Nikita. The girl accusing McGregor.* Not everyone knew, but enough did. So I'd retreated, pulled myself away.

But when McGregor officially launched the pub in July 2021, as Covid restrictions lifted, it felt like another blow. He was back, woven permanently into the fabric of my neighbourhood again. It was a nightmare. This proximity hit like a wave, sweeping away months of progress – small victories I'd made in confidence and mental health were knocked back in an instant. Thoughts of him being nearby made my skin crawl.

I'd always carried the fear deep in my chest that it wasn't over, and I had told the guards about my concern for my safety. Yet what could they do? They couldn't offer a constant presence outside my door.

'You wouldn't want that, anyway,' they said, as if they knew my mind better than I did. So I poured another glass of wine and waited for the dullness that would pass for peace. Alcohol was my anaesthetic. I was numbing the fear and pain.

But Gary was slowly getting through to me. Now I didn't instinctively reach for a bottle every night. Sleep still didn't come easily, but some nights were more manageable than others.

The problem remained that I couldn't feel comfortable in my own home. I felt like an outsider in Drimnagh now, peeking out behind the blinds at a scary world I didn't belong in. My house on Errigal Road had become more of a hiding place than a home. Fear never left. The neighbourhood I'd grown up in felt sinister now, and I felt exposed. But I had nowhere else to go.

18.

Mediation

The call came in the New Year of 2021. My solicitor explained that before the civil case could proceed to trial, we were required to attempt mediation. He explained that it was a confidential process in which both parties used a mediator to help resolve the dispute. The courts preferred that both parties engage in settlement efforts outside of trial, if possible.

I didn't know what to expect of the process and was full of nerves. But Dave assured me that even if McGregor were attending, I probably wouldn't see him. The mediation was held in separate rooms near the Four Courts.

By then, I had learnt the key differences between criminal and civil cases. A criminal case is brought by State prosecutors and An Garda Síochána against the defendant. The purpose of a criminal case is to punish offenders and to protect society.

A civil case is between a plaintiff (me) and a defendant (McGregor). The purpose of a civil case is to resolve a dispute and compensate the injured party. For me, it was always about justice and vindication. If I couldn't have McGregor jailed, I wanted him held accountable, shamed, and the damage he did to me acknowledged. I wanted everyone to know the person Conor McGregor was.

My legal team – four or five people, including Dave – sat in one room with me. McGregor's legal team occupied their own room down the hall.

It was only at the mediation that I properly appreciated that the central aspect of this approach to 'resolving' the case was a compensatory settlement and an exchange of demands – all conducted within a confidential bubble.

I hadn't discussed a compensation amount with Dave at that time. Not once throughout the entire process were specific figures mentioned. I'd seen figures published in the newspapers that my legal team were purportedly suing for. But these vast numbers were a fantasy. Dave knew it was never about money for me and that the financial aspect of the civil case made me uncomfortable from the very start.

He assured me that this mediation was the standard procedure before commencing High Court proceedings and that the courts strongly encouraged all parties to attend. But to find myself involved in negotiating a financial settlement that day made me very uneasy.

My barrister, Siún, shuttled between our room and that of the mediator's. She'd carry an offer for a settlement or some comment. Then she'd leave again, negotiate and come back with a different number and other demands.

Tears pricked my eyes. Although I understood this was the process, and that the professionals around me were doing their job, as a victim of sexual assault, it felt wrong. No price could be put on my trauma.

I sat in the middle of it all, shivering despite the warmth of the room. The process is built on strict confidentiality, so I can't share specifics, but the whole situation made my blood boil. I felt like a commodity in a deal designed to silence me and make me go away. The entire experience felt dehumanising.

One of my legal team, Geraldine, asked if I'd like to go for a walk. She could see I was feeling overwhelmed. I left the room in relief, walking around the block to steady my breathing. I felt sick.

By the time I returned, Dave had reached his limit too. He grabbed my files from the table and turned to me.

'We're not doing this anymore. I'm not putting you through this. We've tried mediation. It's over.'

We got up and left the building. The mediation was a farce,

but it was done, and I was glad. I never wanted any secrecy or deals done behind closed doors. I wanted justice. I wanted my day in a courtroom to tell the world what Conor McGregor had done. I wanted to speak out. The problem was that I still didn't know if I had the courage to do that.

19.

Home Invasion

Friday, 14 June 2024

A sound blasted through the house as loud as a gunshot. My eyes snapped open to darkness, my heart hammering. Gary leapt from the bed. I'd never seen anyone move like that. One moment he was beside me – the next outside our bedroom at the landing railings, his silhouette black against the dim light from downstairs. His voice cut through the silence as I knelt on the bed, blinking, confused, terrified.

'GET THE FUCK OUT OF THIS HOUSE! GET OUT NOW!'

I stared at Gary's bare back, my mind struggling to catch up. His words made no sense. '*Get out?' Who was he roaring at?*

Then I knew. As Gary reversed into the bedroom, three black-clad figures in balaclavas climbed the stairs, watching us, their backs pressed against the wall, moving sideways, slow as a nightmare. Only the whites of their eyes were visible in the darkness. They weren't rushing. They weren't sneaking. They had forced open the front door and were advancing towards us with the deliberate pace of men who knew we had no way out.

My burning anxiety now gave to a level of terror I never thought possible.

Only hours earlier, I'd thought my day couldn't get any worse. My morning had begun in a waiting room in town, my stomach in knots, preparing to meet a psychiatrist whom McGregor's legal team had hired.

Another psychiatrist, Dr Ann Leader, had already diagnosed me with PTSD. Her area of expertise was sexual abuse victims, and she had examined me and prepared reports for my legal team. McGregor's team wanted its own psychiatric assessment.

I didn't know what I was facing, and I was afraid.

'Do I have to do this?' I pleaded with one of my legal team, Diane.

'Yes, you need to do this,' she said.

I took a deep breath and resolved to go. Whatever the defence's legal team threw at me at their client's bidding, I would comply. The years since Covid had sharpened something in me. I'd grown stronger, steadier. My resolve to face McGregor in the courtroom had hardened. I still trembled at the thought of a trial and had sleepless nights every time I spoke to my solicitors about it, but I was determined to continue nonetheless.

I'd walked into the city centre offices of the consultant psychiatrist shaking, braced for hostility. I felt sure that he'd write a report saying I was lying. But when I sat across from him, his first words were: 'I'm just doing my job. It doesn't mean I believe or disbelieve you. I just have to do my job.' That helped a little.

I had to tell him every detail of the assault. Halfway through, the feeling of being back in the moment overwhelmed me, and panic hit, leaving me struggling to breathe. His reaction was swift and kind, and he waited to settle my nerves.

I don't know what the psychiatrist wrote in his report, but I doubt it was helpful to McGregor's team, as they never called him as a witness.

When I left his office, Gary was waiting for me. I wrapped my arms around him, still shaking, and he held and reassured me. We went to a pub nearby to eat, but I couldn't taste anything. The session had triggered me, and everything I'd tried to put behind me resurfaced. We drove home in virtual silence.

The afternoon passed in a haze. Mam collected Freya from school. Gary and I settled in for the day with her, trying to find a sense of normal. Despite my stress from the psychiatrist's visit, these days I didn't take as long to steady and I knew I would bounce back soon enough.

The civil case against McGregor had been scheduled to begin a month earlier, in May, but his legal team had asked for a postponement. They claimed the trial would clash with his preparation for an MMA fight in Las Vegas in June. The judge granted their motion to delay the trial and rescheduled it for November instead.

I was gutted. I didn't want the trial hanging over my head for another six months. As it happened, the delay was unnecessary because McGregor cancelled the fight, claiming he'd sustained a broken toe in training.

After the psychiatrist's visit, I'd gone to bed early, around eight or nine. Freya went to bed around ten, and Gary came up later.

Then, at around 3 a.m., came the unearthly bang – my front door being broken down – and the three men in balaclavas ascending my stairs, cornering us. Gary retreated slowly into the bedroom, wearing only boxer shorts, still roaring at them to get out. I was on my knees on the bed in pyjamas, frozen. The men reached the landing outside the bedroom door, standing there in a line, a wall of black.

At that moment, one thought exploded through my paralysis: *Freya.*

'Please!' I jumped off the bed; my voice came out loud, raw and desperate. 'Please, my daughter's in the other room. She's just a little girl. Please, I'm begging you.'

I moved toward them without thinking, leaving Gary behind me, my hands reaching out in supplication, screaming, 'Please, my little girl! She's only a little girl. Please!' All thoughts of my own safety or even Gary's were gone.

I had edged my way to my bedroom door. Freya's bedroom door was right next to mine, right beside them.

'SHUT THE FUCK UP!' one intruder roared just as Freya opened her door. She looked out, her twelve-year-old face pale in the darkness. She saw the men, and our eyes met for one terrible second before she slammed shut the door again. That glimpse of terror nearly killed me.

'Please, she's just a little girl—'

'SHUT THE FUCK UP! GET THE FUCK IN THERE!'

The intruders' eyes were all fixed on Gary. He was a threat that they needed to take care of. The guy nearest me shoved me into Freya's door. I wrenched it open, stumbled in and slammed it shut behind me, throwing my weight against it. I pulled Freya into my arms and pressed my hands over her ears, as if I could obliterate what was happening in the next room.

Thumping. Struggling. Shouts. The sounds of bodies hitting walls and the floor. Three men against one. I held Freya tighter, my whole body shaking. They were going to kill him. I knew they were going to kill Gary, and there was nothing I could do but protect my daughter for as long as I could. Until help came. This was all happening so fast. I had no plan except to keep Freya alive until help came.

The sounds grew louder, more violent. I felt sure they were murdering him. Then, impossibly, the row began to move away from us, toward the stairs. Gary was somehow forcing them back. How he managed it, I still don't know. He was fighting and kicking, and they were moving down the stairs. I could hear them descending, the chaos moving downward, and then—

'NIKITA, RING THE GUARDS! RING THE GUARDS NOW!'

His voice. I could hardly believe he was still alive.

'Freya!' My hands fumbled towards her in the darkness. 'Your phone. Ring the police!'

I started pounding on the bedroom wall, the dividing wall between the neighbours and us, screaming at the top of my lungs.

'HELP! HELP US! HELP US!'

I ran to the bedroom window overlooking the back of the house, pounding the glass with my fists, pleading with someone, anyone, to help.

Freya stood in silence, the phone pressed to her ear, her young voice steady as she gave the emergency operator our address. So calm. Too calm. The shock had completely locked her down.

I heard more roars. Glass shattered somewhere below, and I went for the door.

'Mam, don't go downstairs!' Freya cried. 'Please don't go down.'

They were breaking the windows, the door, trying to get back in. More crashes, more breaking. Gary's voice rose again, strained with effort as he held the front door closed against them.

I pulled Freya close and opened the door. 'We're going to scream "The police are on their way." One, two, three … THE POLICE ARE ON THE WAY! THE POLICE ARE ON THE WAY!'

Our voices screamed through the house, through the broken windows, into the night. And then, cutting through everything, the men's response came from outside: 'YOU'RE NOTHING BUT A RAT. YOU'RE DEAD. WHEN WE SEE YOU NEXT TIME, YOU'RE DEAD.'

An engine roared to life, tyres squealed and then silence – the chaos, the fury, the smashing and crashing and screaming left with them.

'They're gone,' Gary called up, his voice hoarse.

I bolted from the room, flew down the stairs with Freya crying, 'Mam don't leave me!' ringing in my ears. My instinct was to run for help before they came back.

I ran to my neighbour next door to the left of me, but I couldn't get her garden gate open; my hands were shaking too badly. I ran across the road to my other neighbour's house. She opened the door straight away, and I fell into her hallway, onto the floor, sobbing, the words tumbling out incoherently.

I ran back to my house, and other neighbours were arriving. The guards were arriving now too. I collapsed onto my couch, and someone sat beside me, a hand on my shoulder. I remember voices murmuring comfort, but I couldn't hear through my own crying. Freya was removed from the chaos and taken to a friend's house, where her dad collected her. Someone checked on our little dog Daisy, who had been in the bedroom too. She was stone-deaf, thank God, and slept through the entire attack.

All the time, I remember Gary talking to a guard, his eyes scanning the room and watching me. Still on alert; still protecting us. I could see he was in pain, in shock. He had hurriedly dressed when the intruders fled, but when he lifted his shirt to investigate the source of a nagging pain, he realised they had stabbed him in the stomach.

We hadn't realised the intruders had been brandishing a knife. He was stabbed multiple times and had scratches and other injuries on his legs and arms. But the deepest puncture wound was in his stomach.

I had been refusing an ambulance, but now we had no option. By the time we reached the hospital, my right hand had swollen grotesquely, black and blue down the outer side, from my knuckles to my wrist. The hospital at first thought I'd broken bones in my hand while I'd battered the neighbours' doors and windows, screaming for help.

It took nine or ten stitches to close Gary's stomach wound. We sat together in the harsh hospital light, holding hands, barely speaking. What was there to say? Gary had come close to being murdered in my home. Even after he had fought the intruders down the stairs and slammed the door shut on them, they returned with another weapon.

We know they took something from the boot – a baseball bat or a crowbar – to smash the double-glazed front windows and the door. They had made a second attempt to attack us.

To this day, I believe the intruders were taken by surprise when they found Gary in the house. They had probably heard that Ste had moved out and came expecting to find me alone or with my child, so they only brought one weapon between them. They did not attempt to rob the house. Gary and I both believed those men had invaded my house to intimidate me – or worse. We also feared that this was only the beginning.

The hospital released us near noon that day. My friend Emma collected us and drove us home. When we pulled up, I saw my mam in the front garden, sweeping up glass from the broken windows. She looked small, older somehow, moving methodically back and forth, doing her best to clean up the devastation.

The attackers had shattered all three double-glazed windows at the front of the house. They had punched or yanked out the front door's glass panel on the upper half of the door. It lay shattered on my driveway. Someone had put boards across the openings, like temporary patches on vicious wounds gouged into the home.

The intruders had used a knife to get into the door lock before kicking it in. 'Popping the lock', the police said. The blade was found discarded in the hall, its tip broken. It had still been sharp enough to penetrate Gary, but God knows how bad it could have been if the tip hadn't broken off in the lock.

I had to force myself to step inside the house. I only went in long enough to grab the photographs from the wall: baby pictures of Freya, photos of my late nanny, pictures of my mam and of me as a child. My hands moved automatically, taking down frame after frame. I wasn't coming back. I knew that with absolute certainty. This house was finished for me.

A detective arrived. He took Gary's statement first, then mine. I told him Freya wasn't to be questioned. She was too young and already traumatised. The detective agreed without argument.

I explained about the upcoming trial as the detective's face remained professionally neutral.

'Seriously, would you live here? Do you think it's safe for us to come back here?' I asked him.

He looked at me for a long moment. 'I don't want to tell you it's safe and then have something like this happen again. I can't give you a yes or no.'

I heard what he didn't say: *Run. We can't protect you.*

Gary's cousin Janice arrived that evening. 'You're coming to live with me. That's it. You're not staying here.'

We didn't argue. We left that house that day, and we never lived in Drimnagh again.

20.

Collapse

I woke up feeling *wrong*. My body felt disconnected from me, heavy and uncooperative. When Freya arrived, I forced myself out of bed but couldn't manage anything more than sitting in my pyjamas.

'I'm sorry, I'm not great today, Freya,' I said.

The words came out flat.

'I have anxiety. I'm having a bad day.'

It was almost a month after the home invasion, and I was far from alright. Freya knew. Everyone knew.

'It's okay, Mam. Don't worry.'

Overnight, Gary and I had become refugees in the spare bedroom of his cousin Janice's apartment. When Freya arrived to stay twice a week, she took our bed, and we slept on an air mattress in the sitting room. For more than a year, that air mattress became our second home.

The days that followed the invasion had blurred together in

a haze of panic attacks and sleepless nights. My mental health that I had been so carefully reconstructing now fell apart at the seams. I was back where I started years earlier. If anything, I was worse. I couldn't eat. I vomited so violently that Janice had to help me off the bathroom floor. I couldn't see a future beyond the fear.

Every night, I was convinced they were coming back, that they'd find us, that they'd finish what they'd started. Gary's mental health was shattered too, and he was sleeping with a hammer beside the bed. Gary is the strongest person I know, but it was weeks before he felt well enough to return to work.

Days after the attack, Janice and my mam brought me to see my GP. I still couldn't even dress myself, so I arrived in my pyjamas and had another panic attack at the surgery. The GP prescribed me olanzapine, which was a more potent drug than the sertraline he had increased in dosage after McGregor's assault. It's used to ease manic episodes or severe racing thoughts.

Meanwhile, the guards had not found a trace of the intruders. They'd smashed their way into my house with balaclavas and a knife, stabbed my partner, terrorised my daughter and called us rats before vowing to kill us. And they'd vanished into the night, back under whatever rock they had crawled out from. Their accents told us they were local, but that was all we knew.

From the neighbours' Ring video doorbell, the guards could see one man emerging from their car and flicking a cigarette butt onto the ground. The gardaí had hoped to get DNA that would trace him, but the results came back inconclusive. They traced the car to a certain area, then lost it. The case went cold.

A week after the attack, my solicitors Dave and Diane asked us to come to their offices. Leaving the apartment felt impossible – the road outside was too exposed – but I forced myself out. I was convinced they were planning to quit the civil case. Of course they were. Who would want to be involved after what happened to Gary and me?

I felt a fraction better when Diane met us with her magnificent smile, hugs and a big bouquet of cheerful flowers. We went to a hotel around the corner for a private chat, and I was reassured that they just wanted to check in with us to make sure we were okay. I didn't tell them I couldn't imagine surviving another five months until the trial. Or having the strength left to face Conor McGregor in court.

Now, nearly four weeks on from the invasion, I sat on the sofa on a Saturday morning, willing myself to appear normal for Freya's sake. She wasn't blind. I had lost weight, my skin was pasty and my hands constantly trembled. I hated that Freya was seeing me like this.

The panic attack had arrived without warning. One moment, I was gazing at the television; the next, a wave of pure terror crashed over me.

'This is bad.'

My voice came out strangled as I reached for Gary.

'Hey, relax, love,' he said, hugging me. 'You'll be all right.'

'Get me sugar,' I whispered as the room spun. 'Just get me sugar.'

I crammed sweets into my mouth to raise my blood sugar. I bit into an apple because chewing can lower cortisol levels. I peeled oranges and held them to my nose. I'd been told the scent could distract the brain from panic. I staggered to the sink to splash cold water on my face and arms. I tried several recommended grounding techniques to shut down a panic attack. Nothing was working.

My breathing came in short gasps. My body shook violently, my teeth chattering so hard they audibly clicked. My heart pounded: boom, boom, boom. Sweat soaked through my clothes while my skin went ice-cold. I was dying. I knew it. My head grew too heavy to lift, and I curled over on the couch, the floor heaving below me.

Gary saw my eyes rolling, my tremors and sweat. He looked panicked.

'Please, please help me, Gary. I'm begging you,' I cried, as my vision narrowed. 'I'm going to die here.'

Freya was on her feet, frightened.

'Ring my mam an ambulance!' she screamed. 'She needs an ambulance!'

It felt like a heart attack – I felt numbness in my arm and pressure crushing my chest. My pulse was racing toward something catastrophic.

Gary already had his phone out.

I've had asthma all my life. Emergency services told Gary to give me my inhaler to help me breathe until they got there. He was waiting outside when the paramedics arrived. He gave them the entire story – the court case, the home invasion four weeks ago, my deteriorating mental health and the medication I was taking – as he led them inside.

They took a few vitals and said I needed to go with them to the hospital.

'No!' I pulled back. I wanted them to fix me in Janice's apartment. I couldn't go outside. 'Please help me here. I'll go to see my GP on Monday.'

Maybe I would. I was almost agoraphobic by then, terrified to go outside.

The paramedics were adamant that my heart rate was too high, and I needed treatment at the hospital. But the ambulance itself had become another trauma, a place associated with the worst times of my life. I refused to go. I had expected the paramedics to come, do something and leave. I hadn't thought that they'd want to take me away.

But my body was telling me everything I needed to know: the shaking, the breathlessness, the teeth clenched so tight that my jaw ached. It was an emergency. I needed help.

Gary climbed into the ambulance with me. Freya fought to go too, but she had already seen too much. Janice's daughter and her boyfriend arrived to mind her.

Machines beeped as they attached the monitors. My heart rate was so furious and fast that the beeping sound itself became another terror.

'I'm dying … I'm dying.'

'You're not dying, Nikita. It feels like it, but you're having a panic attack.'

They explained my heart was racing beyond my body's ability to slow it down on its own. My body was running its own marathon, fleeing from invisible terrors.

The ambulance drove me to Beaumont Hospital and brought me straight through to a treatment area. A nurse began blood tests, asking questions and monitoring my heart. My heart rate refused to drop. Time passed in a blur of waiting, sitting and waiting among other patients. The doctor who assessed me was understanding and caring.

'Your heart is still racing. This is your body's "fight or flight" response, and we need to help your nervous system settle down.'

She said she would try a medication designed to help quiet the physical symptoms I was feeling.

'It will help your muscles relax and bring your heart rate back to a normal rhythm so you can feel more like yourself.'

'Give it to me now. Just give it to me,' I begged.

The tablet did nothing. My heart rate stayed elevated. I got up repeatedly to go to the toilets, where I dry-heaved and splashed water over myself. When I wasn't hyperventilating I took sips of water, my hands shaking. My body was in shock and something fundamental was misfiring.

Is the doctor wrong? Maybe this isn't a panic attack, and I really am dying.

'Gary, am I okay?' I grabbed his arm. 'Am I okay?'

'You're okay, Nikita. You're all right.'

I asked again and again. He kept answering, kept reassuring.

An hour later, Gary pleaded with the doctor for more medication for me. The second dose took an hour to work, but the grip of panic finally loosened. My heart rate reduced and my body relaxed.

The doctor diagnosed mental exhaustion and a severe panic attack. She warned that if it happened again, I had to come straight back to lower my heart rate. The hospital sent a letter to my GP. He increased my olanzapine dosage. One month after the home invasion, my body had finally broken down under the stress of it all.

I crashed after the hospital that day. Everything ached. My muscles screamed from hours of trembling. My jaw throbbed from clenching my teeth. I was utterly spent. That night, for the first time since the home invasion, I slept the deep, heavy sleep of complete exhaustion.

Gary watched me spend days crying, unable to leave the house. I couldn't even do therapy. I couldn't talk to anyone. Trying to form the words made me spiral into another panic attack. He had watched my life remain in suspended animation in the years since I had given the guards my statement.

I knew his life was on hold, too. He stuck around when many others would have fled. He wanted me to be free of this as much as I did. But neither of us could breathe easily again until this trial was over. And now, finally, it was within our sights.

21.

Trial Day

Day 1: Tuesday, 5 November 2024

We waited in a private consultation room in the Four Courts, minutes away from the courtroom. My throat was dry, my heart hammering. Gary kept squeezing my hand, reminding me that he was holding on to me.

The trial was about to begin at last. I had waited six long years for this day, yet I felt sick. I fought the impulse to bolt and flee from the place with long, deep breaths.

One of the other solicitors arrived at the door. 'He's here,' they said.

The words triggered a dark feeling inside me, like I was possessed by something cold and horrible. A layer of sweat broke across my skin. I couldn't breathe. My hands began to shake. *Oh, God, no, no.* I was descending into another panic attack.

He's here.

In the weeks before the trial, I met with Susan and Diane from my legal team for a pre-trial walkthrough of Courtroom 24 in the High Court. The idea was to reduce my anxiety by showing me where I'd sit and where the judge and jury would be. The women would show me the set-up and familiarise me with the room.

Courtroom 24 is part of the Four Courts complex, with its own separate entrance on Chancery Place. They walked me through the double doors, through the security scanners and down the corridor. But as soon as I stepped through the courtroom door, my breath caught. The room was small, far smaller than I'd imagined.

The only courtrooms I'd seen before were American ones on my television screen. I'd envisaged a big, spacious room with high ceilings, bright lights and row after row of polished, modern oak seats and benches. This was nothing like that.

I stood in an old-fashioned, dark-wood-panelled courtroom with a public gallery looming heavily above it. The place felt tight and claustrophobic and the gallery felt so close that I could imagine dozens of faces peering down at me.

Diane gestured around the space and walked me through the geography of the ordeal to come.

'The jury is on your left-hand side. You'll sit there, close to the jury.'

The room contained only three long wooden benches,

like pews, with a few rows of seats behind them. My place would be on the left-hand side of the third bench in the courtroom.

'The media will be here on the right-hand side of the judge.'

I stood frozen, taking it in. The jury and media seats, which were on opposite sides of the room, seemed almost within arm's reach. The benches in between looked solid, hard and unforgiving.

'It feels like a church,' I said. 'Everything reminds me of the inside of a church.'

Diane's hand swept around to show me where McGregor would sit. He would be in the row behind me throughout the trial. I stared at the space between where I would sit and where he would be. No distance at all – just a few feet.

'Why am I that close to him?' The words came out before I could stop them. I couldn't understand why they allowed an accused man to sit so close to his victim. But the space in the court was confined, so that was the way it was.

I left the courtroom feeling more unnerved than ever. Diane offered to bring me back again so I could grow accustomed to the space. I declined. I'd seen enough. The next time I entered that room, it would be for real.

In the weeks running up to the trial, I had also met with Diane at her office on Saturdays. She advised me to review statements – mine, McGregor's and Lawrence's. She told me to take notes and refresh my memory.

One day, she sat me down in the office. She had the CCTV footage taken on 9 December 2018 at The Beacon Hotel. The detectives had only shown me stills when they had questioned me. A criminal trial had loomed then, and being a witness to my own assault, they couldn't let me see the CCTV.

Now the video was in my solicitors' hands. They had held it back from me as long as possible, knowing that it would be painful to watch. And I'd resisted watching it. Seeing myself in a normal wedding video was unbearable enough. I didn't want to watch myself drunk, or see myself with McGregor and James Lawrence again. I didn't need those painful reminders.

'There's no point because I can't remember, and I don't want to see myself like that.'

'Sorry, I know it's hard,' Diane said gently, 'but you have to watch it because you'll be facing the CCTV in court.'

So I'd watched. At times, I had to close my eyes. My stomach twisted as I saw myself being affectionate with James Lawrence, my arms around him. Pecking his cheek. The discomfort was physical. It hurt me to watch the video. I didn't recognise the person I saw. I watched a woman who was very drunk, stumbling and vulnerable. I searched the footage for memories, but they refused to surface.

The drunk girl falling around in the car park and in the lift was a stranger to me.

Diane did her best to help, but even if I asked, she couldn't practise or rehearse cross-examination with me – the kind I'd seen on American TV. Coaching and witness preparation is completely prohibited by law. I didn't feel ready for what was coming. After seeing the CCTV, I didn't think I ever would be.

Clíona, my support person from the Dublin Rape Crisis Centre, grasped my hands on the first morning. 'Look at me, Nikita, I'm going to hold your hand every step of the way,' she said. 'It won't be easy, but you're going to get through it.'

And she did. Every single day, walking in and out beside me, at my side throughout court proceedings. She remained anonymous even though her face appeared on the news broadcasts most days. Without Clíona, I couldn't have survived the ordeal.

The wait in the consultation room on the first morning was finally broken. 'It's time,' said the solicitor. And there we were, Gary and Clíona on either side of me, as we walked to the Chancery Place entrance, passing banks of cameras, and in towards Courtroom 24.

Outside, there was a throng of media. A few of them glanced at me as I walked past – just a flicker of eyes, nothing more – then looked away. That first morning, they didn't know me. I was nobody. Anonymous. The way I wanted to be.

Nevertheless, I felt myself tremble from head to toe as I walked up the concrete ramp to the courthouse entrance. At my first glimpse of Lawrence and then McGregor, I fell to pieces. I darted, then crawled up the stairs and cowered in the toilets for the next thirty minutes. I despaired, considered fleeing the Four Courts, and then somehow mustered the strength to continue.

I couldn't conceal my fear or control the visible shaking as Clíona led me to my seat on the left side of the third wooden bench. I clenched Gary's hand on one side, Clíona's on the other, every muscle rigid and shuddering. I didn't look left or right. I just sat on the bench, frozen, braced for an attack.

From that first moment entering the courtroom and for the remainder of that entire trial, fear haunted me. I felt threat all around: the danger that someone could lunge forward and kill me right there inside the courtroom; that someone would walk in off the street and shoot me. The feeling pervaded outside the courthouse too: would someone try to kill me on my way in or out of court? That courtroom was a pit of absolute terror from the start.

Senior and junior counsel filled both sides of the first two benches. McGregor's and Lawrence's counsel sat in the two rows immediately in front of me, occupying the left-hand side of both benches. My senior counsel, Ray Boland and John Gordon, sat on the front-row bench on the right-hand side, with their junior counsel, Siún Leonowicz, behind them in the second row.

Diane sat at a desk below the judge, facing my senior counsel as the instructing solicitor. On my right, sharing my bench, sat my solicitor Dave and his team – Paddy, Geraldine, Maria and

Susan. Behind me were several rows of chairs. James Lawrence was sitting directly behind me, so close I could almost feel him breathing down my neck. It was a disorienting and unpleasant arrangement.

I tried to create distance by sitting on the very edge of my bench, leaning forward and angling myself sideways. But he was right there – just at the corner of my vision. I couldn't twist to my right because McGregor and his dad, Tony, were sitting on the same row of chairs as Lawrence, but behind my legal team. McGregor was still only a matter of feet behind me. Anytime I glimpsed him, his expression seemed stone-cold. He looked straight ahead, chin tilted upward as if he were the only person in the room – or as if the room itself were beneath his contempt. I did my best to avoid seeing him. Every time I did, my stomach heaved.

The court registrar stood and called out clearly: 'All rise.' Everyone in the courtroom stood as Mr Justice Alexander Owens entered. The official announced: 'The High Court is now in session.'

Judge Owens wore the traditional curled horsehair wig and billowing black gown, with a wing collar with stiff white bands at the neck. He sat at the bench, elevated, the focus of the room. He had a reputation for being stern and, looking at him, I knew he wouldn't stand for any nonsense in his courtroom. He even described himself as 'a pedant and a stickler' during the trial.

To my right, I saw the rows of media occupying ground-level seats. The constant click-clack as they pecked away on their laptops filled the courtroom. The public gallery loomed above and behind me. The jury of eight women and four men had already been empanelled and sat in a raised box to my left, waiting.

My senior counsel, John Gordon, began by telling the jury that this case offered me a 'route to vindication'. He told them I was 'no angel and doesn't pretend to be an angel'. He said I was 'out partying hard'.

'She had lots to drink. Her spirit of choice is Bacardi. She also had some beer and she also had some cocaine. Prior to this, she was on medication [...] It is important that that background is known to you so you understand the entire mix of stimulants that were going through her system.'

He talked about the evidence they would see of my attempt to fight off McGregor.

'[...] this was some effort. You will see her hands and her wrists are black and blue. You will also see that on her left breast there is a scratch, a bloodied scratch. The reason for the bloodied scratch is because she was wearing a watch and she had her hands up in front of her trying to keep him off, and as he pressed down on her, she scratched her breast, a most unpleasant scratch ...'

My barrister also said my conduct after the alleged assault would seem 'extraordinary'.

'She didn't rush to dial 999. She didn't rush down the corridor to get somebody in the hotel. She was, of course, full of drugs, and she proceeded in what seems to have been a state of elation, shock maybe. We have all come across the concept of a delayed shock ...'

He explained I made no complaint against James Lawrence until I learnt months later that he claimed to have had sex with me twice on the night. But he said I had 'no recollection of such an event ever happening'.

'Contrivance? I don't know,' he said. 'It is for you to decide.'

He spoke about how I arrived home as 'a gibbering wreck'. And more evidence from the ambulance personnel showed that I was 'an absolute wreck – constantly weeping, shivering, in pain and unable to get comfortable'.

'In the face of this, Mr McGregor tells you this was a consensual encounter. That they were just having fun. And a bit of rough sex. That's his answer. What did I say about your common sense? [...] What he is saying to you is that she consented; she gave him licence to carry out what has to have been a really brutal assault on her body [...] so he says she woke up and asked him for more.'

I shifted in annoyance when he said the defence would also claim I told Lawrence that I enjoyed having sex with McGregor. I couldn't imagine any woman saying that to another man.

Mr Gordon also read out part of the defence's argument,

which said my compensation claim was 'tantamount to an attempt at extortion' and was 'false, malicious and patently maintained in bad faith'.

'That really puts it up to my client. She's a gold digger. She's a fraud,' Mr Gordon said.

I winced several times through my counsel's opening remarks, and that was one of them.

'The defence are alleging that Ms Hand is a gold digger,' he repeated.

The judge added: 'It is a try-on.'

'A try-on, exactly, and that this is all for monetary gain [... Yet] she didn't go to a solicitor until after the DPP had decided not to prosecute.'

Dr Daniel Kane, the gynaecologist who examined me in the Rotunda Hospital on 10 December 2018, was called as the first witness in the trial.

Reading from his report, he said, 'Nikita Hand said that there was kissing, vaginal penetration with ejaculation, that no condom was used. There was also oral penetration, that is penile oral penetration, and digital penetration of the vagina.'

He spent an entire nine minutes listing the 'multiple body injuries' he noted during his examination.

He noted an abrasion on the right side of my jaw, which had been bleeding. A purple bruise on the right of my neck 'that looked like a love bite'. On my right arm, he saw three purple bruises consistent with 'fingertip bruising', a bruise midway down my forearm and two separate purple bruises on my lower arm. He found purple bruising on the knuckles of my right hand, which was tender on examination. On my left arm, he saw a purple bruise, and on my upper arm, two separate bruises on the elbow joint. He noted an abrasion on the elbow with three separate, linear abrasions below this, and four separate bruises on my lower arm.

As the doctor continued listing my injuries, Gary had to wipe his eyes. He squeezed my hand in support but grew more emotional as the evidence continued.

He found a purple bruise on my right shoulder and a purple-blue bruise on the right side of my upper back. He noted 'extensive bruising' on my buttocks, with three separate bruises consistent with a handprint on my left buttock. He found purple bruising on my breasts and a 9 centimetre scratch on my left breast. He saw two separate purple bruises on the left flank of my abdomen; four separate purple bruises on the front of my right thigh. The doctor also noted two separate purple bruises on my right kneecap and bruising on my left thigh. He said four of my acrylic nails were missing.

Dr Kane told the court I was menstruating at the time, and I was very distressed about the tampon and anxious for its removal.

He explained how, sometimes, because of discomfort during these exams, a decision would be made to bring a patient into the operating theatre and to use a general anaesthetic. In this case, they agreed with me to remove the tampon from me without it.

'The tampon was wedged in the right side of the fornix [a furrow surrounding the cervix of the uterus] so it was up at the very, very top of the vagina,' he said. 'In order to be able to remove it, I used a thing that we use in gynaecology called a polyp forceps.'

Upon its removal, he observed that it was breaking apart. He did a digital exam and found a tear or an abrasion on the back wall of my vagina.

Dr Kane told the court that of the 340 forensic examinations that he had performed, this was the first and only time that he had ever encountered a retained tampon after sexual intercourse.

He summarised, saying significant injuries had been identified and that he would categorise them as moderate to severe.

His evidence contained private, intimate medical information, which no woman would want revealed in a public courtroom. I wanted it to end, but I also knew that when he finished his evidence, I would be up next as a witness. Panic clawed at me. *I can't do this.*

I rattled in my seat throughout as Gary and Clíona gripped my hands. But when the court called my name shortly after 3 p.m. on the first day of the trial, something in me shifted. A sudden burst of energy surged through me. Nanny's voice came into my mind as clear as if she was right beside me in the seat – *Go on, love. You* can *do this*. It gave me the strength that lifted me to my feet.

To get to the witness box, I had to exit my seat and walk behind my bench, passing Lawrence first and then McGregor. The hair on the back of my neck rose as I walked past McGregor, knowing he only had to lift his hand to touch me. I walked up to the witness box, swore an oath and shook as I poured myself a glass of water from the jug provided.

Every eye in that room was fixed on me. The judge. The jury. The media. The people in the public gallery glared down at me from the courtroom's heights. All of them were watching. I was sure they could hear my heart like a drumbeat through the room.

I could hardly bear the weight of the collective scrutiny. But I was there. I had made it into the witness box. And I knew the first part would be the easiest as Ray Boland, one of my counsel, led me through what happened, step by step.

Mr Boland asked me about the night of the salon Christmas party with my friends. He asked me to outline the messages I had exchanged with McGregor that night. He asked about the alcohol and cocaine. I answered truthfully.

I was asked if McGregor brought anything out of James Lawrence's house.

'Conor brought a bag of cocaine that he said was cocaine [...]

He gave me some cocaine and gave some to Danielle [...] I only remember me and Danielle doing cocaine. I don't remember seeing James or Conor doing it at all.'

He asked for details of our arrival at the hotel. I recalled being in the penthouse's sitting room and drinks being brought up.

We just got in. We were just kind of looking around, still having fun like laughing and joking, the mood was fine [...] I remember vodka, Bacardi and mixers. Full bottles of spirits and mixers and glasses. Large bottles.'

My heart started to beat heavier just as we reached the part where Conor and I were alone in the bedroom. The prospect of relating that part of Sunday, 9 December, to every stranger in the courtroom made my stomach turn.

'I remember being in the bedroom alone with Conor and I remember just standing beside the bed and he was standing here and he was coming onto me. He started to try kissing me and he was like rubbing my face. I knew what he was looking for so I turned around and said to him, "I don't feel comfortable, Conor, no, I know your girlfriend's family, I know of Dee, my partner is best friends with your partner's brother."'

I continued, the ball of anxiety in my throat growing bigger as we got closer to the part where McGregor raped me.

'I was trying to kind of talk him around, that I didn't want anything, you know, I didn't want to have sex or I wasn't there for anything like that. I was there to have a party and have a good time. Instead of making it really awkward, I tried to talk him around.'

'Okay, and what happened?' said my counsel.

'He just wasn't taking no for an answer and he then pinned me onto the bed, kept telling me to "relax, baby, relax" and rubbing my face.'

'And what happened then?'

'He pinned me right down to the bed [...] I remember just putting my arms up to keep him as far away from me as possible.'

'Were you both fully dressed still at this stage?'

'We were both fully dressed.'

At that point, the judge noted it was 4 p.m. and concluded the first day's proceedings.

When I left the building, I was still shaking, but this time, everyone knew what I looked like. Cameras followed me down the street, clicking in my face. It felt chaotic and invasive.

Clíona led Gary and me to our waiting taxi. Dave had arranged for the same driver, Paddy, to bring us to and from the Four Courts every day. As soon as the taxi pulled away from the courthouse, I exhaled. Relief flooded through me. *I'm out. I survived day one.*

We didn't go straight home. We were terrified someone would follow us and discover where we were staying. So Paddy dropped us off at a hotel near where Janice lived. Then Janice arrived to pick us up and drove us the rest of the way.

Back at Janice's apartment, I peeled off my suit, hung it carefully for the next day, threw my shirt in the wash and collapsed onto the couch in my pyjamas. I sat there, shaking my head, fury rising in me.

'I can't do this again tomorrow. I don't want to do this anymore.'

I was angry and frustrated. Why were McGregor and Lawrence within grabbing distance of me in the courtroom? Why did I have to walk past both of them on my way to the witness box? I was terrified at the prospect of further describing the worst thing that ever happened in my life with both of them in such close proximity.

I was discovering what rape victims endure when seeking justice. During the assault, I was violated by one man. But in that packed courtroom, I was about to be emotionally stripped before strangers. I felt vulnerable, exposed, with nowhere to hide.

22.

Rage

Day 2: Wednesday, 6 November 2024

'Now, where we left it yesterday, I think you said Mr McGregor had you pinned on the bed. Would you continue from there?'

My counsel addressed me in the witness box. He made it sound so simple. *Continue from there* … But to speak the words aloud meant going back into that room, back onto that bed, that weight crushing the air from my lungs. My heart pounded and my throat closed. I swallowed once, twice.

'You can speak into the microphone,' he said.

I tried to find the words that would lead me through without drowning in tears. The courtroom had gone deathly quiet, expectant.

'I'm trying. I'm sorry. I'm just getting a bit upset, I'm sorry …'

What is the truth of what happened to me in that bedroom with McGregor? I told the bare bones of it that morning in

Courtroom 24, as my barrister prompted me, his voice reaching me from somewhere far away. He asked questions that I knew he would, and yet at times I still couldn't force the words out. I replied in spurts punctuated by sobs and tearful requests for breaks, granted by the judge.

Years earlier, I had told what happened to detectives who later arranged my words into a tidy sequence of events: A was followed by B, then C happened. The silences, the sobbing and the parts where I couldn't breathe were sanitised from the typed black-and-white statements.

The real truth of what happened is buried deep inside me and comes back unbidden when I lie awake at night, or when I'm somewhere quiet, and my mind travels to places I never mean to go.

I'm standing near the foot of the ornate bed in the middle of the hotel room. The surrounding decor is bare, white, minimalist. McGregor is standing right in front of me and, with a shock, I recognise his intent. He's coming on to me, trying to kiss me. He's smirking as he moves forward, and my hands are raised to my collarbone, my palms pushing flat against his chest, holding him back, panicking a little inside.

I don't want any of this. I don't want him. But his eyes are fixed on me, leering. His flushed face, with its pronounced jaw, and his sweaty chest are pushing towards me. I'm not really afraid, though. Not at first. I'm mostly cringing inside, embarrassed.

Does he think I'm here for this? Have I done something to let him believe that? My mind is suddenly alert. How do I tell him he's got the wrong idea without offending him? I'm not attracted to him, not even a little. I admire him because he's from our area and has done well for himself. I'm attracted to the idea of Conor McGregor, the famous person, the celebrity, but not *him*.

I feel a small, cold sliver of shame. How do I explain that without looking shallow and foolish? How do I tell him I was flattered that someone famous responded to me on social media? Or that meeting him is a story to share with the girls back in the salon? In my head, I have already been imagining telling everyone: *Guess what? Danielle and I went partying with a celebrity after you went home …*

This was only ever intended as a laugh, but now that this man is up in my face and still pushing into my personal space, it doesn't feel funny anymore. He's stroking my face now.

'No, I don't feel comfortable, Conor,' I say. 'I know of Dee. I know her family.' I tell him that my boyfriend, Ste, is friends with Dee's brother.

I'm nervous, so I jabber. I want to slip away from this situation without causing a scene. I want to talk him around, be nice to him, be his friend. Reason with him. Remind him of his partner and mine.

'No, Conor, no, look, I don't feel comfortable …'

His hands are on me. 'Relax, baby.'

Him calling me 'baby' makes me shudder. It's sleazy. He's caressing my face again, still advancing, pushing his chest against me, leaning on me, pushing me backwards, further back and back. I'm trapped between him in front of me and the end of the bed behind my knees.

Relax, baby.

He's stroking my face again. Heat prickles in my cheeks – part embarrassment, part the dawning recognition that he is not taking no for an answer, part anger as he continues to push himself against me. I stop being polite.

'Get away from me, Conor,' I say, trying to shove him away now. 'No! Get away from me!'

But he's a powerful man, and I am tall but have never been in a gym in my life. His pure muscle leans onto me until he topples me back onto the bed. He follows, allowing his full weight to land on top of me. The impact knocks the breath out of me.

'Relax, baby, relax.'

His hands are everywhere, and his weight on top of me is stopping me from inhaling properly. Panic is making breathing difficult too. It's hard for me to speak. My hands and arms, which were trying to separate me from him, are now trapped between us, my fists pinned to my chest. I am struggling to free myself from under him, struggling with everything I have. As I drag my left arm, the watch on my wrist digs into my skin and scores a deep scratch on my left breast.

Get off me, please. Stop, I can't breathe. I want to say this, but I don't have the breath to speak. Everything is rushing through my mind now as I gasp for air and try to free myself from under him. Panic turns to anger, as he's pulling, tugging at my clothes so hard that I can feel him tearing at my skin. He struggles to remove my jumpsuit, secured by a button at the back of my neck. I can only move my head, so I bite him. In the struggle and the panic, I don't know where it lands.

'Yeah, go on. I love that,' he says.

A chill runs through my veins at those words. I find the space to shove him, but he has only raised himself to tug at my clothes. Everything feels chaotic and violent. 'Get off me!' It's a gasp rather than a roar as I struggle to get out from under him.

But he pins me down again completely until the only part of me that can move is my head. I bite again. I don't know where. I remember a lump of flesh in my mouth, on my teeth.

This time I see his eyes bulge and his complexion turns crimson. Then he's behind me, I don't know how, but he's gripping my neck in a chokehold with his elbow. I'm facing the headboard, dark velvet cushioning set in a decorative silver frame. The back of my head is locked tightly to his chest. I can't breathe. He tightens his hold even more, yanking my head and neck upwards under his chin as if he's hanging me. I don't struggle. I can't. I think I'm going to die, but then his arm relaxes its grip.

Relief. I'm gasping for breath, rasping, struggling for my life, but afraid to fight him now, or to try escaping his grasp or this bed. I say and do nothing; I stay quiet and still, but his arm flexes around my neck again. He yanks me up in another chokehold in the crook of his arm. My heart is hammering in my chest as he cuts off my airway again, my neck squeezed hard.

I think I'm going to pass out, but he releases his grip again. I splutter and gasp. The effort to breathe is huge. He's enjoying this control, only allowing me to breathe when he wants; letting me go just long enough to stay alive before overpowering me again.

I am frozen in terror. He may break my neck or choke me to death while toying with me. I have no time to think, to recover. He cuts off my airway again with another yank. This time, the seconds tick on, and on, and he doesn't release his grip. My vision blurs.

All I can think of is my daughter Freya. *My God, he's going to kill me. He's going to kill me, and I'm never going to see my little girl again.* A strange sense of resignation comes over me, and my overriding sorrow is that I will never see my seven-year-old again. When he releases my neck the third time, I am no longer the same person. I am gone.

'That's how I felt in the octagon; I had to tap myself out three times,' he says.

His words roll around in my head because it seems like a fucking mental thing to say. Tapping with the hand on the mat in MMA means conceding defeat. Now, I do the same. I concede defeat.

'Please, I'm begging you, please,' I croak. 'Swear that you won't do that again. I'm sorry. I won't tell anyone. I promise.'

'If you don't do that to me,' he says, 'I won't do that to you.' He's talking about biting him.

Tears are rolling down my cheeks. I'm still trying to breathe, pleading, telling him how sorry I am, trying to remain calm, anything so he won't put me in another headlock. So he won't choke me to death this time. So I can get home to my child.

He pushes me back on the bed and clambers on top of me, kneeling on my front, on my breasts, crushing me. He's triumphant, grinning at my pain, my fear and my inability to breathe. He's holding me down now with his weight on my chest. He's enjoying watching me struggle for breath.

I am spent, like my power has been stolen. I will not beat this man. One crack of my neck, and I will be gone in seconds. I let him do whatever he wants. I give up on the girl I used to be. I give up trying to save her dignity, trying to protect her body. I concentrate on breathing, on staying alive.

He pushes me, drags me, pulls my jumpsuit off, tears at me, grabs, lifts my flesh from my bones as he yanks my clothes from me. He is shoving my head down toward his penis, trying to force me to do things I don't want to do. I try to pull back, but he wrenches my head any way he wants. *Please let this end.*

As he manoeuvres me and forces his penis inside me, it's odd, but I don't feel him. It's like it's happening to this other girl, another person who's not me. What's happening is too terrible to stay for, so I've left. I'm floating.

I see the ceiling and his face above me. His mouth and hands are on my body, wet and heavy. It means nothing. I have no feeling. I am looking at myself instead, observing this other girl who is separate from me.

I am not the same person who entered this room. I am not Ste's girlfriend. I am not Freya's mammy anymore. I am an empty shell; completely numb. I can see what he's doing, but my body is something apart from me. I am detached, feeling nothing. My body is hers. I can see him pummelling and shoving and pounding her.

His expression is aggressive, furious. He's full of rage. But I'm watching everything happen to another girl who looks like me. He's on top of her, violating her body. He's doing whatever he wants to her, but she feels nothing.

His tattoo, the black monster wearing a crown, hovers over her face. She can see his mouth moving, grimacing with effort. She sees his red, sweating face and chest. His hands are on her buttocks now, pulling her around onto all fours, pushing into her, dragging her legs in every direction, arranging her limbs to his satisfaction. She is his rag doll.

I don't know how long he's been doing this to her – to me – because time moves strangely now. He is still writhing on this girl, still crimson-faced and angry, taking a long time to finish. It's okay, though, because the girl is very far away.

It could be forever – it feels like forever – before he finally rolls off her. Then it is over; it is done. The girl gets up and sits at the edge of the bed. She's carefully calm. No tears. No scenes. Everything is okay. She is quick to pull her clothes back on, but he reaches out for her and pulls her back before she can leave.

'Lie down here with me and sleep for a while.' Whatever he tells the girl to do, she will do. She lies down. Somehow, strangely, she falls asleep.

For most of the second day in court, I recount the physical details of what happened in that room: *A was followed by B, then* C *happened.* I sob endless tears, while the man who did this to me is near touching distance, watching, chin tilted upwards, eyes full of cold contempt.

23.

Cross-Examined

Day 2, continued: Wednesday, 6 November 2024

I returned to the witness box after lunch without my glasses and discovered that the sea of hungry eyes around me had disappeared. As long as I didn't wear my frames, the world stayed a non-threatening blur. My glasses were for long-distance viewing, so without them everyone became soft, featureless, moving smudges, except the judge and the senior counsel in front of me. I never wore my glasses in the witness box again.

I sat in the witness box as the screen in the courtroom flickered to life. My counsel was showing a montage of the CCTV put together by the defence, the one that Diane had made me watch before the trial. Even then, in the privacy of her office, my stomach rolled as I saw myself, a grainy figure lurching through the underground car park. That person wore my jumpsuit, but I didn't recognise her.

Now the footage played again. The courtroom had gone quiet except for the sound of coughing in the gallery and the tap, tap, tap of the journalists on their keyboards. On the screen, I looked silly, hyper, drunk. Heat crept up my neck. I could feel the jury watching – not the screen, but me. Watching me watch myself.

My counsel showed footage of McGregor, Lawrence, Danielle and me going down in the lift to the car park around 6.15 p.m. The footage conveyed a completely different mood to the giddiness of our arrival in the morning. Here everyone was quiet. I'd been hyper when we first went up. Not so now. I wasn't sure what had happened to me, but some part of my brain knew something was wrong and was trying to make sense of it.

A report* commissioned by my legal team, by clinical psychologist Dr Kevin Lambe, commented on this: 'The atmosphere is muted and the plaintiff and her friend, Ms Kealey, while smiley, appeared dazed and confused.'

Much of the video showed Lawrence and me in the car park and lift after McGregor and Danielle left. I learnt later that McGregor's other car was parked there, but there was no sign of the driver, who was in the hotel.

---

* This was a pre-trial report in an advisory capacity, and was not tendered in evidence. It does not represent findings of fact or legal conclusions.

'Without a key card for the room, they can't get beyond the ground floor, and they eventually figure that out and go to the reception,' my counsel said. 'Do you remember any of this?'

'No.'

'You appear to be on the floor of the lift there. Do you have any recollection of that?'

'I have no memory of any of this at all.'

'It looks like you are carrying one shoe and a drink in your left hand. We can see your watch on your right hand.'

My toes curled with embarrassment throughout the forty-five-minute-long video. It had been painful enough to watch it on my own. To watch images of myself stumbling around, in front of a courtroom packed with strangers, was excruciating.

'I am very nearly finished with you now, Ms Hand,' my counsel added. 'I have an intimate question to ask you. In terms of having periods and having sex, what would your approach be in general?'

'I wouldn't have sex on my period, especially if I had [inserted] a tampon.'

Cross-examination by McGregor's senior counsel, Remy Farrell, began after 3 p.m. His smile was so disarming that I returned it, thinking that perhaps this wouldn't be so terrible after all. How naive I was. At times, the cross-examination would feel nearly as bad as the assault itself.

From the beginning, McGregor's counsel painted me as a party girl, someone who was always out on the town. He quoted from my statement to gardaí, in which I said I had around nine bottles of beer, three Bacardis and some cocaine that night.

'It's just yourself and Danielle at seven in the morning. You were the hardcore of the party, as it were … It is quite clear that this was a fairly significant night out, some people might call it going on a bender; would that be fair?'

'Me and Danielle going out with Conor was like a moment of madness to be quite honest with you.'

'So when you would go out, you would hit it fairly hard.'

'Not every single time, but sometimes I would, yes.'

He read out a message that I'd sent to Ste in the salon.

Is it okay if I go out with everyone today? They are all going out, we are still in the salon partying. But they are all going out in a while. I want to ask is it okay XXXX.

'By this stage, it was only yourself and Danielle [… and] you had already been in contact with Mr McGregor, isn't that right?'

'I didn't want to tell Ste the truth, that is the truth of it. So I just said me and everybody else […] I didn't want to tell him I was actually going to a party with Conor.'

'You are looking to deceive Ste as to what your actual plans are […] You are lying to him about where you are going, who you are going with and who you are going to meet, isn't that correct?'

He kept the spotlight on the messages I'd sent to Ste. My lies to Ste were more 'gold' for the defence.

He read out the message I'd sent Ste from The Beacon Hotel after I'd been raped:

All great, I am so drunk ha ha in The Goat. xxx.

I told him I had remembered nothing at that stage. Counsel retorted that I could perfectly function if I could lie to Ste again via text.

His cross-examination continued for what seemed like endless hours, dissecting my confusion about the hotel's location. How could I possibly have mistaken The Beacon for The Morgan in town?

'I think The Morgan hotel is on Fleet Street; isn't that right?'

'Yes.'

[...]

'I think Fleet Street, am I right in saying it is a cobbled street, it is one of those Temple Bar streets; isn't that right?'

'Yes.'

[...]

'A lot of people might be surprised somebody mistakes Sandyford, where The Beacon is, for Temple Bar?'

'It was just the interior [I confused], that's all.'

He tried to use my confusion as an example of another lie. He returned again and again to Temple Bar's cobblestones, as if the street's construction should have penetrated my drunken brain.

'I mean you don't dispute what's on the CCTV?'

'I just can't remember [...] You can see I'm a very drunk woman. I don't remember any of that whatsoever.'

[...]

'At the time I wasn't wondering where I was going. I wasn't asking. I was just in a car. We were having a drink, we were having a laugh. I thought we were going to a party. But I didn't say where are we going, no.'

Mr Farrell continued to question the confusion over The Beacon and Morgan hotels.

'You told Ste you were in The Morgan bar; isn't that right?'

'That is where I thought I was because the interior of the hotel is very similar to The Beacon Hotel.'

'You have been to The Morgan before, obviously?'

'Yeah, I have.'

McGregor's counsel pivoted, his tone shifting. 'You have obviously [been] in the hotel rooms?'

The implication hung in the air: with other men.

'I have, with Ste, yes.'

I would have liked to expand that I had been there once for Ste's twenty-fifth birthday, and we stayed in an ordinary room. I'd been pregnant with Freya then and could have shown him the photos.

He reminded me that I told Ste I couldn't tell him who had raped me because 'he would kill me'. Mr Farrell asked if I meant McGregor would kill me, and I said yes. He then said I had mentioned nothing in my garda interviews about McGregor threatening to kill me.

'Is that something that happened or didn't happen?' he asked.

I said I couldn't remember him saying that he would kill me. He didn't give me a chance to explain that I believed McGregor had nearly killed me in The Beacon, and I had promised I wouldn't tell anyone. I had been convinced that he would finish the job if I told people.

Mr Farrell began leading me through the untruths I told my boyfriend when I came home, describing them as 'a web of lies'.

'So you weren't telling the truth when you said, "I was in The Morgan Bar"?'

'Bar, yeah.'

'And that was a conscious misdirection on your part, a conscious untruth?'

'Yeah. I thought I was in The Morgan Hotel, but I was telling Ste I was in The Morgan Bar. I didn't want to tell him the truth.'

'You told him you were there with Danielle, Jade, Ger, everybody from work?'

'I did say that, yes.'

'And they were all in the penthouse; is that correct?'

'Yes.'

'Why did you tell him that?'

'I didn't want to tell him the truth. I lied to my boyfriend, it is just as simple as that.'

'I know, Ms Hand, but I am trying to figure out why you told the lie?'

'Because I didn't want to tell him the truth [...] Me lying to my boyfriend doesn't take away what happened to me. Lying to your boyfriend is not a crime, but what happened to me is a crime.'

I did everything I could to avoid telling Ste the truth that it was Danielle and me and two men in that hotel room. Who would want to admit that to their boyfriend? I wasn't the first girl or guy to lie to their partner, and I certainly wouldn't be the last.

But McGregor's counsel made it sound like the worst crime in the world. The words 'lying' and 'liar' became a regular refrain, a weapon wielded against me.

'We know you have told a very significant number of lies, and we are going to go through some of them in this transcript.'

'I agree with you; I did lie to my boyfriend.'

He read a text in which I claimed I was sharing a taxi home with Eimer. 'You're telling lies to Ste.'

I wanted to scream. I told a lie, trying to paint the mistakes I made in a softer light and save my relationship. That was all.

I had one strategy during the trial: to tell the truth. I knew once I told the truth, I could face any question, and he could never trip me up. I could not present myself as the perfect witness, but my truth would never change. I just had to keep repeating what I remembered, what I knew to be true.

But the strategy was to consistently hammer me for lying. As part of McGregor's defence, the barrister was focusing on painting me as dishonest in front of the jury. This line of questioning hurt a lot.

But whatever he said, I spoke the truth. No matter how bad it made me look – from admitting that I took cocaine, that I went back to a hotel room with two men, that I lied to my partner, stayed out all hours, drank too much – no matter how it made me appear, I didn't care. I told them the truth, regardless of how bad it looked.

All I wanted was for everyone to know the whole truth of what happened in the bedroom of that hotel penthouse that day.

24.

Torture

Day 3: Thursday, 7 November 2024

The cross-examination from McGregor's counsel continued. It was relentless, one question melting into the next, McGregor's counsel's voice drilling into me until I could barely remember my own name without second-guessing it.

My trembling fingers often reached to squeeze the folded fabric in my pocket, Nanny's multi-coloured headscarf. It stayed hidden on my person, my secret anchor and source of comfort, every day of the trial.

Please, Nanny, give me the strength to get through this. Please God, give me the strength …

When I wasn't rubbing Nanny's scarf, I rotated her gold

engagement and wedding rings around the fingers of my right hand. I needed to feel her close.

I felt as if the defence wanted to break me, and I hated them for it. I broke into pieces again and again during the trial, then reassembled myself and returned to the witness box. I had to remind myself that McGregor's counsel was doing his job. He wasn't the monster. I squeezed my nanny's scarf again and prayed harder.

He reached the topic of arriving at my manager Eimer's house on the night of the rape.

'You don't remember then telling her you woke up with two bodyguards coming into the room?'

'No, I don't remember that.'

'You don't remember telling her that you jumped up and ran out because you thought you were going to be gang-raped?'

'No, I don't remember that.'

Maybe I had said that, or maybe Eimer misunderstood me. I wasn't in my right frame of mind. Things weren't actually coming back to me correctly. Maybe I was trying to explain the incident that happened before McGregor assaulted me, when I found myself in the bedroom with three men and felt panicked and left.

'You don't recall telling Eimer Brennan that you ran off because you were afraid you were going to be raped by the security guard?'

'No, I don't remember that [...] I was all over the place. I was obviously very confused at that point [...] I was just after being brutally raped and battered. Things slowly came back to me.'

He asked me about the messages that I'd deleted in the days afterwards.

'I deleted some, and I told some of my friends and family to delete them because I was afraid.'

'So, it seems that you deleted some of your text messages but not others; isn't that so?'

'I deleted a good bit, but the guards got some of it back because I handed over my phone for evidence.'

He also quizzed me about the double doors between the bedroom and the living room in the penthouse. The defence tried to claim that the doors between the two remained open throughout our stay at the hotel.

'I am going to suggest to you that the way that these doors were was that you couldn't actually close them over fully, or you couldn't engage the latch?'

'You probably could have just closed it over, and it stayed that way,' I said. 'It probably just didn't lock.'

[...]

'So you are not going to disagree with others who say the door couldn't close; is that fair?'

'I can't disagree with them, no, because I don't actually have a physical memory of the door being locked or closed.'

I spent that lunch break crying in the consultation room. I

knew many rape victims were on the stand for hours or even a whole day. At most, they were in the witness box for two days. It wasn't normal for a victim to be in the witness box for three days.

I kept asking, 'This must be the last time, right?' And Clíona would reply encouragingly that it should be. But the defence kept me in that witness box for four torturous days that week.

The isolation from my own solicitor Dave and his team made it worse. From the moment I took the witness box for cross-examination, a wall went up between my legal team and me. My solicitors couldn't speak to me. Senior counsel couldn't speak to me. The rule applied to everyone – Dave, Diane, my barristers and everyone on my legal team – no contact about the trial, nothing, until I left the witness box.

I couldn't ask whether I was doing okay or whether they thought I was performing well. I could receive no reassurances, no feedback nor advice. To be honest, nothing could have prepared me for the reality of what I was facing. I had no concept of how much it would affect me, how traumatising the court case itself would become.

Back in the courtroom, later that day, the torture of cross-examination continued.

'I think you made it clear you weren't looking for sexual activity or romantic entanglement or anything of that sort?' said McGregor's counsel.

'No, I wasn't.'

'On the CCTV footage […] I want to put this as delicately and as inoffensively as I can, it would appear to suggest that you were interested in romantic entanglement?'

[…]

'Yes, but I can't remember any of it.'

[…]

'I presume you, like everyone else, saw the footage where you appear very affectionate towards Mr McGregor? […] The first thing you did when you got into the lift there [when he was leaving the hotel] was to go over and hug Mr McGregor, isn't that right?'

'I didn't see myself hugging.'

'Did you not watch his footage?'

'I thought he had his arms up.'

McGregor's arms were stretched across the mirror in the lift, taking up most of the space, and you can see me move towards him. I wasn't hugging him.

'Just play it back again. I thought he had his arms widened,' said the judge, agreeing with me.

'We will just look at it again then,' said Mr Farrell, replaying the CCTV. 'That seems to be you hugging?'

'You can't see that very clearly, that I am hugging.'

'All right, you disagree with that. We will keep our eye on the bottom right-hand corner, you seem to almost give a little kiss to the back of his arm at some point.'

My head lowered for an instant, and they decided to describe that as me kissing his arm.

'I don't know what I am doing there.'

McGregor's counsel said it was 'blindingly obvious', but that wasn't how it looked to me.

I said the CCTV showed a 'very drunken woman who didn't know what she was doing', adding that I 'should have been looked after, should have been brought home' in that state.

He referred to a call logged on my phone at 6.27 p.m. to McGregor. 'You don't remember that at all?'

'No, I have no idea why I called. I can't remember.'

'This is a point in time when he has left the hotel?'

'Yes.'

'You see that in the CCTV. And this is the man who has brutally raped you, but that is gone from your mind at that point; is that right?'

'Yes, I remembered when I got back up into the hotel with James, and that is when it started coming back to me, but I didn't remember absolutely every detail.'

'You are looking to have a chat with him at 18:27, just after he has left, but you have no recollection of that?'

'I don't know why I rang him, but there was a lot of hanging around, as you can see in the CCTV footage. So I know James took my phone out of my hands on the CCTV footage at one stage as well.'

[...]

'There are twenty minutes, half an hour in and out through the doors and all the rest of it. No memory of that?'

'No, none whatsoever, none. And it is very hard watch for me, and I don't want to have to go through another forty minutes of that, sorry.'

'Why is that hard for you to watch, Ms Hand?'

'Because I can't remember and it is not me, it is not my character. It is not who I am. I don't want to have to look at it again.'

'It is absolutely you, isn't it?'

'It is me, but it is not my character, and I don't want to have to look at it again; it is very disturbing for me.'

'Can I suggest another reason it is very disturbing for you, Ms Hand,' he said. 'Everything in that CCTV footage flatly contradicts the story you have told; isn't that right?'

'I don't agree with you.'

'You don't agree?'

'No. That CCTV footage doesn't take away what happened to me in that room with Conor. I know what happened to me – I was brutally raped and battered. I know what happened to me, and that bit of CCTV footage does not take away from what happened to me. I need to have a break, I'm sorry.'

Later, the CCTV also showed me in close physical proximity to Lawrence, touching his arm, my movements unsteady and gaze unfocused.

McGregor's counsel leaned in again.

'And again I want to put this delicately. I don't want to put it in any way that you might find offensive, but you certainly seem to have romantic designs on Mr Lawrence at various points?'

'At some points of it, yes, I saw that.'

[...]

'There is a point where I think you seem to be kissing him?'

The words caught in my throat.

'Yes, it looked that way.'

'So we have to consider what you say, that you had no interest in romantic entanglement, in light of that. You are just wrong when you say that. Isn't that right?'

How could I explain? I'm the kind of person who hugs everyone, who becomes even more tactile with alcohol. I don't believe I was making advances on Lawrence. I thought he was being nice, kind. Psychologist Dr Kevin Lambe described me on the CCTV as 'dazed' and 'falling into' Lawrence. He'd also noted how Lawrence 'had a habit of looking at his reflection and quaffing his fringe'.

The defence skipped CCTV footage that didn't fit their narrative. In one excerpt, I tried to leave the hotel, and Lawrence seized my arm, pulling me back – that didn't make their highlight reel. Neither did the scene where Lawrence punched the elevator wall in frustration, while I stroked his arm, clearly unsettled by the aggression.

To the defence, the CCTV was gold dust. Mr Farrell's voice cut through the courtroom again and again: 'You're saying you were raped and beaten, yet you're behaving like this afterwards.'

Since the day I had first seen the CCTV footage in my solicitor's office, this question had burned in my mind. For a long time, I was in the dark, trying to understand why I'd acted that way after what happened. Why was I oblivious to what McGregor did for so long?

My legal team had consulted experts on this. Dr Kevin Lambe's report suggested I'd experienced dissociation during the assault – my consciousness shutting down like circuit breakers flipping. 'Dissociation' would have helped explain the silence during the attack, and the strange calm that followed. I shut down to protect my body from trauma. This resonated with me strongly. And indeed, over this past year, intensive therapy I've done with the Dublin Rape Crisis Centre has helped me understand more about trauma and memory. People often talk of fight or flight, but there is less understanding of how many people freeze or operate on autopilot after trauma.

During the court case, my solicitor Dave had also considered calling Dr Abbie Maroño, who specialised in explaining the freeze response and emotional shutdown to American juries. 'Victims don't follow the same script,' she had explained. 'The brain simply stops processing pain when it becomes too much.'

In the end, my team decided against using experts from this

field. They believed they should concentrate on the medical evidence instead. They were right – because we won. But I wish those experts had taken the stand. Their words might also have explained the amnesia I experienced after being assaulted.

McGregor and Lawrence's counsel played the CCTV footage again. And again. Pausing. Rewinding. Replaying. The same questions circled back like vultures.

I sat in that witness chair for hours, watching forgotten fragments of the worst night of my life projected for dozens of strangers; a woman I didn't recognise performing actions that were alien to me.

'I don't remember,' I repeated as he continually asked me what I was doing in this frame or that frame. 'I'm going to keep telling you, I don't remember.'

Even the judge had intervened. 'She's told you she can't remember. There's no point making her watch it again.'

Finally, I broke down in tears and refused to watch anymore. I'd reached my limit.

'I keep telling you I don't remember. So you can keep asking, and I'll keep answering the same thing. But I'm not watching it anymore.'

I sat there, defiant, refusing to look at the screen. I stared straight ahead and felt again for my nanny's scarf. *Please, Nanny, give me the strength to get through this.*

25.

The Recording

Day 3, continued: Thursday, 7 November 2024

The sound of Ste's pleading and my voice, drowning in tears and anguish, filled the courtroom later that day. Each word of Ste's recording of us during the early hours of Monday, 10 December 2018, cut me like a knife.

I hadn't listened to the entire tape because I couldn't bear to. It brought me back to that awful night, hours after being raped. Now, as McGregor's barrister broadcast forty minutes of unadulterated pain through Courtroom 24, I felt like I was being tortured. I put my head in my hands in the witness box as a mixture of shock and shame flooded my veins. I felt sweat collect on my legs and under my arms.

It was unbearable to have this intimate and fraught episode of my life replayed in front of strangers in a courtroom.

Five minutes after Remy Farrell started the tape, the tissues in my hands had disintegrated, fallen to damp shreds in my fingers. Streams of tears ran down my face and into my bare hands as I cried along to the sound of myself sobbing six years earlier.

'Look at my knuckles from fighting' were my first words on the recording.

'My body is sore,' I said. 'I'm so sorry. I'm so sorry.'

Ste: 'Okay. Okay.'

'And I bit him. I bit him.'

Ste: 'Put them clothes on.'

He was trying to get me into my pyjamas.

'Eimer kept saying to go home to Ste and tell Ste what happened.'

Ste: 'Nikita, just put them on, will you?'

'My body's sore,' I sobbed.

Ste: 'Shh.'

'I'm so sorry.'

Ste: 'Yeah, just tell me what happened. Okay, put that on you. Let me go and close it for you. Let me close it for you.'

'I have to tell my mam.'

Ste asked again to tell him what happened.

I told him that after the salon, Danielle, Jade, Ger and 'everybody from work' had gone into The Morgan Bar and into the penthouse there.

As Ste demanded to know who my assailant was, I repeatedly told him I couldn't say.

'He choked me and told me he'd kill me [...] Just please, just let me get my head straight.'

I explained that I had started my period and that my tampon was stuck inside me. I said I would go to St James's Hospital the next day. I begged Ste not to involve the gardaí and to stop asking me questions.

'The only thing you should be doing is supporting me right now. You haven't even put your arms around me.'

Despite my upset, I feared the foundations of our relationship were already crumbling.

'I'm not a slut if you think I am. I'm not like that.'

And I said over and over: 'You're not going to think the same of me anymore. You're not going to look at me in the same way again.'

Ste shrugged off my worries. He was focused on finding out who was responsible.

'This isn't a shut up and say nothing situation,' he said. 'This shit doesn't happen anymore. This thing about keeping quiet about stuff is not happening [...] I don't know what happened. I want to know who invited you up to The Morgan penthouse.'

I could hear myself growing angrier as Ste continually asked questions and said he was trying to process this.

'Process it? Process it? How do you think I'm fucking feeling?' I responded. 'How do you think I feel right now? [...] I said get off me. Look at my knuckles from fighting back […] He was choking me, and I couldn't breathe […] three times he done it to me [… I] thought I was dead …'

My head hung in humiliation in that courtroom. The emotion in the recording was raw and unfiltered. The sound quality was perfect. Crystal clear. And the man who'd done this to me, who'd caused me to cry hysterically that morning, was sitting mere metres away – no doubt blank-faced and emotionless.

The exchange between Ste and me continued, seemingly forever.

'Fuck off, Ste. I'm after being raped. Fuck off […] I'm after being sexually abused. Fuck off, right? Fuck off […] Put your arm around me and ask me am I okay. That's what you should be doing […] I'm hurt. I'm black and blue, and all you care about is you.'

I pulled my hair forward, creating a curtain, trying to block out the world, trying to create some small barrier between myself and all those watching eyes.

I wanted to scream: *Stop! Just stop!*

I lifted my head. 'I need a break.'

The judge immediately agreed. The recording wasn't an easy listen for anyone else in the room either.

But instead of fleeing the room, I sat frozen in the witness chair, unable to move. Clíona came up to me and led me toward the exit. She gripped my hand, but my panic was rising.

To get out, I needed to pass McGregor and Lawrence and push my way through members of the public crowding the door. I couldn't do it. I broke down completely. The words tore from my throat. The entire courtroom heard me shatter.

'I can't do this! I can't do this!'

Listening back to the audio had felt like being transported to my sitting room in the early hours of 10 December, hours after being raped. The original trauma and all the memories that I never wanted to be reminded of again hit me.

That conversation was deeply personal, talking about being sore, about my period, about the tampon – all things never intended to be heard by anyone else but Ste and me. I found it degrading beyond words to have everyone eavesdropping on something so deeply personal. It felt like being stripped naked in public while everyone stared at me.

When the judge allowed a break, I wanted to bolt from the courthouse, quit the trial and never come back. Instead, Clíona led me to a small room outside and began working her calming magic. 'You have only fifteen minutes of the tape left. Let's get through those fifteen minutes, and then you're done. You'll never have to listen to it again.'

'I can't! I can't do any more.'

Gary came into the room, a wreck, distraught from witnessing what I was going through. He paced up and down, full of emotion at watching his partner being destroyed day after day in the witness box.

'I can't. I can't do it,' I said over and again.

I wanted Gary and my mam to put their arms around me and walk me out of that place, telling me it was okay, that I didn't have to do this anymore. But they couldn't take me, and I couldn't leave. I did the only thing I could. I caught my breath, wiped the tears from my eyes, composed myself and returned for the next round.

26.

Backfire

Day 4: Friday, 8 November 2024

Before evidence could even begin the next morning, the jury foreman handed a note to Judge Owens. The judge's face darkened.

'The jury has stated that at the end of the proceedings yesterday, members of the jury noticed somebody in the public gallery using a mobile phone, pointing down at the jury,' he said. 'They are concerned about videos or photos of the jury being circulated to the public.'

He said he couldn't verify what had happened without an investigation.

'I am going to arrange for a guard to be stationed up in the public gallery to make sure that there is no prospect of that particular matter happening again. It is a contempt of court to take photographs of the jury, and there will be steps taken to deal with that matter in the event that anybody is suspected of it.'

He also decided that the courtroom, in particular the public gallery, was overcrowded and ordered that anyone without a seat had to leave.

The alert that someone had been recording the jury was not an isolated incident. The judge confirmed that a screenshot of the court had been circulated the previous week. He said he took 'a very dim view' of it and called it a clear contempt of court.

'Members of the jury, you're entitled to know these things have taken place,' he said.

Each interruption like this sent an icy jolt of fear through my chest. I feared that someone would share images of the jury on WhatsApp groups, where people would start naming them. Every jury's safety depends on its anonymity. If the jury members' identities had been leaked, the entire trial could collapse, wasting all those hours of testimony. We – I – would have to start again. My worst nightmare.

I felt for the jury, for what they risked simply by performing their civil duty. If their faces got out, there were people out there who might target them.

Real or imagined, I certainly felt intimidated most days in the courtroom. On one occasion, I entered the hallway in the Four

Courts and a man rose to his feet in front of me. He squared his shoulders and glared at me, his arms folded across his chest. I recognised him: he was a Drimnagh local, a McGregor supporter. There was no mistaking which side he was on.

When I gave evidence about McGregor, the same man began pacing at the back of the courtroom. Without my glasses, I couldn't see his expression, only the blurred outline of him moving. That constant stalking behind the benches was meant to distract me, to break my concentration and unnerve me. My solicitor, Dave Coleman, realised what was going on and had the man removed. Some people believed that if they scared me enough, I might stop giving evidence.

Another morning, someone played the dance track 'Dirty Cash' on their phone behind me over and over until the court was in session. When McGregor was being cross-examined on the stand, a person came up behind me and called me a liar in my ear. I experienced several instances of what you could only describe as intimidation.

McGregor's counsel continued cross-examining me on day four, focusing on the lies I'd told in Ste's recording. Throughout the recording, I'd only heard my rising frustration. My sadness. My pleading for help. I'd listened to my description of being choked, fighting back and biting my attacker. Everything I'd later tell the guards was captured in Ste's recording.

I heard myself telling Ste that my throat was sore. The struggle. The pain. If the recording and the CCTV from The

Beacon Hotel had featured another woman, I would have thought: *God love her, that poor girl needed help*.

It took my mother to finally see through the crisis clearly, when I went to her house the next morning. She cut through everything else and recognised the single essential truth: her daughter needed help. My mother didn't care about the hotel, the drugs or the man. She saw her daughter covered in bruises, bleeding and in pain. Nothing else mattered to my mam apart from getting me proper medical help.

I didn't consent to Ste recording that conversation, and I never consented to the recording being aired in the trial. McGregor's legal team demanded it, believing it would help his case. They used it to try to prove that I was a liar. But I believe playing the recording backfired spectacularly for them.

The entire room could hear the emotion contained in that recording, the vulnerability and profound hurt I was feeling. Even though I was still extremely drunk, the audio referenced the truths that I have always spoken about, such as having been choked three times. It showed I did not make up details in the cold light of day.

The court heard everything that happened when I arrived home only hours after McGregor attacked me. Although listening to that recording in the courtroom was a traumatic experience, it may also have saved me. The jury heard it. And they knew what they heard.

27.

Bowed Not Broken

Day 4, continued: Friday, 8 November 2024

Courtroom 24 was never designed for crowds. In most other civil cases, a handful of spectators would have drifted in and out, their presence barely noticed. But McGregor's name had changed that. Crowds young and old packed the public gallery each morning, many leaning forward, straining to catch every word that rose from the courtroom floor below. When the judge wasn't sitting at the bench, people's heads hung over the balcony's edge, peering down to glimpse McGregor.

Given the shortage of space, my legal team had advised me not to encourage friends or family to come, as it wouldn't be comfortable for them. So I told Gary's cousin Janice, who had become a close friend, and my mother that it was okay to stay away. My aunties. Friends. Gary and I said we'd get through it together. Most days, Mam came anyway, and when I glanced over my shoulder, I'd see her reassuring wave. Two of my uncles came nearly every day; their familiar faces helped too. Other days, my cousins and aunties arrived.

However, I hadn't seen my daughter Freya all week. Another two weeks would pass before I would hold her again. I'd told Ste I needed to focus entirely on the trial, that I couldn't manage the questions she'd ask, the explanations she'd need. She was old enough now to understand, and what was being discussed in a public courtroom was nothing that a teenager should hear. We spoke on the phone every day. That had to be enough.

After lunch, on my fourth day in the witness box, James Lawrence's senior counsel, John Fitzgerald, started his cross-examination of me. His voice cut through the room, telling everyone that his client was in court not because of anything I said, but because of something Lawrence said himself.

Lawrence had placed himself in the firing line by claiming that we had consensual sex twice after McGregor left the hotel. My team argued that I did not consent and was incapable of consenting to sex with him, and therefore he had raped me.

Even though my legal team took a case for sexual assault against Lawrence, they also argued he invented the story to damage my credibility and help McGregor's claims that we had consensual sex. Lawrence's senior counsel had argued several times during the trial that our case against his client was contradictory.

'Detective Sergeant Woods said to you, "Did anything happen between you and James in the room." You said, "No. Just talking …"' Lawrence's counsel said.

I confirmed this. He then said I was shocked when gardaí told me Lawrence claimed to have had sex with me twice that evening.

[…]

'Do you not believe him?'

'I think he's lying,' I said.

'You think he's lying about having sex with you?'

'Absolutely.'

He played another excerpt of the CCTV footage of me coming down in the lift to the car park of The Beacon Hotel with Lawrence at 6.51 p.m. I had a drink in my hand, I was hugging Lawrence, and at one stage I was biting his ear.

I squeezed my eyes shut in humiliation.

'So you don't agree with my suggestion that you don't look remotely like somebody […] who has been hit by a steam train of her memory of having been violently raped?'

He showed another clip of Lawrence and me leaving the hotel for the last time after 10 p.m. He again put it to me that I didn't look like someone distressed at being violently raped earlier that day.

'I look very, very drunk and I am hitting off walls and stumbling, I can see that,' I said.

He showed more CCTV footage.

'You're kissing Mr Lawrence [...] he's not kissing you.'

My stomach rolled again as I said I had no memory of it. That woman in the CCTV might as well have been a complete stranger to me.

He switched back to earlier in the day.

'At some point, you and Mr McGregor went from the first room into the bedroom [...] to have sex.'

My chest rose and fell rapidly. 'No.'

'... the door was open. You could be heard clearly [...] moaning noises. Noises that clearly indicated you were having a good time and not a bad time.'

I shook my head.

'Ms Kealey said that you were going to regret this because you'd just bought a house with your boyfriend [...] And while you were in that room with Mr McGregor, having pleasurable sex, Mr Lawrence and Ms Kealey began to have sex in the other room [...] you were coming in and out of the bedroom and you saw what happened on a number of occasions?'

My voice rose in exasperation. 'This is another made-up story!'

'This went on for some time. Long enough that Mr Lawrence had sex three times with Danielle. Long enough that he could see through the open door – you, naked, on top of Mr McGregor. Having sex for a second time.'

'Lies.'

'You called Mr Lawrence a "dirty bastard" for performing oral sex on your friend.'

My face contorted. 'That's disgusting [...] I don't agree with that.'

My God, they've concocted a complete story between them, I thought. But they'd had plenty of time. McGregor raped me on Sunday, 9 December 2018, and neither of them was interviewed by police until over a month later.

Lawrence's counsel claimed I only became upset after I had sex with Lawrence for the second time and asked him what I was going to say to Ste about the bruises on my arms.

'I probably did say that [about the bruises].' Through the fragments, I recalled my worry at the time about how I would explain the bruises to Ste. But for the hundredth time in that trial, I had to repeat I was very drunk and had little memory of this time.

Mr Fitzgerald said I was 'attempting to edit Mr Lawrence out of this case, and he has brought himself back into it'.

He insisted I did remember having sex with Lawrence, but that it 'wasn't a good look' for someone accusing another man of rape to have had consensual sex with another man afterwards.

I said an emphatic 'no' to that.

Lawrence's counsel said he was finished with his cross-examination. It was now my own counsel's turn. Ray Boland stood. He read out a statement from McGregor's barrister to me:

'"I am suggesting to you that you largely took your own clothes off; he took his clothes off and you took yours off."'

My counsel showed photos of the jumpsuit and underwear I'd worn the day McGregor attacked me. They were torn and shredded.

'That tear on the right-hand side of your jumpsuit – was that present when you went out that night?'

'No.'

'And then the last photographs also show damage to the straps of your underwear?'

'Yes.'

'I take it you say that damage wasn't there when you went out that night?'

'No.'

'Can you help the jury as to what caused that damage, to both the jumpsuit and to the underwear?'

'Pulling.'

'And pulling by whom, when?'

'Conor, aggressively.'

'Okay, and when did that occur?'

'When he was attempting to rape me.'

When the judge finally said I could step down, my legs were like jelly. After four days of torture, at 2.30 p.m. on Friday, 8 November, I was done in the witness box. My heart hammered, but my spine stayed straight. I was proud and relieved to have survived everything McGregor and Lawrence's legal team had thrown at me. My solicitor and our team had to stand to let me get to my seat. Dave's hand landed warm on my shoulder as I passed him.

'Well done!' he said.

Those two small words warmed my heart. Dave had become something like a father figure over the years, so his approval meant everything. It was also the first time he'd been able to communicate with me for the entire week.

But what made the moment really sing was simpler than that: McGregor sat directly behind Dave, close enough to see his hand on my shoulder; close enough to hear those two words and close enough to watch me walk past with my head high, still standing tall and unbowed, despite his best efforts to floor me.

28.

White Coats and Professionals

Days 5: Tuesday, 12 November–
Day 6: Wednesday, 13 November 2024

As the second week of the trial began, the hustle and bustle in and around the court intensified. Crowds packed the back of the room and around the door and queued for the public gallery. Many, no doubt, were expecting to see McGregor on the stand.

However, they were to be disappointed as my legal team devoted Tuesday and much of Wednesday morning to evidence from medical witnesses and other experts.

Paramedic Neal Dempsey's voice was steady and factual, describing me as 'visibly upset' with 'visible marks in or around' my throat when he and his Dublin Fire Brigade female colleague attended me at 8.40 a.m. on Monday, 10 December 2018.

'She became a bit more distressed on the way to the hospital,' said Mr Dempsey. 'She was having what was the premise of a panic attack, just faster breathing, faster heart rate and just generally distressed.'

He spoke about giving me a sick bag. He said it appeared as though I was going to vomit and that my chief worry was the tampon and the 'pains she was having in that area'.

We saw CCTV footage of his colleague, Eithne Scully, examining me in the ambulance outside Mam's home before she drove to the Rotunda. The video evidence showed her examining my lower limbs and thighs. My counsel stopped to point out the bruising evident on the footage.

'The patient was very withdrawn, very agitated and upset,' Ms Scully said. 'There was some bruising around her neck at that point before I examined her [...] She was very bruised. I haven't actually seen somebody so bruised in a long, long time. Not that intensity, the amount of bruises on a person.'

My GPs from Walkinstown Medical Practice were called to court. Discussing my private medical records in public seemed so invasive, but they had no option. Everything had to be laid bare in this legal process.

Dr Emma Quinn spoke about my attendance at the practice for neck pain and tenderness nine days after the assault.

'I diagnosed internal bruising, which would be something that would be there for a few weeks after an injury,' she said.

GP Frank Clarke, who'd known me since I was a child,

discussed how he had prescribed sertraline before the assault. He described it as 'an extremely commonly prescribed type of medication' for people to manage anxiety and depression.

'She would tend to be anxious and withdrawn and would struggle with confidence, and that kind of medication would be used,' he said.

He checked his notes as he talked about certifying me as unfit for work in May 2019.

'[Hairdressing] is a kind of performance-oriented thing. You need to be confident; you are dealing with people all the time. You are [...] trying to be cheery about what you are doing, positive. She wasn't really coping with that. She felt very, very conscious of what had happened to her [...] She was scared of being identified because she felt unsafe.'

He explained prescribing olanzapine for the first time that year, without revealing the reason for it – the home invasion five months earlier. My counsel had only made a vague reference about my 'distress' that was 'triggered by a very difficult event'.

'Obviously, the incident has nothing got to do with Mr McGregor,' he had said, giving no further detail. (The issue of the home invasion was discussed in the absence of the jury after my GP gave evidence. The judge said he had issued a ruling concerning it at the beginning of the case. As a result, the jury would learn nothing about that attack as it was not part of the evidence.)

'Olanzapine is a major tranquilliser,' my GP now said. He explained that it is used to treat severe mental illness like psychosis and mania, 'but in smaller amounts [...] is very, very helpful to deal with an acute surge of panic and distress and sleeplessness as a result of more severe anxiety symptoms, or PTSD in particular. This is for somebody who is having night terrors, panic, and much more severe distress.'

He gave his professional opinion on my issues with alcohol.

'Nikita isn't an alcoholic [...] If you have an underlying tendency to be anxious, alcohol is very helpful because it reduces anxiety. The thing that people don't realise, though, is that it causes more depression.'

He told the court that meeting my partner, Gary, had been a 'very positive thing' for me.

'She brought [consuming alcohol] back under control, with the help of her partner.'

I glanced at Gary beside me and squeezed his hand in acknowledgement. It was one of the few occasions in that courtroom that I actually smiled.

Dr Ann Leader, an eminent psychiatrist for almost half a century, gave evidence on my behalf. She specialised in working with survivors of sexual abuse. She told the courtroom I was a 'good communicator, a clear historian and a sincere person'.

McGregor's counsel rose to his feet immediately, stating he wanted to address an issue in the jury's absence. After a discussion between the judge and legal teams, Dr Leader was ordered by Mr Justice Owens to 'stick to psychiatry' and not express her views about my sincerity.

But the words had been uttered – and by one of the most respected professionals in her field. I was glad everyone heard her call me 'a sincere person' after it being implied I was a liar so many times in the same room.

'She felt she had been permanently damaged by what happened,' Dr Leader told the court. 'She could not sleep or eat properly [. . .] She spent a lot of time in bed, and she told me she wanted to die. She could not function normally. She returned to work but could not cope. She felt dirty, ashamed and guilty.'

She traced my first episode of PTSD back to The Beacon Hotel and what happened that day.

'She described becoming depersonalised,' she said. 'When somebody is undergoing a severe traumatic event, it is quite common that they detach themselves from it because it is so shocking and so traumatic that they are not able to process it . . .'

She concluded I had 'very pronounced and classical symptoms' of PTSD and I would continue to experience significant psychological problems into the future.

DNA specialist Dr Charlotte Murphy from Forensic Science Ireland read her clinical evidence.

'[Nikita] says that Conor McGregor had vaginal sexual intercourse with her, digitally penetrated her and put his penis in her mouth, all without her consent. She has no recollection of having sexual intercourse with James Lawrence. She was medically examined approximately ten hours after the alleged incident.'

Dr Murphy then gave evidence of semen swabs taken from my body and clothing. She found DNA profiles matching Conor McGregor's on my clothes and underwear and on 'high vaginal, vulval and perianal swabs'. Lawrence's DNA was not present in the swabs, but added that if a condom was used, there was less likely to be semen.

She also told the court that the straps of my jumpsuit were ripped from the front of the outfit. This appeared recent, was not normal wear and tear and was caused by pulling, she said.

Property valuer Patrick Sheehan was brought to the witness stand by my other barrister, Siún Leonowicz.

Dave had spoken to me about what I wanted to achieve from the case. I was clear: I wanted to hold Conor McGregor accountable. I wanted justice. It was never about money. Yet I also wanted to move on, restart my life, far from Dublin 12. I could never again live in the area where I'd grown up.

'In an ideal world, I'd like a small home, like the one I lost, but anywhere else,' I told Dave.

He had sent a property valuer to my former home as part of a compensation claim seeking the costs of relocating away from Drimnagh. The property expert said he valued the house that summer at around €430,000.

She asked him to outline his research into similar properties in areas outside of Drimnagh. He said he looked at the Shankill and Cabinteely areas about twenty minutes away.

'We looked at a number of properties there, and I suppose they were all coming in €500,000 and under €700,000 in that area.'

My former boss, John McMahon, co-owner of Gerard Paul Hairdressing, was called as the next witness. He told the court that I returned to work after the assault in February 2019.

'She worked four days a week for a time, but she struggled. She worked, but there were no-shows like two days a week sometimes, and then eventually she resigned in May 2019.'

'She was good, and she knew she was good,' he said.

Asked about my earning potential, he said he expected me to build up a clientele.

'Essentially, we pay 25 per cent, so if she were taking in, say, €3,000 a week, she would get €750 [...] Tips are all based on personal relationships, but I mean, €100 would be low enough.'

After leaving the witness box, he came to the bench where I sat and put his hand on my shoulder and wished me the best of luck, a gesture of support that I appreciated.

My legal team also hired occupational therapist Elva Breen to prepare a report evaluating my capacity to return to work. She said she saw evidence of PTSD and psychological issues when she assessed me in 2020 and 2024.

She told the court I was on disability allowance and related my attempts to return to work after leaving Gerard Paul.

I had worked for a cleaning company at a college in 2023, which I'd enjoyed. The repetitive motions of cleaning allowed me to tune out in a pleasant, mindless way. It was also mindful because it anchored me, forcing me to focus on something other than my anxieties. I handed in my notice when I became overwhelmed by panic attacks ten months later.

I returned to hairdressing in 2024, working in a salon in Walkinstown that I could walk to every morning. This was February, four months before the house invasion, when we were still living in Drimnagh. But the reminders were constant, and it became too much to cope with.

'Did you hear Conor McGregor is building all those apartments?' a client said on one occasion, as she got a full head of meche highlights. I hoped she hadn't noticed my stricken expression in the mirror.

'No, really?'

'Yes, eight storeys high. Spending millions on it, I hear.'

I steered the conversation in another direction. Holidays were usually a safe topic.

'Are you planning to go anywhere this summer?' I asked another woman having a root touch-up.

'I've just been away on a girls' weekend – a big group of us, and guess who one of them was? Conor McGregor's mam …'

Another girl whose hair I was curling told me that McGregor's friends had been in her house till 6 a.m. that morning.

I left after six weeks. It had been foolish ever to think I could work in Dublin 12.

The occupational therapist concluded that I needed to work in 'a safe and predictable environment' [...] 'where there is routine' [...] 'A customer-facing role will be very challenging for her.'

The defence had spent days discrediting me, suggesting I had orchestrated sex with McGregor and simply regretted it and then lied about it. But that day, a succession of professionals built up a wall of evidence that supported everything I said.

My legal team called Peter Byrne, an actuary, to provide evidence of the value of my lost earnings to date and possible future loss of earnings.

The calculations were all very convoluted and varied. In the end, he estimated my gross loss of earnings from shortly after the assault to just before the High Court case as approximately €136,000. Projecting into the future, he said that if I didn't work again, my net loss would be almost €600,000.

I didn't need actuaries with diagrams to explain my losses to me. Neither they nor property valuers could ever measure what I'd actually lost. They were only doing their job, but I knew the true cost. My many heartbreaks could never be calculated in the debit and credit columns of an accounts ledger.

No one could quantify how hard it had been to see my position at the hair salon filled by another girl. Or know the loss of my independence when I had to let my car go.

How could anyone estimate the emotional cost of leaving a house that I'd made into the home of my dreams? Or measure what it cost me to watch the neighbourhood where Mam lived, and I grew up, become out-of-bounds to me – associated only with terror?

What price could be put on a family life that was completely fractured? Since moving into Janice's home, I only had my daughter Freya two nights a week. Losing the ability to be the mother I wanted to be for my child, my everything, could never be counted.

As for my wellbeing, my peace of mind? Since December 2018, I had been a shell of a person, living a half-life. Could a dispassionate professional put a price on shelving six years of my life, waiting to have my day in court? Or on sitting in that court day after day, feeling stripped and exposed, listening to outrageous lies while strangers judged me?

Even losing my little dog was a heartbreak that no money could ever compensate for. Daisy couldn't get along with Janice's dog, so my mam was caring for her instead. But Daisy was thirteen, confused and upset, always looking for me. She was the best dog in the world, and I missed her terribly.

Hearing men estimate the costs of this assault in cold, hard cash, I didn't know whether to laugh or cry. I could list exactly how much I'd lost, and money meant absolutely nothing in comparison.

29.

The Reluctant Witness

Day 6, continued: Wednesday, 13 November 2024

'Judge, my client isn't here this morning,' McGregor's counsel said on day six of the trial. 'He had food poisoning overnight. I am hoping he will be here later on.'

McGregor had failed to show up on the day we expected him to start his evidence. When I looked over my shoulder, I could see his father, Tony, sitting in his usual place behind me. There was an empty seat beside him.

Part of me wanted to cheer aloud in the courtroom. The crushing anxiety of being in the witness box may have ended, but the thought of McGregor and Lawrence taking the stand made me feel ill. Knowing that together they would paint me in the worst possible light was another form of torture. McGregor had not shown up, and I was relieved.

Danielle was the first witness to be called on behalf of the defence. We had sent a few messages after that day in The Beacon. We had also exchanged 'Happy Christmas' sort of messages on Snapchat for a while, but I eventually stopped all contact. Not out of anger – I had nothing against Danielle. But she had become something else: a reminder. Every time I saw her name, that night came flooding back. It felt like touching a live wire. We'd been colleagues working in different salons, nothing more. Once I stopped working at Gerard Paul, even that weak connection was gone.

As she walked to the witness box that day in Courtroom 24, it was the first time in years I'd seen Danielle. Our eyes never met. She had been called as McGregor and Lawrence's witness, not ours. From what I understood, she hadn't wanted to come at all, and her demeanour told the same story. Danielle appeared uncomfortable in the witness box.

I understood the discomfort she must have felt at having to appear before a roomful of strangers to discuss an episode of her private life. I never wanted to drag anyone through this. But all these people – Danielle, Eimer, everyone connected to that night – were pulled into the machinery of the trial.

She began explaining that she did not know me well, as we had worked in different branches of the Gerard Paul hair salons.

McGregor's counsel did his best to draw her out. But Danielle repeated many of the same phrases I used: *I don't remember. I didn't hear anything. I didn't see anything.*

She didn't know why McGregor had driven us around for around two hours before taking us to the hotel. She said she remembered going into various housing estates and that she and McGregor 'didn't get along very well at the start'.

She didn't remember what the problem was.

She said she received an Instagram message from me at the Rotunda Hospital, where I told her I had been raped. She admitted she had been 'surprised' to hear that.

'I know Conor McGregor and Hand went into the other room. I saw them go in. I didn't know what was happening in there. She came back out, and everything was fine. This was just before we left. Everything was fine; I didn't notice anything that happened. No one seemed upset.'

'I suggest to you that Ms Hand was coming in and out of the bedroom in the suite?'

'Throughout the whole day, yeah.'

'And that she didn't appear distressed?'

'No.'

McGregor's counsel asked Danielle about me supposedly going into the sitting room, witnessing a sex act and calling Lawrence a 'dirty bastard' or something similar.

'I don't remember.'

McGregor and Lawrence's senior counsel showed her CCTV footage of us in the hotel lift, but she couldn't remember the scenes either.

'I think you had sex with Lawrence, isn't that correct?' Lawrence's senior counsel, John Fitzgerald, asked.

'Yes,' said Danielle.

'Am I right – that was three times?' Mr Fitzgerald was referring to Lawrence's statement to the guards.

'No, once.'

'You think it was once, okay. I put it to you that you both heard noises coming from the next room that suggested that Ms Hand and Mr McGregor were having sex in the next room?'

'No, I can't remember.'

'And that you said something to the effect of "she is going to regret that because she's bought a house with her boyfriend"?'

'I can't remember.'

'And why did you lie?' he asked, referring to her original statement where she said she had no sexual activity with Lawrence.

'Because I didn't feel it had anything to do with the case.'

She spoke about leaving the hotel with McGregor.

'My phone was broken, so I asked Conor if I could get a lift with him as I lived nearby,' she said. 'He didn't agree at first, but I asked the driver, and then he agreed. Nikita and James were supposed to get into the other car and go home. I said goodbye to Nikita and gave her a hug. She wanted everyone to stay, but I can't remember why.'

She spent seventeen minutes in the witness box before lunch and another thirty minutes after the break.

McGregor's lawyer noted Danielle wasn't 'hugely enthused' to be in court. When the judge summed up her evidence, he called it 'minimal' and warned the jury not to speculate about what she might have said if she'd been more forthcoming, 'or on the rack in the Tower of London'.

The knot in my stomach tightened when McGregor suddenly showed up at the Four Courts after lunch and took his seat beside his dad. The glee I'd felt earlier evaporated, and I braced myself for the worst as his counsel prepared to call him to the witness box.

30.

McGregor Takes the Stand

Day 6, continued: Wednesday, 13 November 2024

I made my decision the moment I saw McGregor stand that afternoon. I wouldn't look at him. Not once. I stared at the bare courtroom wall ahead. I looked at Gary's hand holding mine, or Clíona's hand. I looked anywhere but in his direction. I didn't want to see that face. It was bad enough listening to that voice telling a string of falsehoods.

In the witness box, he swept his absence away, saying he had been 'a little under the weather last night'. His senior counsel, Mr Farrell, brought him through his version of the events of that weekend in December.

'Nikita and I are from the same area. She is from Drimnagh,

I am from Crumlin. I didn't know her personally. I knew of her, I'd seen her around and we would be in the same circles,' he said. 'Nikita used to follow me on Instagram and send me messages, and sometimes I responded.'

I felt almost sick when he said my name. He implied I was constantly messaging him and we were 'chatting online'.

His counsel asked how we had first been in contact in October 2018.

'I am not 100 per cent sure. I believe she gave me a compliment of some sort, and I just said, "Thank you." And that was the beginning.'

He described Saturday, 8 December.

'I would have trained that day. I would have been just resting in my house after training and, obviously, it is Saturday in Dublin, seen what, you know, keeping my options open, maybe something might come up [...] At that time, I was in an estate called Ladycastle in the K Club.'

He said that evening he went to District 8 at the former Tivoli Theatre, where DJ sets were being played. The event organiser invited him on stage, and he said he took a picture with the DJ and the crowd and posted it to his Instagram stories for the public to see.

'Something I'd do often,' he said. 'Ms Hand responded to that picture that I put publicly; she responded privately. She sent me a picture of herself in a red jumpsuit on the evening [...] slightly provocative, and began asking me where I was and also letting me know what she was doing. We began talking then [...] it was a nice picture; I liked it.'

The word 'provocative' was like another gut punch. He was implying I sent the photo to arouse him, but I'd posted the same photo on my private story, which many friends and family members could view. I wouldn't have been sending it to everyone if it had been 'provocative'.

It wasn't like the unsolicited nude photos that he allegedly sent to American rapper Azealia Banks, which she shared online in July 2025. I was wearing my Christmas party outfit, a high-street fashion jumpsuit.

At around 2 a.m., McGregor said he and his friends, including James Lawrence, went to Krystle nightclub on Harcourt Street. He said everyone had rounds of drinks and 'a bit of cocaine was produced'. He said he received 'a slew of messages' from me, but didn't respond because he was with friends.

This was also untrue, but he painted me as an obsessive fangirl, pursuing him. He said they stayed out 'ridiculously late [...] 7 a.m.' in Krystle. He drove around with friends, including Lawrence, to see where to go next. 'I think Mr Lawrence was either dropped home or he jumped out.'

He said I told him to meet us at the salon. He said he 'knew of' me but had never met me, and had never met Danielle, so he had no plans about what to do afterwards. At around 10.15 a.m., McGregor and his driver arrived at the car park of the Goat Bar.

'I actually was of the belief I was going to their party. You know, there was conversation on the phone, we were joking about getting my hair done, obviously going into a salon. I thought I was going to the salon to their afterparty. But when I pulled up, they were outside the car in a blink.'

He never believed for one minute that he was going to our party. I had made it clear that Danielle and I were the only ones left, and we wanted to go to an afterparty.

'When Nikita came into the car, she was very bombastic and very, you know, energetic [...] They dived into the vehicle, and I felt myself going back, like this, against the window. I was kind of unsure what to do, so you know, we just drove around.'

Hearing him describe me as 'bombastic', my eyes rolled in my head. Again, he was trying to portray me as a party girl. When I went home that night, I Googled the word to see its exact meaning. I was right. He was trying to describe me as someone loud and ridiculous.

He downplayed the incident in which he erupted in fury at Danielle in the car. He said there 'wasn't really a disagreement'.

'Maybe Danielle thought I was showing off my watch or being a show off. I didn't feel that was the case. It wasn't necessarily a disagreement. I did not know the two ladies. I hadn't really decided what I was going to do. I also thought I was going to their party, then they are in my car, and now they are slagging me and making fun of me and whatnot. I was kind of like, right, it is early morning. I will just go home now, and let's call it a night [...] I was going to drop the ladies off and then make my way. And then, Nikita was "no, no, stop. Let's keep going, let's party away", and we all got along then perfectly. There was no problem.'

He said he collected Lawrence at his family home because he had 'two girls, two boisterous ladies, full of energy, and I needed to level it out, you know, make it a party, that's what they wished for, a party. And I thought James was perfect. Nikita knew James as well, so we made our way to James's.

'I end up going into the house. "James, I have got two lovely ladies here, real friendly girls. Do you want to have a look out the window? They are asking for you." You know, "do you want to come out and have a party, a little bit of buzz". Eventually, I got him on board, a little somewhat reluctantly, and then he came out.'

He directed his car to the hotel where he'd booked a room hours earlier, around 4.30 a.m. We arrived at The Beacon fifteen minutes after the room was ready for check-in at noon. He said his security went to get the key before we headed to the room. He said we walked into the penthouse full of 'energy, happiness and excitement'.

He told how he ordered vodkas and beers, and he set up Bluetooth to play music through the television. 'There was Bacardi as well,' he said. 'Nikita loves Bacardi, so that was got for her.'

His counsel prompted him about the bathtub.

'Nikita went up and jumped into the bath. So I heard a thud into the bath from the top end of the bath [...] It was a thud. I thought maybe she had probably hurt herself. I went over, and she tried to play it off by pretending to swim, a playful pretending to swim. I found it amusing. I thought it was strange. She was in fully clothed. She was in her high-heeled shoes.'

He referred to me in high-heeled shoes several times. I left the salon carrying the heels. In the car, I wore his designer runners, and in the CCTV footage, I was either barefoot or carrying my shoes.

He was asked where he first touched or kissed me.

'The car. Straight away.'

Then he said it soon started again in the hotel.

'So I just, kind of getting a bit more closer and having a buzz, you know. We were kissing and whatnot and then, you know, and all the rest of it.'

My stomach heaved as he began repeating the lies in his statement about how I pursued him for sex.

'I went into the bathroom. I didn't tell anyone nothing. I just went to the bathroom in the bedroom, and Nikita followed me in ...'

I had had enough. I would not listen to his lies. I rose from my seat but struggled to get past the crowds jamming the door. I couldn't get out of the courtroom fast enough. I thought I might get sick if I had to listen to more of his fiction.

Afterwards, I read how he reinvented a brutal rape scene and turned it into a story where I initiated sex and was an 'enthusiastic' participant in fully consensual and 'athletic' sex.

'I know I was there in the toilet. I know I had my zip open. I believe I did, yeah. So, as I was in the bathroom, Nikita was in and out of the bathroom and in the bedroom and very boisterous, very energetic and very enthusiastic. As I had began to walk out of the bathroom and was putting up my trousers, we began kissing and a bit more passionate, a lot more passionately and then it began to take off from there.'

'I am going to have to ask you to give us chapter and verse on it, Mr McGregor,' said his counsel. 'So when you say it took off from there, what exactly do you mean?'

'She performed oral sex on me at that moment. At that time, we were both clothed. I obviously had my trousers down, and then we began to take off our clothes. I took off my top, took off my runners. She took off her onesie thing, you know, took her shoulders out of it,' he said, apparently moving each of his shoulders to mimic the act of undressing.

Evidence already given the day before, from those who examined my torn outfit, made a mockery of the claim that I removed my own 'onesie'.

'That was it. We were both naked then in the bedroom, and we moved to the bed then,' he said.

He claimed that Danielle and James were on the nearby sofa bed.

'They were just three feet away […] The door was open.'

'Some people may find it unusual that you would engage in sexual activity in a bedroom with the door open,' said his counsel. 'What would you say about that?'

'You are not really thinking at that time. You can't see the sofa bed, so it wasn't like they were sitting there looking in. There was no thought about closing the door. It progressed very quickly.'

'You are going to have to tell us exactly what happened.'

'We began engaging in sexual intercourse, fully consensual. We began in the missionary position. So the sex was enthusiastic, and it was athletic, and then we were in the missionary position. Then at one point her legs are on my shoulders and still in the missionary position, and then another time, another time I am upright and her knees are towards her chest, and my hands are on the back of her thighs. That was the course of our missionary. Then she wished to get on top of me, so I said, "No problem". She moves to being on top of me. We have sex where she is on top of me now. It went through a multitude of these positions, you know, bent over and back again, and it went on for a bit.'

He said he could also hear James and Danielle having sex.

'Ms Hand has given evidence that she had a tampon inserted in her vagina, is that something you felt or noticed?'

'No, there was no tampon. In broad daylight, there was no tampon. There wasn't, not from what I could see, not from what

I could feel, and there was no blood, there was no discussion of a tampon or nothing. There was no tampon.'

I came back into the courtroom at that stage, hoping he had finished. Instead, I re-entered the courtroom just as he said he slept until James and I woke him by pulling his legs and giggling.

'She propositioned me again. She jumped onto the bed and began performing oral sex on me again, and we began to have sex again, this time her solely on top of me.'

He was asked about the timing of these supposed sexual encounters with me.

'All in, I was in the hotel room for about six hours, I believe. We began having sex the first time maybe an hour and a half in, and that would have probably went on, on and off, stop and start for maybe an hour and a half or so. I would have slept then for about an hour and a half, two hours. It was a good, deep sleep. I was out. I awoke, and they were still going, which I was a bit taken aback by. So then we had sex again. It wasn't as long as the first time, and I was ready to go.'

He said that I wanted to keep the party going.

'I just had nothing left, I was no good to no one, and I wished to leave. Then I was kind of just hanging around, and then I just decided I am going, so I just walked out.'

He added later: 'Nikita was keeping the door open and trying to pull out of my arm, "stay, stay, stay" so I am like this getting pulled out of the car. I say, "Look, I am going", and I beckoned my driver to drive, and then that is it, we exited.'

'Did you see any bruises on Nikita?'

'No bruises, whatsoever [...] Not an iota of distress was seen.'

He said he saw the chatter on social media afterwards about an assault and a sports star. He said he remembered initially saying, 'It's definitely not me.' When he started hearing his name, he said it felt like 'the most scary thing I have gone through in my life. I wanted to get everything correct ... I had been advised to go to a solicitors, jot down all my notes, everything that happened, show everything I have and all the rest of it.'

My senior counsel, John Gordon, rose to cross-examine McGregor in the late afternoon.

'Mr McGregor, you have just said that your reaction to all of this was "to show them everything I have".'

'Yeah.'

'Why didn't you give the guards your phone?'

'They didn't ask.'

'Are you sure about that?'

'Positive.'

'Okay, why didn't you offer it?'

'I was taking the advice of my solicitors.'

'So your solicitor advised you not to make your phone available; is that correct?'

'Not necessarily that, but he did not advise me to – it just never came up.'

'What do you mean it never came up?'

McGregor's counsel objected, and the judge said McGregor could claim privilege in relation to his solicitor's advice.

'Of course he can, absolutely,' said Mr Gordon. 'But what I want to know is why he, given that he says he was so anxious to assist, he didn't personally want to give his phone to the guards. Why didn't you?'

'Because the phone wasn't present during this incident. The CCTV was present, and the taxi footage was present, all of this stuff that was very important to the case, you know. My phone wasn't.'

I wondered why he and Lawrence hadn't been asked to hand over their phones. I handed over my phone, as did Ste.

'I am upset over that, to be honest,' he said. 'I want every single shred of evidence to be put before this court.'

McGregor was growing increasingly annoyed as my barrister questioned his cooperation with the guards. I could hear it in his voice, rising and getting louder. The atmosphere in the courtroom was tense. Everyone was silent, straining to listen to every word he had to say. Then he erupted.

'I want the statement of the taxi driver that saw your client frolicking,' he said, his voice now raised.

Referring to James Lawrence, he added, 'She was sucking his fucking dick in the back of the thing; it is a crazy carry-on.'

The entire courtroom felt his contempt. My eyes widened, and my head swivelled towards Clíona. 'What the hell ...?'

I didn't notice how the jury reacted to his aggressive comments. I was in too much shock. It was the fury and hatred behind the remark that scared me. His tone triggered me, reminding me of the McGregor who attacked me in The Beacon Hotel. The judge ordered him to restrain himself.

McGregor was referring to the taxi driver who'd collected Lawrence and me from the hotel around ten that night. The driver, who was from Pakistan and didn't have fluent English, claimed in his statement that he'd heard me performing oral sex in the back of his car. This never happened.

Most of that journey exists only as black fog. All I remember was being woken by the driver demanding money. However, the truth was I'd fallen asleep on Lawrence's lap.

Thankfully, Lawrence even mentioned this in his statement. 'She was lying down on my lap, and the taxi man kept looking back, probably thought that she was doing something sexual.'

The taxi driver's entire statement was confusing and contradictory. Not even McGregor's side called him as a witness.

McGregor would have known every line of Lawrence's statement, but that didn't stop him from trying to muddy the waters in the courtroom with a vile lie. He wanted to make dirt of me in public and didn't care how he did it. I was upset afterwards that no one explained what lay behind McGregor's outburst in court. RTÉ even reported his words that 'she was sucking his fucking dick in the back of the car'.

His lewd lies did him no favours, however. One reporter wrote about how 'the feeling of contempt and horror at the things Mr McGregor was saying and the way he was saying them, radiated from the jury box where the eight women and four men sat'. Another wrote, 'His comment and the aggressive and contemptuous tone in which he said it drew gasps in court from onlookers and from the jury.'

My counsel continued cross-examining McGregor.

'Mr McGregor, you are aware that my client gave her phone to the guards?'

'With the deleted messages, yes.'

'[...] And you are aware that she allowed to have them recovered?'

'Some, but not all.'

'She facilitated that?'

'Some, not all.'

'Isn't that right?'

'Some, not all.'

'Okay, and you are aware that your counsel has used them extensively in cross-examining her?'

'Yeah.'

'Isn't that right?'

'Mm-hm.'

'But you chose not to make your phone available?'

'No, there was not a choice. It never presented itself, and I am upset over that.'

'You are upset about it?'

'Yeah.'

'Would you like to give it now?'

'It is a different phone, but, yeah, if you want it, pal, no problem.'

I heard the sneering disrespect in his voice.

My counsel continued to quiz McGregor and asked him about losing a fight against Khabib Nurmagomedov in Las Vegas two months before he raped me.

'And how were you beaten in the fourth round?'

'A neck crank.'

'To the untrained eye, you were put in a headlock.'

'Mmm.'

'He put his arm around your neck and basically began to suffocate you. You couldn't breathe, isn't that right?'

'Mmm.'

'And ultimately, you had to tap to stop it?

'Yes.'

'Or you would have died?'

'Mmm. If I had of went to sleep, the ref would have stopped this.'

[...]

'This was a very distressing event?'

'It is a fight; it is a sporting event. You win some, you lose some in the martial arts game.'

'[...] from the beginning of her recounting of her experience with you, my client has described how you put her in an arm lock. Isn't that right?'

'Full of lies. Your client is full of lies. Everything is a lie, Sir.'

He brought up Eimer's evidence and reminded the court that she was the very first person I'd seen after the assault.

'Eimer Brennan recounts how, when Nikita arrived that evening, she described having been put in an arm lock by you. And she also says that after this, you said to her, "Now you know how I felt in The Octagon when I tapped three times." You said that?'

But McGregor snarled back.

'I mean, how anyone could believe that me, as a prideful person, would highlight my shortcoming. It is not in my nature. It is a full-blown lie among many lies.'

'Within literally a couple of hours of this happening, you're saying that she is so devious that she has made up this patent lie? You know that the only evidence in this court is that my client knew nothing about the rules of your game?'

He replied: 'Your client was present in Las Vegas in 2015 for my inaugural UFC World Title win. So, your client is well aware of the sporting aspects of mixed martial arts.'

He falsely insinuated I was in Las Vegas for his fight.

My counsel replied: 'Her evidence is that she wasn't at the match.'

That was the moment someone came up behind me and said the word 'liar' in my ear. I jumped with fright, and Gary's head whipped around. He had heard it too. There was nothing we could do about it without creating a scene in the courtroom.

McGregor continued to deny that he had put my head in an arm lock.

'It's a lie, and it is almost a fantasy in my head. It feels very like a fantasy.'

'You have heard the evidence that she was found to have bruising on her neck?'

'I heard the SATU guy say it was consistent with a love bite, yes.'

My counsel replied that my GP gave medical evidence of internal bruising. But McGregor continued saying it was a 'love bite' because those words were mentioned on Dr Kane's report from the Rotunda as a description of one bruise mark.

'Tell me this, where do you think she got all the bruises?'

'Well, I would say one off the bat, when she swan-dived into the bath and then, you know, you are out three days, absolutely three days.'

This 'three-day bender' was another lie he tried to spin. I left the salon on Saturday night at around 7 p.m, and the taxi driver's meter showed he dropped me off at Eimer's house on Sunday at 11.24 p.m. Her statement says that she poured me a glass of wine that I didn't drink – twenty-eight hours had passed, not seventy-two.

'Well, she said it herself, she went into the bath, walked across a stone layout in full heels and jumped into the bath. She is out three days. You take knocks and bruises. I tell you where she didn't get them – from me.'

The high heels were mentioned again, perhaps because they sounded 'provocative'.

'Are you saying that she didn't get any bruises from her encounter with you?'

'I will say the sex was athletic. It was physical. The sex with me now, not the sex with Mr Lawrence. I don't know about the sex with Mr Lawrence.'

He was making sure to remind the jury of his and Lawrence's fiction that I'd had sex with both of them that afternoon.

He had his own explanations for my bruises and injuries.

'I didn't cause them, so I was shocked. It was only upon piecing the evening back together and then thinking of all the events, and you know, the demeanour, and you know, seeing the CCTV footage and thinking of the bath and then thinking of the fact that three days across a multitude of different parties.'

McGregor listed the 'multitude of parties' as Airfield, the Goat Bar and the salon.

'Then you start to piece it together, and I'm not so much [shocked].'

My barrister told the court that James Lawrence was only mentioned during McGregor's third written statement, many hours after he read his first on 17 January 2019.

'Was that to suggest that maybe somebody else had caused these injuries?' Mr Gordon asked. 'Was it in your mind that Mr Lawrence might be the patsy?'

McGregor began stumbling over his words.

'Ehm – I am not – I don't believe so, and I am not sure. I was just – I don't know. I said my piece, and then I took my advice from my lawyers.'

'Was it in your mind that Mr Lawrence might take the fall for you?'

'Whoever could believe in something like this, to take a fall for something like this? How silly. What do you mean by this?'

[...]

'Your immediate reaction to seeing these was shock and to disassociate yourself completely by suggesting she had sex with someone else?'

'I didn't cause those bruises, and I asked the question: did she have sex with someone else [...] it seems that she most very well did.'

'Did what?'

'Had sex with somebody else on the evening in question.'

'Okay, so we are now onto the third person; is that right?'

'Your client had sexual relations with multiple people a multitude of times throughout that course of that three days – bender we will call it, yes.'

The judge interjected. 'You said that Mr Gordon's client had sex with multiple people?'

'Yeah, yeah, she did,' said McGregor.

'Who?' asked Mr Gordon.

'Myself and James, that I am aware of.'

'Are you speculating that she had sex with somebody else?' asked Mr Gordon.

'No. Well, I don't see – I don't see unless she had sex maybe in the Goat or the Grill or Airfield or the salon.'

'So you are speculating?'

'No, I am not speculating, that is not what I was speculating. I was just saying she had sex with multiple people; two people, you know, at least.'

Every chance he got, he used his platform in the witness stand to blacken my name as much as he could.

When it was put to him he came onto me, and I remonstrated with him not to do it, he replied, 'Lies, more lies.'

The trial finished for the day just before four, when McGregor requested a bathroom break after one hour and ten minutes on the stand.

I left the courtroom feeling degraded. His lies were already out there, reported in the media and read by my family and friends, and by people I'd never met.

I went back to Janice's apartment, feeling low. I felt completely stripped again after listening to him lie about having 'athletic' and 'enthusiastic' sex with me when he had raped me. I felt soiled and dirty.

Gary was trying to lift my mood, asking me if I would like this or that, and I was snapping at him in return. The truth was, I was annoyed at myself and taking it out on Gary.

Why the fuck did I put myself in that situation? I thought. *If I hadn't gone to the hotel, I wouldn't have to listen to him talk about me the way he's talking. I would never have been in that courtroom today. I wouldn't have to be degraded publicly like that.*

I felt a maelstrom of emotion, and most of it was negative and directed at myself. I didn't want to get out of bed the next day and face more shame and humiliation. I never wanted to see the inside of that courtroom again.

31.

No Comment

Day 7: Thursday, 14 November 2024

I didn't look, but I could hear McGregor's discomfort, his shifting in the witness box.

My senior counsel's voice soared through the packed courtroom as he spoke about McGregor's first statement, submitted in writing to the gardaí during his arrest on 17 January 2019.

'After you read that statement to the guards, the guards asked you some questions?'

'Yeah.'

'And I think your answer to the questions was "no comment"?'

McGregor's counsel shot up to object to the line of questioning, and the judge sent the jury out. An anxious hour followed. I wanted the jury to know exactly how McGregor had treated the investigation. The judge finally ruled with my counsel saying McGregor opened the door to the 'no comment' line of questioning by conveying to the jury that he provided full cooperation to the guards.

So when the jury returned, my counsel posed the question again to McGregor.

'Is it the case that in answer to every question that they [gardaí] asked you, you said "no comment"?'

The room was silent.

'This was the first time anything like this had ever occurred to or happened to me, and I was beyond petrified.'

McGregor was rattled.

'I went to a lawyer's office. I gave them my series of events in what had occurred, and then, with the seriousness of these allegations and accusations, I just took their advice from there on.'

'So is the answer yes, that you did say "no comment"?'

'In periods during the interview, I said "no comment", yes.'

'And I think you were asked over 100 questions?'

'Okay.'

'And you said "no comment"?'

'To some. I said what I was advised.'

[...]

'Beyond giving them that statement that day, you were not prepared to provide the guards with any further assistance; is that correct?'

'You know I would have loved to go to the top of a mountain, you know, with a microphone and shout it from the hilltops but, you know, with the seriousness of this allegation and how afraid I was, I spoke to my lawyers, I said my series of events so it was fresh and dialled in and then I just took their advice from there on in.'

'I see. So are you saying that, but for your lawyers, you would have been fully cooperative with the guards? Is that what you are saying?'

'[…] I was just taking the advice at that stage, you know. It was out of my hands. I was so nervous, I did not know what to do. It was alien to me; the first time anything like that had ever happened to me in my life.'

My counsel invited McGregor to read out the first statement he had also read aloud to gardaí in January 2019:

> *We started kissing and then moved on to start having sex. It was a long session. The sex was quite physical, and we had sex in multiple different positions. For instance, at one point, we were having sex, and she had her legs on my shoulders. I then had both my hands on the back of her thighs while she had her knees bent up in the air […] I eventually did wake up, and then she wanted to have sex with me again.*
>
> *[…] She jumped on top of me, and we started having sex again with her on top of me. We moved back again into*

that earlier position [...] At different points, I remember her saying to me, 'fuck me, fuck me' to encourage me. On both occasions I could tell Nikita was enjoying it and she was moaning with pleasure.

When he had finished reading, my counsel reminded McGregor that Detective Ger White tried to question him.

'[The detective] asked you, "How do you know Nikita Hand?" And your answer was, "no comment".'

'I was just going by the advice of my lawyers at that stage in a state of shock and fear.'

'[The detective] asked: "Is she from the same area as you in Crumlin?" Answer: "No comment." And it went on like that for at least 100, maybe 150 questions. Isn't that so?'

In fact, it was over 200 questions. I counted.

The detectives also asked McGregor that day: 'How is it possible those injuries can be caused by consensual sex? This is the chance to say or explain ...'

Again, his response was: 'No comment.'

When he read out his second written statement later that night, he posed the question to investigators: 'Are you sure she did not have sex with anyone else?'

The guards then responded: 'You're asking us, are we sure she didn't have sex with anyone else. Have you any information you would like to pass on to us?'

He responded once again: 'No comment.'

Later that night, detectives interviewed McGregor again under caution, and for the first time, James Lawrence was introduced into his statement.

'I am certain that Nikita was at all times consenting to what we did together, and I believe Nikita had sex with James Lawrence after I left the hotel,' he read out.

'How are you aware James Lawrence had sex with her?' the detective asked.

'No comment,' he replied.

'You say you believe it. How do you believe it?'

'No comment.'

'Did he tell you he had sex with her?'

'No comment.'

Judge Owens interjected in the courtroom to say that everyone had the right to answer 'no comment' on the advice of lawyers, and that the jury could not draw an inference from that.

'You don't owe an explanation to anybody,' he said to McGregor.

McGregor's reaction may have been legal, but it still begs the question: why didn't he defend himself and cooperate with gardaí? Was saying 'no comment' to 200 questions the first reaction of an innocent man? Even simple questions, such as 'Are you the owner of Proper [No.] 12 Whiskey?' received a 'No comment' reply.

Most of these weren't trick questions. These were the sorts

of things you'd tell a stranger at a bus stop. He had so many opportunities to cooperate, but didn't. Instead, he handed over bad fiction in the form of prepared statements.

My counsel asked McGregor whether he was aware that Lawrence used the same solicitor's firm as he did. McGregor eventually admitted that he 'possibly' paid Lawrence's legal fees.

'I'm not a million per cent. I get staggering legal bills,' McGregor said. 'I don't check them all.'

The judge intervened, saying: 'It is a very simple question. Did you pay Mr Lawrence's legal bills?'

'I believe I did,' McGregor responded.

My counsel put it to McGregor that he said I was not wearing a tampon when he had sex with me. He reminded McGregor that Dr Kane said he removed the tampon, which was 'wedged' at the very top of the vagina, using forceps. Then my counsel turned to Dr Charlotte Murphy's DNA evidence.

'To put that in simple language, she found your DNA in precisely the same location where Dr Kane found the tampon.'

He added: 'Well, we know that she had a tampon wedged up at the top right-hand corner of her vagina, I think that is a fact we all agree on?'

'Yeah.'

'How do you think it got there?'

'Not from me, not with me,' McGregor said.

Mr Gordon asked McGregor whether he recalled requesting

his security to book the penthouse at The Beacon at about 4.30 a.m. on Sunday, 9 December 2018.

'I can't recall the exact times, possibly yeah,' McGregor said.

He confirmed he had been to The Beacon Hotel before.

'If you go out on a Saturday evening and if you are up until the early hours of the morning, I would usually get a hotel room to, you know, to sleep and rest and wake up and shower, eat and get dressed in something fresh before I go back into the normal world, if you will. It would be a thing I would have done back then for sure.'

[...]

'So I must suggest to you that in fact the reason that you would hire hotel rooms at nighttime is with the intention of bringing girls back for sex?'

'No,' McGregor responded. 'I would bring back, certainly get one [room] maybe for a party or an afterparty or have the option but also just to, just to get myself rested and refreshed and wake up and have the breakfast and use the gym and that would be more the reason.'

My counsel said McGregor was at the nightclub with a group of girls, and that the girls decided to go home.

'So here we are, it was around half seven in the morning, and the girls were gone; isn't that right? After that, you make contact with Nikita Hand?'

'She was making contact with me, and it was at that time I engaged; I engaged back.'

Mr Gordon asked if McGregor had told me he was going to bring me to a party.

'I was invited out to the salon,' McGregor said. 'They were having an afterparty. It was an after-after party, a post-Christmas party celebration, and I was out already. I still wished to party. There were even jokes that I was going to get my hair done.'

Mr Gordon said McGregor ultimately knew he was going to The Beacon Hotel.

'Not necessarily, sometimes I would book rooms and not use them,' he said. 'I could've ultimately decided to go to my home or to my mother's home.'

'The purpose you had reserved the suite was to have sex?'

'The purpose was I would have a place of rest, and if I wished to have an afterparty. If sex was to happen, if I was lucky enough, maybe, I am not going to say [...] But I don't get a room just to have sex.'

He added: 'Back then, six years ago, that would've been what I would've done.'

The entire courtroom was silent as he continued, everyone listening intently.

My counsel said Danielle and I were in the car for a long time. He suggested McGregor was buying time until the hotel room became available at noon.

'There was no waiting around or trying to buy time or anything like that, no.'

The legal teams finished with McGregor before lunch. He had completed an hour and a half on Wednesday and a half day on Thursday.

One of McGregor's security, Denis Dezdari, was called after him.

My counsel asked Dezdari why he requested the hotel staff to clean the room at 2 a.m. on Monday, 10 December 2018?

'I am just wondering why you would be concerned with cleaning up the room or getting rid of glasses or tidying the room?' Mr Gordon asked. 'Why would you do that? Would you always do this after a McGregor party, you clean the room?'

'No.'

'Why were you doing it on this occasion, do you know?'

'I can't say I did or I didn't, you know. I don't remember.'

Counsel told him he had confirmed this in his statement to the guards. The guards also confirmed with the hotel that Dezdari had the room cleaned at 2 a.m., rather than wait for the regular cleaning rota in the morning.

32.

Lawrence Under Oath

Day 7, continued: Thursday, 14 November 2024

'You can see from the video … she was kissing me, slapping my arse, biting my ear, coming on to me.' James Lawrence leaned forward in the witness box, his words spilling out in a torrent. I hadn't expected it, but his evidence was almost as bad as McGregor's.

Lawrence's senior counsel, John Fitzgerald, had filed several motions to dismiss the case against his client, arguing that it was contradictory. It was certainly confusing.

I never believed I had sex with Lawrence. The forensic professionals found no physical or DNA evidence of it having happened. But Lawrence inserted himself into the case once he claimed to the gardaí, in his statement the day after Conor

McGregor's, that he had sex twice with me after McGregor left the hotel.

In the original investigation, gardaí looked at the evidence of my bruises, my intoxication on the CCTV and decided no woman in that state would or could have consented to sex. They tried to build a case against Lawrence and sent it to the DPP.

When the DPP declined to prosecute and a civil case became my only recourse, my solicitors had to do the same. They included Lawrence in the civil suit because the court needed to formally test and rule out his involvement, so that my case against McGregor was not undermined by Lawrence's statement to police. If sex happened twice, as he claimed in that statement, I was incapable of consenting to it, and he had therefore raped me.

'This is one of the difficulties of this trial,' the judge said in the jury's absence as he addressed my counsel, Mr Boland. 'Because, let's face it, your client's position in relation to this is that none of this happened at all.'

'Correct,' replied my counsel.

The judge added: 'And that all of this thing [was] to get Mr McGregor out of a hole.'

I'd already bumped into Lawrence a few times in the Four Courts, usually near the toilets. But I never needed to worry about him. Every time he caught sight of me, he fled in the opposite direction. He stayed well away, except in the courtroom where he sat behind me every day of the trial, usually on his own.

As each day in the courtroom passed, he seemed more agitated and exasperated. He would sigh loudly or mutter. He kept leaving his seat during the proceedings and, minutes later, I'd hear him coming back again. He was up and down to his legal team every time there was a break. His restlessness distracted me, keeping me constantly aware of him. I had to lean a little further forward on my bench to put space between us.

'There's no way he's going into the witness box,' I said to Gary and Clíona. 'He can't sit for five minutes.'

I was wrong. He sprang up to give evidence when he was called at 2.30 p.m., two hours after McGregor's time in the witness box ended.

From the beginning, his words came rapid fire, tumbling over each other. The judge and his own senior counsel stopped him many times, asking him to repeat himself and slow down, as no one could keep up.

'I counted fourteen times myself, maybe if you go over the video. You'll probably count more. I rejected her fourteen times. I turned away from her fourteen times. She was chasing me around the lift. She lifted me into the lift. I didn't lift her. I didn't assist her. It was all her pushing on me [...] She put moves on me. But I rejected her, I rejected her, I rejected her, I rejected her ...'

Despite being asked to slow down, Lawrence kept at it, each

accusation launched before the last could settle. He couldn't expel his stories fast enough, words he'd seemed to have been storing for years.

He kept repeating that the CCTV verified everything he said. I saw the CCTV too. I had to watch it through a gap in my fingers, and I never want to see it again. But I saw a very drunk woman careening around the car park, the lift and the hotel reception.

I saw this girl, who looked like me – who was me, but was also lost to me – kiss Lawrence on the cheek. I saw her arm around him and his arm around her. I saw her biting his ear. But that girl reminded me of those inebriated girls who stagger up to you after a long night, grip your arm and say things like, 'You're so lovely. Has anyone ever told you? You're so lovely.'

I was stumbling around, lost, looking for a steadying hand, for someone to look after me; nothing like the sex-hungry predator that he and McGregor tried to portray me as.

Even the judge commented (in the absence of the jury): 'This woman was intoxicated at the very least [...] She was certainly not behaving normally.'

Yet Lawrence gave evidence that I 'peer-pressured' him, in front of McGregor's driver, to return to The Beacon Hotel to have sex after we left in the car the first time.

'We got to the car park [...] She was kissing me, asking me to do stuff like that. I told her I wasn't going anywhere. I was completely done with the night.'

He claimed I wanted to go to the Marble Arch pub.

'I told her I wasn't going to bring her anywhere. I had no shoes or socks on. I was done. I wanted just to go home. She continued to kiss me and stuff like that. I then looked and seen Gezim was looking. He is the driver of the car. He was looking in the rearview mirror, and he was asking me what I was doing [...] She was asking me what I was doing. I felt, not embarrassed, but basically peer pressure. She is doing it in front of another man, and I felt a little bit belittled.'

He said the driver dropped us back to the hotel.

'I asked Gezim had he got condoms. He then gave me two condoms. We got into the lift and went up [...] We were kissing in the lift on the way up. We were kissing from the lift, kissing through the corridor, we were kissing when the door opened [...] We had sex on the same bed that me and Danielle had it.'

Without being asked, he recited the positions we were in for this made-up sex.

'I started off in the normal position, basically me on top of her. We continued like that for a while. Then Nikita asked me would I like for her to get on top. I told her, yeah.'

He insisted I instigated everything.

'She kept me going, kept me going, in front of other people. She peer-pressured me into going back to the hotel. You mightn't believe it because I am a man, but that is the way it was.'

He also talked about the sex he claimed to witness between McGregor and me. He claimed the door between the bedroom and the sitting room was open.

'One thing I can one hundred per cent stand by is that the door was open the whole night,' he said, adding he heard 'sex noises' and could hear me 'moaning'.

I felt sickened with his fictional description of me 'bouncing' on McGregor as we had sex.

'You can see from the bathroom straight into the room where Conor and Nikita [were] having sex, and Nikita was on top of Conor having sex. She was on top of him, bouncing on top of him.'

'Okay. Can you remember what Ms Hand was wearing?' Lawrence's counsel asked.

'She had nothing on her at this time. She was completely naked on top of Conor.'

The second bathroom in the sitting room was surrounded by glass, like the bedroom ensuite. But it would have been difficult for him to see from the second bathroom into the bedroom. According to garda evidence given in the court, the sitting room and bedroom were separated not by one, but by two back-to-back doors, which opened into each room. Given the angle of the bathroom that Lawrence used, both of the doors into the sitting room and the bedroom would have had to be pinned wide open for Lawrence to have seen the bed.

I didn't remember that there were two interconnecting doors, but I remembered that a door between the two rooms was closed, and I testified to that. Danielle's statement in 2019 said the door had been closed over but not fully shut.

I knew my barrister would get his turn. He'd cross-examine him, pick apart his story. But it was hard sitting there, hearing a made-up version of events, designed to make him and McGregor look like the victims.

Lawrence's counsel asked when he realised that I was accusing McGregor of rape.

'Almost instantaneously. The next morning, when we woke up, there was articles left, right and centre on the internet. I think one of the major newspapers in Ireland had printed it – "sports star was in a rape allegation" and whatever. It was on every page.'

'Did you think that referred to Mr McGregor?'

'I didn't first off, and then as I read on through the day, I read on that it was two girls in a hotel, it was more and more close.'

'Okay. And did you discuss with Mr McGregor what you would do about this?'

'I didn't discuss the night or anything like this. I decided I would do the same as him, go and seek legal advice because I had been with the same girl.'

[...]

'What did you do on the solicitor's advice?'

'I went and I gave a voluntary statement to the police about the night. That was it.'

'Okay. Do you know what a patsy is, Mr Lawrence?' his counsel asked.

'No.'

'A patsy is a fall guy, somebody who takes a dive for someone else?'

'Right.'

'Are you being a fall guy for Mr McGregor?'

'Never in a million years. What man would put himself up for the rape of a woman?'

Lawrence spoke to the guards early in the investigation, but only provided pre-prepared statements after that, answering 'no comment' when questioned later:

'You're friends with Conor.'

'No comment.'

'But I just want to know how was it decided to go back to The Beacon?'

'No comment.'

The jury never heard this, as my counsel could not question him on this. However, my counsel began punching holes in some of Lawrence's evidence almost immediately. Lawrence had portrayed himself as a sober witness when his counsel was examining him.

'I don't go out that much and I'm not much of a heavy

drinker so I'd have a few vodka and Lucozade, but I wouldn't go overboard [. . .] I'd always have me senses about me with drink,' he said about his Saturday night out with McGregor.

He talked about his sobriety again when he described arriving at The Beacon Hotel.

'We all had drinks. I'm not much of a drinker. I poured myself a drink and was having a sup of that.'

But my counsel referred to his first statement to gardaí, in which he said he returned home after being out in Krystle with McGregor on Sunday morning, 9 December, and that his mother gave him €20 to pay for the taxi. The statement read: 'When I left Krystle, I was bad on the drink. My Ma told me when I came back, I got money and gave the taxi €20.'

'So you came home drunk?' Mr Gordon said.

'Yeah.'

'And you got up again two hours later, I think, isn't that right, around 10 [a.m.]?'

'Yeah.'

'So, you had two and a half hours sleep or thereabouts?'

His counsel had also asked him if he took cocaine.

'I have never taken cocaine, and I didn't take cocaine,' he said. 'Drugs have had a bad effect on my family, and I stayed well away from them.'

'You have heard the evidence that you came out of the house with a bag, or sorry, that Mr McGregor came out . . .'

'Yes, that's a lie. It didn't come from my house. I am standing by that. I do not do cocaine. I have no involvement with cocaine, whatsoever.'

What Lawrence failed to mention when he said he 'stayed well away' from drugs was that he was facing drug possession charges at that time. Gardaí had searched him and found him in possession of MDMA, commonly known as ecstasy, during the Electric Picnic festival in Stradbally, Co. Laois, a year earlier, in September 2023.

Lawrence continued claiming he had sex three times with Danielle before having sex twice more with me. My counsel questioned the frequency of sex he had with Danielle in the hour available.

'How many times did you have sex with her in total?'

'I had sex in total with Danielle three times. I can remember this for a fact because I used all three condoms with her.'

[...]

'So, between you getting the condoms and [when] Conor wanted to leave, was there about an hour?'

'I am not sure on the times.'

[...]

'And you are telling the jury that you had sex three times with Danielle Kealey?'

'Yeah, that's a fact.'

'In an hour?'

'Fact. I don't know the time difference, but I definitely had sex with Danielle three times.'

'You will recall that she was cross-examined on this and that she says she had sex with you once?'

'She also said she didn't have sex with me at all,' he retorted.

My counsel continued, referring to evidence from one of McGregor's security guards.

'He gives evidence that he checked in [on the hotel suite] from time to time, isn't that right?'

'Yeah.'

'And on no occasions when he checked in did he see you apparently having sex with Danielle. He seems to think that when he did call in, you were dressed.'

'Probably was dressed, yeah. I wasn't walking around in the nip after having sex anyway. I am not sure I even had my clothes off, could have had my bottoms down, I am not sure.'

'So you say you had sex three times?'

'Yeah.'

[...]

'Did you ejaculate on each occasion?'

'Yeah.'

'You did?'

'Yeah.'

'Okay, this all happened within an hour?'

'Yeah.'

'So, within this hour, the two of you dressed yourselves after sex on three occasions?'

'Yeah. It doesn't last that long if you are having sex. Who is to say it lasted this time, or for this long? The first time is five minutes, still another fifty-five minutes to go. First time is ten minutes, still forty minutes to go.'

Lawrence became rattled when quizzed on the bruising on my body. He raised his voice as he insisted he had seen no bruises.

'You said you had sex in the missionary position and then you had sex with her on top of you?'

'Yeah.'

'May I suggest to you that if you did all of that you would have seen all of those bruises?'

'That is what you suggest. I am telling you what I seen.'

'What are you saying you saw?'

'She didn't have any bruises on her at all, [especially] none of the bruises that were shown in them pictures.'

'You are saying she had no bruises at all?'

'I didn't see any of them bruises whatsoever. I didn't see a bruise on her cheek. I didn't see a bruise on her boob. I didn't see any bruise on her, apart from the one she pointed out on her leg or her arm … Like I said, it was a small bruise. I don't know where she got the bruising from. She didn't get it from me.'

[…]

'Would you agree that this has all the hallmarks, all of these marks, of a violent assault?' Mr Gordon asked.

'I have also seen, when I go out on a night out, or my partner goes out, or anyone goes out on a night out, you could end up injured or marked,' Lawrence replied. 'I don't know how she got the bruises. Like I said, she didn't get them from me, and as far as I know, she didn't get them from Conor. I didn't hear anything from the room other than pleasurable sex.'

[…]

'Would you agree that, however she got them, she got a bad beating?'

'Like I said, I don't know. I don't know where she got them. I do not know. How do you know she got a bad beating?'

'The photographs.'

'That doesn't mean she was beaten. I am not a bruise expert, neither are you. You don't know where they came from, and neither do I.'

My counsel asked Lawrence about me breaking down in tears that night.

'Not broke down, not broke down […] She teared up a minute or two for a second. Like I say, I asked what was wrong with her, but she wouldn't tell me. It started annoying me because I was thinking, "Why is the girl having sex with me and then having a little tiff about it?" And then she explained to me that it was the bruise thing. She asked me, what is she going to tell her boyfriend? She is looking to tell her boyfriend another lie.'

'In any event, you had sex with her again at that point, you say?'

'No, I didn't. I said she became upset after the second time having sex. We had sex, we had food, and we had sex again. The second time we had sex, we were all done, and all finished, she had a tear in her eye. She instantly dried it back up. Everything was all good. In the lift, you can see her again kissing me, hugging me, the nicest fellow again. Everything is all good again, she is in a happy mood again.'

He insisted at every opportunity that McGregor had done nothing.

'We were four foot away from Nikita at all times. I was four foot away from Nikita at all times. Like I told you already, I don't care what man it is, it could be my brothers, it could be anyone, I would not let any man do anything to any woman, nothing, nothing. Not a slap, not a bleedin' pulling the hair [...] If I thought he bleedin' slapped her once, I wouldn't be here.'

'Tell me, what's your attitude to having sex with girls who are drunk?'

'We all had drink on us, we were all in our right state of mind. If you look at the videos, Nikita didn't remember this, and she didn't remember that, but she is well able to text her boyfriend Ste. She was well able to lie to her boyfriend.'

[...]

'Did you notice that she had a tampon?'

'No, she didn't have any tampon in her. If she had had a tampon in her, she could have said that. I wouldn't have had sex with her. When I put my penis in Nikita, everything was seemingly fine, the way it is with any other girl. I started off on top. I started off on top, yeah, and then she asked me would I like for her to get on top. I said, "Yeah," and she got on top, and that is where she finished. There was no moaning, no pain, no nothing, she was all good; it was all good.'

He spent about two hours in the witness box and, with no further questions, the hearing was adjourned at 4.30 p.m. until the following morning. Day eight would be brief: a single medical witness took the stand, followed by legal argument, and the court adjourned within two hours.

I left the court on day seven, however, feeling as if I'd been mauled and trampled upon again. I felt stained with the lies he and McGregor had delivered to a gallery full of strangers and to the world. The only saving grace was that I knew I had told the truth, and it was almost over. The pair of them had done their worst and I was still standing; sick and shaken, hollowed out, but standing.

33.

Closing Speeches

Day 9: Tuesday, 19 November 2024

Loathsome. The word rolled around in my head. It seemed odd to hear the person paid to defend McGregor accuse the jury of possibly loathing the sportsman. Yes, his senior counsel did this.

'For all I know, most of you may well have [had] negative views about Mr McGregor before you even sat on this jury,' he said. 'You may have an active dislike of him. Some of you may even loathe him.'

McGregor's counsel continued in this surprising vein during his closing submission.

'Mr McGregor is someone who is probably hard to avoid. He is somebody who elicits strong views; some people very much do not love him, there is no getting away from that [...] It might be something of a euphemism to say that Mr McGregor has a forceful personality ... We have ears, so when Mr McGregor gives his evidence and refers to "two lovely ladies", we do hear the intake of breath coming from the jury box.'

He continued: 'Many of you may also have considered it ill-advised for Mr McGregor to have described Ms Hand and Ms Kealey as being somewhat "bombastic" when they got into the car.'

For the first time, I was tempted to glance over my shoulder to see how McGregor was handling this barely concealed criticism of his performance on the stand.

'You may also be unimpressed with the picture of a man who leaves the family home on a Saturday, goes into town and ends up drinking with women in hotel penthouses. These are all aspects of Mr McGregor's behaviour that are unlikely to endear him greatly to you.'

Mr Farrell leaned in towards the jury box.

'But I'm not here to ask you to like Mr McGregor. I'm simply here to ask you to actually look at the evidence. I'm not asking you to invite him to Sunday lunch. I'm simply asking you maybe to interrogate your own views in respect to Mr McGregor.'

He was effectively saying the defendant may have come across as unlikeable and rude, but that could not be part of the jury's consideration.

'You do not give a verdict in accordance with your gut

reaction, with your feelings, with the fact that you might not like Mr McGregor,' he stated.

McGregor's counsel was clever. He was charging them to be a fair-minded group that could acquit a man they might loathe if the evidence against him was weak.

He then talked about the issue paper: the final list of questions the jury had to answer to reach their verdict.

'You have the issue paper. The legal way it is framed is to say, "Did Mr McGregor assault Ms Hand?" In reality, the case is about rape. Rape is a form of assault, and it's only if you answer that question, say "yes", then you go on to consider the other consequences, the damages and so on.'

Then McGregor's counsel turned his attention to me, describing my evidence as 'a very carefully curated account'.

The way he described my evidence was: 'I am making my allegation, and if you want to cross-examine me or ask me about any other details, I can't remember; I was confused.'

He talked about the CCTV evidence: 'In the aftermath of what she alleges to have been a rape [...] You hardly need me to tell you what that CCTV tends to show.'

I felt my colour rise when he spoke about Lawrence and the CCTV.

'She clearly found Mr Lawrence irresistible. I am not sure what charms Mr Lawrence has that the rest of us don't, but look at that CCTV and just try to figure that out.'

He added: 'There was a whole part of Ms Hand's evidence

where she said "That's not me". It is her. Ms Hand is apparently prepared to sue [Lawrence] for rape in circumstances where she doesn't think she had sex with him and she never thought she had sex with him, so you will just have to make of that what you will.'

He also said I was lying about not recognising The Beacon.

'She does not apparently, at any stage, see the large sign saying "The Beacon Hotel" that is above a door that she went in and out of, I don't know how many times. You can count the number of times on the CCTV footage.'

My throat closed as McGregor's counsel continued on and on. I kept my eyes lowered, looking at Gary's hand or Clíona's hand gripping mine. I couldn't look anywhere else. I was afraid to look at the jury in case I saw them nodding in agreement.

McGregor's counsel was critical of my counsel's decision to introduce a property valuation expert.

'He told you how much it would cost to buy a house in Cabinteely or Shankill, in a nicer area than where Ms Hand was living,' he said. 'I think the amount of €665,000 was claimed in the pleadings. And if you don't understand how any of that could arise in a case of this sort, don't worry, you are not alone [...] It's not normally a feature of compensation claims for people to say, "I'd like a new house".'

I cringed at that. But he did what he was paid to do. He made it sound like this entire ordeal was about money – compensation instead of vindication.

He kept going back to the CCTV where he described me as 'happy'.

'Happy, happy, happy, all the way through, happy, and then – bang! As soon as she knows she has to go home and face the music, that's when the allegation is made. You can't ignore that.'

His entire submission was almost two hours and twenty minutes long. I felt like I had done several rounds in a boxing ring by the time he'd finished attempting to punch holes in my evidence. But I kept revolving my nanny's rings on my fingers, running my fingers over her scarf in my pocket and praying.

Nanny, please give me the strength to get through this.

Lawrence's counsel, John Fitzgerald, gave his closing submission next.

'Mr Lawrence obviously arrives here in a very different way, with none of the fame or perhaps even notoriety that Mr McGregor has,' he told the jury. 'He has lived his thirty-five-odd years in relative obscurity, and I would bargain that after the experience of the last couple of weeks, it is obscurity to which he would like to return after this trial.'

He spoke a lot about the CCTV evidence too.

'This isn't a situation where a man is mauling a woman that you might feel in some way uncomfortable about,' he said. 'In fact, she is initiating the contact. She is putting her arms around him, she is kissing him, she is grabbing his arm on one occasion, putting it around her and, in fact, particularly in the early stages, you'll see he has his hands down by his side. The initiator of the sexual contact here, or the affectionate contact, flirtatious contact, is Ms Hand, and she exhibits no signs of distress, none whatsoever, quite the opposite, that, I'm going to suggest to you, wholly supports Mr Lawrence's account.'

He also questioned my evidence that I began having flashbacks when I returned to the hotel room.

He said the jury should look at the CCTV and referred to a Groucho Marx line: 'Who are you going to believe, me or your own eyes?'

Mr Fitzgerald's submission was mercifully short, ending at 1.15 p.m. that day, after less than forty minutes.

After lunch, my counsel, John Gordon, rose to give his closing submission. He talked about McGregor's 'mask slipping' in the courtroom.

'Having given very bland evidence for quite some time, the mask slipped. He lost his temper. And what did we witness? And you witnessed it – a stream of invective aimed directly at my client across the courtroom. What does that tell you about Mr McGregor?'

[...]

'As I said while I was opening the case, she is no angel. She never pretended to be an angel. She was out for a good time and, indeed, up to a certain point, she had a great time. But things went badly wrong.'

My counsel claimed McGregor had laid his plans for sex at half past four in the morning when his driver had booked The Beacon Hotel.

'At that time, he was in town, I think he was in Krystle with a group of friends. Among those friends were two girls. Krystle went on until half past seven. The girls decided to go home. So here he was at half past seven, eight o'clock in the morning, the suite booked, but no girls. Nikita said in the course of her evidence that she was surprised to hear from him so late in the morning. You are entitled to infer that that wasn't his original plan at all. She was, in fact, the substitute.'

He rubbished McGregor's claims that he often booked a hotel room to wind down after a night out and use the gym.

'That is all risible nonsense, absolute poppycock. He started his evidence by saying that he actually had left his own gym to go to Dublin because he had a good workout. But he ended by saying he might actually stay in town to use the gym in the hotel. Isn't that complete nonsense?'

He was also scornful of McGregor's explanations for my injuries, highlighting that, 'He must drop some more possibilities into the equation. And these are possibilities that he kept to himself until he was here in court. She took a swan dive into the bath. Really? She was out for three days, and she probably got knocked about in Airfield or the pub or whatever it was. Really? Thank goodness you have the common sense to realise that you are being sold a pup by this arrogant man.'

I smiled to myself when he said that. For the first time, McGregor was getting a real pummelling in the courtroom.

Mr Gordon reminded the jury of the professional evidence, citing that I suffered from PTSD.

'The defendants did not call a psychiatrist, but they could have. The defendants did not call the vocational assessor, but they could have. The only reason they didn't call any of these people is that they knew that any of these professional people would actually agree with my professional people.'

He told the court that they could 'assume that Mr Lawrence was in cahoots with Mr McGregor from the word go'. He said he didn't furnish his statement to the guards until McGregor did on 18 January.

'So it's at that point that he drops in the little hand grenade that he had sex with my client as well. He describes it as "soft sex" in his statement to the guards. Why would you throw in the word "soft"? You'd throw it in because you were now aware, since you've seen all the photographs, that this lady had been badly beaten up. You throw in the word "soft" to distance yourself from all of that, but at the same time confuse the narrative, make her out to be an even bigger hussy than you are trying to say she is anyway.'

He described Lawrence's rushed performance in the witness box.

'You have seen the mantra, the rushing through the answers, the repetition of the same thing, the mantra. It is quite clear, again using your common sense, that these two chaps have been in collusion throughout and are continuing to be in collusion.'

He tried to explain some of the inconsistencies in my salon manager Eimer's evidence, about what I told her.

'And of course her account is a bit all over the place when she finally gets to talk to somebody. She is suffering from a fragmented memory. She is all over the place. Why wouldn't she be all over the place? How would you feel if somebody had done that to you? Would you be cool, calm and collected?'

He spent a long time outlining what he described as all 'the irrefutable evidence' that I was held in a neck hold and discussed potential compensation for my injuries.

'My client did suffer PTSD, post-traumatic stress disorder, something which, according to her psychiatrist, is triggered by a violent event, and she is still suffering from it, and she will continue to carry it with her. That's the evidence. And so I would suggest that when you come to these levels of compensation and when you come to special damages, you have regard to this particular evidence.'

He highlighted that McGregor's actions retraumatised me again and again.

'The abuse didn't just happen in the hotel, it didn't just happen during the garda investigation, it continued in the litigation, it continued in the pleadings in this case, and it continued throughout the hearing of this case when you were subjected to arrogant, distasteful, dishonest testimony from the defendant. So the abuse hasn't ended, it's continuing.'

I sat up straighter as I heard my counsel shred McGregor's character.

'Rather than repetitiously calling my client a liar, venomously and otherwise in the course of his evidence, the liar here is Mr McGregor, who doesn't have the courage, who doesn't have the decency to own up to what he did. This is a man who lives by the media, who thrives by the media. What he should have done, if he was a man at all, is apologise to my client for what he did to her that night. But he is not a man; he is a coward, a devious coward, and you should treat him for what he is.'

The words 'devious coward' settled in the courtroom. I felt them in my chest. I sat on that hard bench in the courtroom's silence and took the first real breath I'd taken all day. I wanted to shout *yes* and *thank you* and *finally!* I wanted to jump up and applaud my own counsel.

Mr Gordon's closing submission lasted an hour and forty minutes. He'd unravelled the entire narrative and wove it back into its proper shape. I was relieved. Someone had finally called McGregor out for who he was, and I left that day trembling with something that felt dangerously close to hope.

34.

Judge's Charge

Day 9, continued: Tuesday, 19 November–
Day 11: Thursday, 21 November 2024

The first hour wasn't so bad. I could hold myself upright on the bench in Courtroom 24, attentive, hands folded.

By the second hour, my tailbone started to ache. A dull throb at first, easy to ignore. I shifted my weight to the right. Then back to the left. Rolled my shoulders and stretched my neck as inconspicuously as I could.

Three hours in and I'd forgotten what it felt like to be comfortable. The ache had spread up my spine, settling into my lower back. My hip cramped. My legs felt numb from where they met the edge of the bench. I'd move and realise I had pins and needles that made me want to stand and shake them out.

But I couldn't move. Not really. A slight adjustment here, a subtle shift there; an occasional trip to the toilets with Clíona, moving as if I'd forgotten how to. Anything more would draw attention and look restless. I didn't want to do anything to suggest I wasn't taking this seriously.

So I sat, as my body slowly seized. Everyone else central to the case, including the jurors, had to sit there too. I expected to be riddled with anxiety and terror throughout the process, but I had underestimated the physical discomfort of the courtroom.

The judge's charge, often referred to as the summing up in the UK, was the final address to the jury. It was a marathon event in my case. He started his charge just before 4 p.m. on Tuesday, after my counsel finished his closing summation. And his summing up went on for many hours across three days that week, until near the end of Thursday.

His job was to sum up the case impartially and instruct the jury on the legal principles to follow. He discussed 'the issue paper' – the list of questions the jury must answer to reach its verdict. We heard him explain that in civil cases the jury doesn't have to be unanimous; a majority of nine out of twelve jurors would be sufficient to answer the questions on the paper.

Everything he said had to be incredibly precise. If the judge made a misstep, McGregor and Lawrence could overturn the verdict on appeal. If his tone or phrasing suggested he believed one side over the other, it would provide grounds for a mistrial.

He told the jury that their role was to be 'the judges of the trial'. They must ask themselves the question if they believed 'on the balance of probabilities' that McGregor raped me.

He said the case 'really boils down to who you believe'.

'In my view, one side or the other is telling lies about what happened in The Beacon hotel room,' he said.

He explained that the standard of proof in a civil action is on the 'balance of probabilities' and that, using the evidence, they must decide if it was more likely than not to have happened.

'Does the evidence show me that it is more likely than not that he raped her?' he said. 'If the answer is "yes" in inverted commas, you return a "yes" answer to question one. If you are not satisfied, you must return a "no" answer. The point here is that the obligation of proof rests with Ms Hand to demonstrate the "yes".'

He also explained that the trials against McGregor and Lawrence were separate.

'You have to decide each of the two cases separately, even though they are being tried together and even though the evidence is common to both.'

He talked about the CCTV evidence and Lawrence.

'Does it show her staggering around in a state of incapacity and engaged in silly intimacies which drunks, as we all know, sometimes engage in [...] or does it show preparation for what I might describe as a little bit more, or even full-blown sexual intercourse? Does it show her advancing on him with sexual intent?'

He continued, talking about the 'drunken affection' evident in the CCTV.

'While excessive alcohol may result in disinhibition and displays of drunken affection, hand-holding and all the rest of it, and can certainly inflame tempers and result in lapses of good judgment, you can't proceed on the basis of a presumption that women who engage in such behaviours are sexually promiscuous.'

He told the jury to be cautious about how they think someone who is a victim of sexual assault should behave.

'A person who has been a victim of a stressful event, such as a rape, may respond to that event in ways which may seem strange or irrational. Especially so where a person is befuddled by the consumption of intoxicants such as alcohol and drugs, or may have fallen asleep after an event.'

He urged the jurors not to be sidetracked by 'judgementalism' and prejudices.

'The wearing of clothes that may be revealing or the sending of a photograph on Instagram is not an invitation to be sexually molested,' he said. 'The fact that a woman engages in what you might describe as risky activity, which makes her easy prey for potential predators, such as getting drunk or taking drugs or consuming drink and drugs on top of each other, and all of the above, and wearing a risqué outfit, doesn't mean that they are up for sex.'

He asked the jurors to avoid conclusions based on 'lazy assumptions, victim-blaming, rape myths and so forth'.

He said the jury should ignore evidence about my anxiety and the medication I was taking for depression, saying that there was no evidence that this could interfere with my recall.

'There is a tendency by some people to regard people who suffer from psychiatric conditions as less reliable and to treat their evidence as less worthy of belief,' he said.

By the third day of the judge's charge, I'd stopped feeling like a person. I was just a collection of small aches and pains, stacked on top of each other, trying to remain still. We all suffered on those impossibly hard and unforgiving wooden benches, silently begging for the judge to call another break in proceedings.

He finally invited the jury to retire and begin their deliberations at 3 p.m. on Thursday, 21 November. The trial was supposed to last a week – maybe two at most. No one expected it would stretch across three weeks, starting on 5 November and finishing near the end of the month. I left the court that day with the judge's words rolling through my mind: *It really boils down to who you believe.*

Who would the jury believe? Despite my trembling as I walked out, I felt calmer than I had in weeks. I could hold my head up high because I had told the truth. But would the jury believe me? *It really boils down to who you believe*: eight simple words that reduced weeks of testimony to a simple choice, and that kept me awake for most of that night.

35.

The Verdict

Day 12: Friday, 22 November 2024

The next morning began like any other during the three-week trial. I walked into the courtroom alongside Gary, Clíona and my legal team, and then everything changed in an instant.

Heads swivelled and faces glowered at us. I realised the back of the court was filled with McGregor's family and friends. His partner, Dee Devlin, and his mother, Margaret, sat on either side of him. His father, a sister, a niece, his boxing coach, Philip Sutcliffe, and a large contingent of supporters and friends were packed into the courtroom. I even spotted several of his pub staff.

One hostile expression after another turned on me, hitting

me like a physical blow. Throughout the trial, McGregor had his father as his principal support. Now, he had his tribe, all glaring and surrounding me in the small, claustrophobic courtroom.

I looked away, found my seat on the bench and tried to steady my breathing, but I felt their hard eyes boring into my back.

The judge entered, we all stood, and then he explained that the jury would go away and deliberate. From now on, it was a waiting game. As soon as the judge rose and left, everyone clamoured for the doors.

My team guided us back to the private consultation rooms. We exited the court complex and walked the short distance to the Law Society rooms, which were on the ground floor of another building.

I kept myself together as we marched to the room in virtual silence, but the moment the door closed behind me, all composure disappeared. The stress of the imminent verdict and the sight of so many McGregor supporters was too much. Those familiar tremors convulsed through my body, and I was overcome by a panic attack.

Clíona and Gary held me tight, as if they were trying to keep me from shattering in the room. Dave arrived and read the terror in my eyes.

'I know,' he said quietly. 'It's a shock.'

As Gary, Clíona, Diane and others did their best to calm and centre me, my gaze drifted to the window behind me.

Beyond the Georgian glass panes, I could see the Luas tracks and beyond those stood the Hampton, a Hilton hotel. I took deep breaths and watched people walk to and fro outside. And then I spotted *them*: McGregor, Dee Devlin, his mother, his brother-in-law and his entire entourage all moving as a group towards the hotel, cameras and reporters following alongside, flashing in their faces.

My immediate reaction was to crouch; to hide in case they looked towards the window and saw me. But then I felt anger. So many supporters surrounded the man who had hurt me and lied about me in court. They were going to wait in a fancy hotel where he would no doubt swagger and laugh as they slapped his back and assured him I had no chance of winning.

Meanwhile, I had retreated to this institutional room, where I sat panicking and sobbing into sweaty palms. Terrified. Gary kept squeezing my hand, and Clíona urged me to drink glasses of water. The legal team were back and forth, bringing sandwiches and tea. My mind kept spinning. One minute, I felt certain the jury would believe me. The next minute, dread swept through me – what if they didn't? What if they decided I was lying? Then the world would think so, too.

My phone rang. My thirteen-year-old daughter begged to be allowed to come to court for the verdict. Freya said she wanted to be with me when I got to read my statement afterwards. *If I got to read it.* I had already requested my legal team to make the statement if I lost the case. I didn't know whether I could survive that verdict.

My resolve wavered as I heard Freya plead on the phone. Part of me wanted her there. I longed to hold and cuddle her. But the other part, the protective mam part of me, knew better.

Dave removed the phone and the decision from my hands.

'Freya, it's better if you don't come in. It's not good. If your mam doesn't win, it's going to be very hard for her. And if she wins, she's going to be very busy.' He spoke to her kindly, explaining everything about the process. Once Dave talked to her, she was fine about not being able to be there.

But I felt scared and vulnerable facing McGregor and his gang of supporters in the courtroom. I was intimidated by their stares and their sheer numbers. I dreaded having to return.

I called my mam.

'It's awful, Mam. All his family's here. Pub staff. Friends. It's just me and Gary.'

My mam was indignant and fierce.

'Sure, we're on our way in now. Your family and friends are coming too. We were coming anyway – you didn't even need to tell us. We were waiting until later because we knew the jury would be out. Don't you worry, we're coming!'

Mam's reaction brought fresh tears. I felt like the cavalry was on the way. We had people behind us to watch our backs.

Family and friends couldn't join me in the consultation room, but I became aware they were gathering in the courthouse to wait. A few had to endure insults from McGregor supporters. 'There's them cunts there!' one person said, uttering the words clearly, right into my aunt and cousin's face. My aunt pulled my cousin closer, and my cousin didn't cry until they were out of sight of the perpetrator. During the extended wait, several people said they witnessed Dee Devlin sitting on the bench outside the courtroom. They said she kept her head down the entire time.

At lunchtime, everyone was called back to the courtroom. Dave told me to stay where I was. He didn't want me back in that room until I had to be. The judge said the jury had indicated they intended to continue deliberating until 6.00 p.m.

In the consultation room, the hours crawled by. I paced. Cried. Sat. Stood. Paced again. Cried again. Gary's anxiety matched my own. He was pale, almost silent. We held hands, squeezed tight, and said next to nothing. I couldn't talk, a ball of anxiety in my throat.

When Dave's phone rang, it was well after 4 p.m. and getting dark outside. We expected the call to tell us that the jury hadn't reached a decision, and deliberations would have to continue after the weekend. But that didn't happen.

'The decision is in,' Dave said.

The news hit me so hard I thought I would vomit. I pulled Nanny's scarf from my pocket and squeezed it as if my life depended on it. *Nanny, please give me the strength …*

Clíona and Gary gripped my arms, supporting me. My legs barely functioned. Each step felt like I was walking on a ship's deck in a storm. I sobbed all the way to the courtroom.

I exhaled a little as soon as I saw the reassuring presence of my family and uniformed gardaí. Dave had made a request for gardaí to be present in the courtroom, as he feared some in the court might react badly if the verdict went against them.

I sat clutching hands with Clíona on one side and my mam on the other. Gary sat on the other side of Mam. My family and friends stood to my left, directly in front of the jury.

I couldn't catch my breath. I tried to sip water, but my hands were trembling so violently that the bottle rattled against my teeth. My panic was escalating. A man who had been sitting in front of me throughout the trial turned around, startling me. I knew he was part of McGregor's legal team, so when his eyes looked into mine, I froze.

'Relax,' he said. His voice was kind. 'It's okay. Everything is going to be okay.'

Why is he saying that to me? He was trying to calm me, but he wasn't even on my side; it made no sense. But something about his tone planted a seed. *Maybe … maybe I am going to win.*

When the judge sat, he was aghast at the crowd crammed into the place.

'It is very crowded down at the back of the court there. Can some of you move up to the top, please?'

The courtroom fell silent as a tomb as he began. Then, audible in the stillness, I heard a deep, shuddering breath – loud enough for everyone to hear. I realised it was McGregor. It sounded like he was trying to steady himself. *He's afraid.*

The judge began by issuing a stark warning: 'I want everybody to remain calm when the verdict is given out. I want no scenes. Anybody who makes a scene will find themselves in jail.'

The registrar announced that after six hours and ten minutes of deliberation, the jury had reached a verdict.

'Now, Mr Foreman, have you reached a verdict on which nine of you or more have agreed?' asked the judge.

'We have.'

'Have you recorded a verdict on the issue paper?'

'We have.'

The foreman handed the judge the jury's decision on paper. He began reading their verdict aloud.

The courtroom froze. I sat in the stillness, unable to process the words coming from the judge's mouth; their meaning lost to my frazzled mind. The whole room seemed suspended in time, and everything was frozen, distant and unreal, apart from the panic surging through me and the pounding of my heart.

The judge was saying something. Something about Conor McGregor. Something about assault. Something about me.

I turned to Clíona, whispering, 'What's happening? What's going on?'

Clíona turned to me with tears in her eyes. 'You won! You won!' she hissed. 'They believe you. The jury believes you. Can't you hear him?'

'What?'

'You won.'

The judge had posed the simple question: 'Did Conor McGregor assault Nikita Hand?' The foreman had answered, 'Yes'.

People wrapped their arms around me, patted my back. I didn't know who, and I couldn't tell whose hands belonged to whom. I smiled through the tears. My family was crying too. Gary was crying. Someone was pulling me close. Everything was a blur.

I was told afterwards that McGregor exhaled sharply and doubled over with his head in his hands, shaking his head.

The judge spoke for a few more minutes, and that was it. The verdict was concluded in less than five minutes, and then he rose and left. It was over, and I didn't know what had gone on apart from the news I had won.

My family swarmed around me. My legal team embraced me. And someone – a woman – whispered in my ear: 'You fought this for so many years, and you never stopped, Nikita. You fought it to the end, and you've won.'

I've no idea who said this to me, but I've never forgotten

the words. Some in the media approached and shook my hand. 'Well done. We believed you from the start,' said one.

I felt dazed, as if I were in some strange dream. *I won. I won. The jury believed me. I won.* I said the words over and over in my head and still didn't believe it.

Dave wrapped me in a tight embrace. 'I'm so proud of you,' he said. 'This is all good. I'm so happy for you.' I hugged the rest of my legal team: Diane, Geraldine, Susan, Maria and Paddy. Emotion overwhelmed everyone. I shook my counsels' hands and thanked them. I told everyone how incredible they were. I felt so fortunate to have had these people around me, at my back all these years.

Amidst the chaos, my legal team said I should wait to give McGregor and his entourage time to leave. They didn't want me facing them again. So I sat in the courtroom, still shaking, still crying. Dave hugged my mother and shook hands with all my family members, and then he turned to me.

'Are you ready to make your statement?'

He had already informed the media that I would make one.

The week before, I'd sat at Janice's kitchen table with her, Gary and my friend Emma, writing out what I'd say if the jury's verdict went in my favour. I had felt confident that day, believing I would get to read it.

My pen had moved steadily across the page that afternoon. I had read each line aloud while the others listened. Janice nodded. Gary suggested a different phrase. Emma said, 'Yes, that's good.' Then someone else had said, 'Say that instead.' I'd needed them there, their voices encouraging me when my own certainty faltered.

I patted my pockets and then looked around me.

'I left the speech in the consultation room …'

Paddy from my legal team was already moving, taking off down the corridor at a half-run. When he pressed the folded pages into my hand afterwards, my fingers wouldn't stop trembling.

Emma stood beside me.

'Will you do this for me?' I pushed the pages towards her. 'I can't. I'm too shook up.'

Emma took hold of my upper arms and nearly shook me.

'Nikita, you have to do this yourself. No one wants to hear from me. You need to read your statement.'

I nodded reluctantly.

'All right then, I will.'

How am I going to do this? I thought as we left the courtroom. I was terrified. My spirits rose outside as random people called out: 'Well done, Nikita!' A woman I'd never seen before stood outside the court gate, holding handmade banners. *Simply the Best, Nikita,* read one. 'Oh, can I have that?' I said, momentarily delighted and distracted. The woman had been waiting in a nearby pub or café for the verdict, then rushed to the court the moment the news broke.

But Diane urged me forward. Lights flashed in my face,

cameras surrounded me and reporters pushed close. I could barely see as I walked down the concrete slope outside the court. I clung to Gary's arm. The media had set up a bank of lights, microphones and film cameras in the dark.

'Give her some space!' I remember someone shouting that. 'Stand back and give her some space!'

I looked out into dazzling light, a wall of white glare in front of me. I was completely blinded. My heart pounded in my throat. I had never stood before strangers intent on recording my every word. It wasn't anything I'd ever prepared for in my life. I began reading my statement, my voice quivering and my hands shaking so badly that the microphones picked up the sound of the pages rustling.

I would like to start by saying I'm overwhelmed and touched by the support I have received from everybody. First, I want to thank the Coleman Legal team and my three barristers, John Gordon, Ray Boland and Siún Leonowicz. They have been amazing from start to finish.

I want to thank Mr Justice Alexander Owens, the jury and all the witnesses. I want to thank the doctors and nurses, everyone from the sexual assault treatment unit at the Rotunda hospital for looking after me, and especially my own doctor, Frank Clarke.

I want to thank the Rape Crisis Centre, especially Clíona, who has been by my side throughout this entire period. I want to thank all the guards and the ambulance crew.

I want to thank all the women and men out there who have supported me throughout this trial; for every person who reached out to me, a card, a letter, an email, everything, it hasn't gone unnoticed. Thank you, I really appreciate it so much.

I want to thank my partner, Gary, who has been so supportive for the last four years and has held my hand throughout every day of this trial and every other day.

I want to thank my mam and all my family and friends. Lastly, I want to thank my daughter, Freya, whom I'm most grateful to. She has given me so much strength and courage over the last six years, throughout this nightmare, to keep pushing forward for justice.

I want to show Freya and every other girl and boy that you can stand up for yourself if something happens to you, no matter who the person is, and justice will be served.

To all the victims of sexual assault, I hope my story is a reminder that no matter how afraid you might be, speak up. You have a voice – keep on fighting for justice. I know this has impacted not only my life, my daughter's, my family and my friends tremendously. And it's something that I'll never forget for the rest of my life. But now that justice has been served, I can now try to move on and look forward to the future with my family and friends and daughter.

Journalists began firing questions at me.

'What have the last two weeks been like?

'A nightmare.'

'What is it like finally to be believed?'

'I have no words. It's unbelievable. Thanks so much.'

'Do you feel vindicated now?'

'Yes, I do. I do. Thank you. I just. Okay, I just need to take a minute.'

I needed more than a minute. I was afraid my legs wouldn't hold me up, I was trembling so hard. My legal team pulled me away before the questions could continue.

Security at the court let me walk back through the courthouse – a shortcut so I didn't have to plough through the media. I returned to the consultation room and gathered my belongings. Family members hugged me, congratulated me again and then slowly dispersed.

My mother left with a couple of my friends. Gary and I went with Janice and another friend who was travelling in the same direction. The two guards who had stood watch in the court escorted us to our taxi. Paddy, our regular driver, brought us back to the hotel near Janice's home. Throughout the entire trial, Janice never let the taxi go directly to her address. Nobody could know where we lived.

When we walked into the hotel lobby, the first thing I saw was my face filling the large television screen mounted on the bar wall. I froze, mortified to see myself reading my statement outside the court. Hotel guests and bar patrons glanced at the screen, then at me, still standing in my formal suit, bag in hand.

Gary's sister worked at this hotel, and one of the bar staff approached discreetly.

'If you want to have a drink, we can switch off the news. Nobody will bother you.'

The staff changed channels, and the four of us sat down for a celebratory drink, a glass of Prosecco.

As we raised our glasses, a woman approached our table. 'Are you Nikita Hand from the news? The one who won her trial?'

'Yeah.'

My voice registered caution, but she was smiling, so I wasn't as nervous as I might have been.

'Can I hug you? I followed everything. I'm so proud of you. I feel like I know you.'

Her embrace was brief and genuine. It was lovely. But I was drained – mentally, physically, emotionally. Gary was wrecked too. We finished our glass of bubbly and left for Janice's apartment. That was as much celebrating as we could manage on one of the most significant days of my life.

36.

The Aftermath

When the phone rang mid-morning the following day, I groaned in the bed. My exhaustion felt unnatural – a bone-deep weariness that went beyond physical tiredness. Gary and I were planning to stay in bed all day.

It was Dave. 'Simon Harris wants to ring you.'

I sat up. 'What? The Taoiseach? Why?'

'He wants to congratulate you. On behalf of the country.'

'Really?' I was dazed.

'If you see a number you don't recognise, it's going to be him.'

I answered a call a short while later.

'Hi, this is Simon Harris …'

He chatted to me, warm and friendly.

'I wanted to thank you for your incredible bravery, your

courage,' he said. 'I want to make sure you know how much solidarity and support you have across this country.'

He also said that he wanted me to be aware that the Dublin Rape Crisis Centre had noted that many other women had now come forward in relation to their own experiences of sexual abuse as a result of my bravery. I beamed as he spoke. He was lovely.

Then he asked how I was feeling the day after winning my case.

'Well, I'm still in bed,' I said.

He burst out laughing.

'Brilliant. Stay in bed, you've earned it,' he said. When I hung up, Gary and I stared at each other in disbelief.

'What the hell was that?'

I never expected in my entire life to be in my pyjamas, propped up in bed, chatting to the Taoiseach.

All that day, I felt as if I was in some strange dream-like space. Gary and I read countless news reports and expressions of support. We ordered takeaway and watched the TV coverage. We saw news of a march scheduled for the following Monday to protest the DPP's decision not to pursue criminal charges against McGregor, led by politician Ruth Coppinger. I cried thinking of women and men walking for me, carrying signs. So much intense public discussion and media coverage marked that entire weekend.

The only negative response came from McGregor and his

entourage. The jury had found that Lawrence did not assault me. I had said in the witness box that I didn't believe his evidence that he had sex with me. Following the verdict, the judge remarked that the jury's decision indicated it did not believe Lawrence's claims either.

Yet he and McGregor tried to spin this as a win on social media. They celebrated, triumphant that the jury had *not* believed Lawrence's evidence.

> *I won my case against NIKITA HANDOUT which means the jury believed my story and not that lier (sic), she is now fully liable for all my legal fees and I will be sueing (sic) the LIER (sic) for damages.*

McGregor wrote:

> *Two men falsely accused. One vindicated, the other soon to be! Congrats James Lawrence on absolute exoneration! [...] Absolute nonsense. How these lies were accepted, I will never know [...] The reporting in court a laughing stock to everyone present. As clear as day bias. This is not a court of hard evidence and truth. It is a kangaroo court [...] We are not done yet. Not by a long shot. No chance. On we fight! Justice and truth will prevail! Appeal! Appeal! Appeal! Appeal!*

I expected that from them, but not so much the attack posted online by McGregor's partner, Dee Devlin. She shielded her partner from accountability for his actions, issuing a victim-blaming, slut-shaming message that accused me of a 'three-day bender' with a 'child at home'.

> *Imagine a WOMAN, with her own boyfriend and child, texting provocative pictures of herself to another woman's man with a family and child on the way. This woman claims to know me, yet still went ahead and sent messages and pictures of herself over and over to my man? Really?*
>
> *Whilst out on a 3-day bender, texting excuses to her own child at home where mammy is on Saturday afternoon, Saturday night, Sunday morning, Sunday afternoon, Sunday night into Monday morning.*
>
> *All the while out of her face in a hotel room, dancing around a hotel carpark. What sort of WOMAN are you!!*

I saw the funny side when I read all the comments urging McGregor to give Dee's phone back to her.

Dee added another message:

My sons will be warned women like you exist in the world.

I remember thinking I hoped she would also teach her sons about consent and respect for women.

McGregor's gang couldn't hurt me that weekend. The jury recognised the liar in court, and it was Conor McGregor. My relief was mixed with gratitude for having won. It was such an important victory. The jury believed me – not McGregor and not even Lawrence, according to the judge. Meanwhile, I had named and shamed the man who hurt me. That meant more to me than anything.

My phone rang again that morning, and it was a journalist. I was bewildered as to who gave him my number, but all he'd tell me was that he had gotten it from 'a source'.

'Did you think you were always going to win?' he asked.

'Yes,' I said simply. 'Because I told the truth from day one.'

I also told him that I had pursued the case 'so my daughter does not have to grow up in a world where she has to shut up and say nothing'.

The judge had announced the financial award in the courtroom, but I hadn't heard it properly nor understood it. I hadn't heard or absorbed anything much beyond the verdict.

The award came in pieces – €50,000 for this, €20,000 for that – and I couldn't make sense of the numbers. I hadn't discussed it with Dave either.

I learnt what the jury had awarded me by reading it in the media, like everyone else: 'The jury awarded €60,000 in general damages, damages for loss of earnings of €135,026, agreed medical expenses of €4,557.64, and loss of future earnings of €50,000. Special damages awarded in total were €188,603.60. No aggravated damages or exemplary damages were awarded. The total damages awarded were €248,603.60.'

I would learn later that 'special' damages are quantifiable financial losses – loss of earnings, etc. Aggravated damages mean that the defendant's behaviour, either during the incident or during the trial, has made the plaintiff's suffering worse. Exemplary damages are rare in Ireland, more to punish the wrongdoer than to compensate the victim.

I was on a high from winning the case. The money, a life-changing sum, was just a bonus. It was more money than I'd ever imagined having. My initial reaction was relief that the nightmare was over. The jury believed me. They had rejected McGregor's lies.

I wouldn't have swapped anything for the jury's verdict. It meant everything to me that the world knew the person that McGregor was. For me, it was always about vindication. I had that now.

37.

The Decline

For years, I had dreamt about the moment of winning – pictured myself walking out of that courtroom into brightness, breathing deeply for the first time in a long time. My mental health had been poor leading up to the trial, but I imagined winning would solve everything; that vindication would heal me. The knot in my stomach would loosen. The world would right itself. It didn't happen like that. I won, but that knot tightened.

The week after the verdict, I sat down to read all the letters of support that had been sent to my solicitors and the Rape Crisis Centre. Hundreds of letters and messages, enough to fill a big cardboard box, came from men, women, survivors, victims – a whole cross section of Irish society. Some sent little gifts; one even included a cheque for fifty euro – never cashed – but I appreciated the kind gesture. I was touched and felt bolstered by the heartfelt support and encouragement from strangers. But the feeling didn't last long.

It didn't matter that McGregor received an avalanche of negative press. Hundreds of supermarkets in both the UK and Ireland had removed brands associated with him. Proximo Spirits, the company that bought his Proper No. Twelve Whiskey brand, said it did not plan to use his name or likeness in its marketing going forward.

IO Interactive, the creators of the *Hitman* video game, said it would cease its collaboration with McGregor in light of the court ruling. Even Ireland's National Wax Museum said it was removing its likeness of McGregor. It seemed the world had declared war on McGregor, but I was too busy tearing myself apart to notice.

By the second week after the verdict, the locks on Janice's apartment door had become my horizon. I couldn't step beyond them. If I heard noises outside, I stood at the front door peephole, watching, braced for an imminent attack. If Janice persuaded me into the car, I'd duck down in the seat if anyone glanced in our direction.

Janice did nearly everything now. She'd arrive home, arms full of groceries and my medication from the chemist. She rarely asked if I wanted to come along anymore.

'Someone strange was at the door today,' I said to her one

day when she returned from shopping. 'They rang the doorbell, but I hid.'

I was sitting on her couch, where I'd been since Janice had left me earlier that morning.

Janice set down the bags. 'No one knows you're here, Nikita.'

'What if they've found out where I live? Someone was watching today. They were at the door!'

My eyes moved to the window, then away, as if even looking might give me away.

'Nikita—'

'You don't believe me!' I wasn't angry. More despairing.

'I believe you're frightened,' she said.

A few weeks after the trial, my friend Aideen arrived with her colouring bowls, scissors and brush roll, all energy and determination.

'We're doing this,' she announced. 'You're going to start looking like yourself again.'

I tried. I sat in the kitchen chair, let Aideen section my hair and smelled the familiar chemical tang of the lightener. I badly needed some highlights in my hair, and Janice and Gary assured me it would make me feel better to look better.

For ten minutes, maybe fifteen, it almost worked. I could practically remember who I'd been: a woman who took pride in her appearance, who'd meet friends, who once existed in the world without anxiously watching the front door.

Then my lungs forgot how to pull air, and my hands locked

around the armrest of Janice's chair. Aideen's voice reached me from somewhere very far away, saying my name, then saying it louder. But I had gone somewhere else – trembling violently, somewhere small and dark where my heartbeat was the only sound. The full-blown panic attacks were back.

When I surfaced and started to breathe again, Aideen had left. I learnt later she stood at the lift outside, crying to Janice.

'That's not Nikita in there,' Aideen said to her. 'I don't know who that is, but it's not the girl I knew. She's not right.'

'I know,' Janice said.

'What happened to her?'

'The trial.'

'But she won—'

I sat with my hair limp and wet, staring at nothing in the kitchen. I wasn't the girl that anyone knew. There was an absence where something vital used to be. It was like I'd gone into that courtroom and come out with pieces missing. Pieces I couldn't name, just a hollow where the rest of me used to be.

I had won. Why couldn't I be happy? Why was I filled with so much fear and anxiety? All I knew was that the trial had broken me.

A week after the jury's verdict upholding my civil claim, Mr Justice Owens awarded me the costs of my civil action against McGregor. He had to pay everything.

My legal team had been more concerned about Lawrence's

costs as the jury found he had not assaulted me in The Beacon Hotel. But the judge decided against awarding him costs against me and made a no-cost order, meaning each side must bear their own expenses for that claim.

The judge explained it was 'difficult to see' how Lawrence, a man of 'modest means', had incurred separate legal costs. In this 'peculiar' case, he said, McGregor's defence relied on what Lawrence said. Both men filed a joint defence, were represented by the same solicitors and were 'in lockstep with each other'.

He believed the jury's decision that Lawrence had not assaulted me arose because they didn't believe his claims that he had consensual sex with me after Mr McGregor left the hotel. He said the jury's 'no' answer meant Lawrence had not taken advantage of me while drunk, 'because he did not have sex with [me] at all'.

Winning my court costs was another decisive victory in the run-up to Christmas 2024. I should have been delighted, but that Christmas was another dark blur. I remember little of it. It was just another holiday that I tried to get through for Freya's sake, more forced smiles while she opened presents before leaving for her father's house.

Some news reached me when I needed it most. Christy Moore had paused mid-set at Vicar Street in the New Year and spoken my name, along with the name of Natasha O'Brien – a survivor of a violent assault and a campaigner for women's safety. One of Ireland's best musicians had offered up his song and Bob Dylan's lyrics to two women he'd never met. I couldn't believe it. A music legend had thought of me. He had said my name out loud. It was an unexpected morale boost.

Mostly, I spent days those days in bed, sleeping, hiding. My olanzapine prescription took the edge off my anxiety, but I continued to fall headlong into a spiral of depression. Because I never left the apartment, I couldn't stay off my phone. It seemed like everyone was weighing in on the verdict, and much of the judgment appeared to focus on how I looked. And I read everything. I read comments calling me ugly, fat, slutty, a homewrecker. I kept reading the comments even though I knew I shouldn't.

When I looked in the mirror, I no longer saw a reflection but a bundle of defects that social media had decided on. I saw confirmation of everything people said was wrong with me. Their loathing became self-loathing. The trial almost destroyed me, and now these comments shredded what was left. I felt sick when I saw a photo appear in a newspaper or flashed on TV. My mental health completely deteriorated.

In January, two months after the verdict, I was shaken to read that yet another woman had filed a civil lawsuit against McGregor for sexual assault. An unnamed senior Wall Street executive alleged McGregor had sexually assaulted her in the toilets, following a basketball game at the Miami Heat's Kaseya Center back in 2023.

Court documents filed on her behalf had alleged McGregor acted for 'his own sexual gratification and for the purposes of degrading [her]'. Once again, McGregor vocally denied all claims that he assaulted the woman. (The lawsuit was voluntarily withdrawn in December 2025. No public explanation for the withdrawal was provided.)

I always suspected McGregor would prolong my case, keep proclaiming his innocence and fight until the end. I suspected his ego was such that he couldn't bear to lose a fight, but losing so publicly to a woman must have been especially galling.

'He's definitely going to appeal,' I had said to Diane. 'He's said it on social media. He has the money. He won't care about being back in the news for sexual assault.'

Still, when Dave or Diane broke the news to me in February 2025 that he was formally going ahead with his appeal, it felt like another kick in the face. All I could think of was that I might have to go through this whole ordeal again. I didn't know if I had the strength.

And there was another worry, one that kept me awake at night – Lawrence had also launched an appeal for his legal fees. *Was this ever going to end?*

The judge had ordered McGregor to pay €100,000 of the damages to me, with the remainder deferred pending an appeal. Even though the money now sat in my bank account, I couldn't touch it. I didn't know what would happen in his appeal. What if the Court of Appeal didn't uphold the original verdict?

Dave was confident that McGregor wouldn't win his appeal, but he was always careful to add that you could never tell. Lawrence's appeal was different. He was found not to have assaulted me, so technically, he won his case. Usually, that meant he would be entitled to his costs. If the Court of Appeal agreed, I knew I would lose everything. Maybe even more than everything. I could end up owing money that I didn't have. The €248,000 award would be gone – consumed by legal fees. I wouldn't even have the deposit I'd wanted to save towards a house.

In the weeks after the trial, my phone screen lit up constantly. My mam, cousins, friends; the same names cycling through again and again, trying to talk, trying to help. I watched their calls come through, but I couldn't summon the energy to answer. My mam's texts shifted from worried to frustrated. 'Why are you not even ringing me back?'

I typed and deleted responses three times before finally replying.

'I just can't talk to anyone right now. It's not personal. Don't take it to heart,' I pleaded, knowing she would anyway.

The thought of forming words, of explaining, of simply being in conversation with another human being, was too much. My mind felt fractured, still scattered across the courtroom floor.

38.

Neighbours from Hell

A phone call from Diane, a few months after the trial, began like many of the others: some friendly chat and then a few updates on McGregor's appeal to overturn the jury's verdict. But she had saved something for last.

'Listen,' she said, her voice careful. 'McGregor's legal team has made an application to introduce fresh evidence from two new witnesses to support this appeal. Their names are Samantha O'Reilly and Steven Cummins.'

'Who?'

My head raced. I turned the names over and over in my mind. They meant nothing to me. Diane suggested I search my phone and social media contacts. I came up with nothing there either. I tried Google when I got off the phone. Diane did too, and she was more successful. She found a photograph of Samantha O'Reilly and Steven Cummins among couples posing for a newspaper competition for a wedding at the Red Cow Inn in Dublin. She sent it to me, and recognition struck me like cold water.

'I know them. They lived across the road from me.'

But even as I said it, something felt wrong. At this stage, we didn't know what they claimed to have witnessed, but nonetheless the timeline didn't fit.

'I don't think they lived there then,' I told Diane. 'I don't think they were even there when it happened.'

But I had no way to prove it.

Weeks crawled past while we waited to see their affidavits. When they finally arrived, Diane read them aloud over the phone.

Samantha O'Reilly claimed she'd witnessed everything from her bedroom window, looking into our bedroom through our venetian blinds. She said she saw Ste digging me and kicking and punching me. Or she saw what looked like him doing that to me because she said she couldn't see me on the floor. She said I came out on the road screaming, hunched over like an old woman in pain, and she tried to help me.

Steven Cummins said my screams and shouts from our house woke him, but he told Samantha O'Reilly that it was none of their business. He said he did not even look over to see what was happening.

My mouth dropped open on hearing the statements. It seemed incredible, but McGregor's legal team said this fresh evidence bolstered their client's claims that he was not responsible for the extensive bruising on my body.

Throughout the trial, no other neighbour had come forward with similar information. If anything like that had happened in the middle of the night, everyone would have seen and heard me. The entire road would have known. The statement was completely fabricated.

'The whole thing is crazy,' I told Diane. 'A complete fairytale.'

Of course, I had to tell Ste before the story went public. I dreaded telling him that he was about to be portrayed as some kind of woman-beater and thug in McGregor's appeal. But Ste's response came swift and certain. He basically said we both knew it never happened, so he didn't care.

I promised to defend his name in court and tell everyone that he had never raised a hand to me during our relationship. Ste's recording of him and me from that December night was clear evidence, anyway. In the forty-minute-long recording, he didn't even raise his voice.

I thought the new witnesses' testimony was ludicrous. My legal team didn't think it was a laughing matter, however. Dave and Diane were furious, and their determination to challenge these statements steadied me.

Fear and doubt crept into me despite the absurdity of it all. Maybe people would believe two witnesses corroborating each other. The media coverage of these two new witnesses was huge, and my character was being torn to shreds on social media again. Many believed this proved I'd been lying all along. My doubts about winning the appeal grew and spun around my head.

Around the time that all this was going on, I decided enough was enough. I would not live this half-life anymore, cowering in someone's apartment. I opened my contacts and rang Clíona's number.

'Can I set up a therapy session?' I asked her.

That Thursday, 6 March 2025, I went online and met my new therapist from the Rape Crisis Centre. It was an immediate match. The woman's eyes were kind, and she created space for me to talk without piling on pressure.

'Same time next week?' she asked at the end.

I realised I was already looking forward to it. Each Thursday morning became a place where I could talk and reflect, where the shattered pieces began to be reassembled. Slowly, impossibly, I began to feel normal again. Not the same as before – that person was gone – but someone new. I was healing. I started to feel glimpses of happiness again.

On the morning of the appeal, Tuesday, 1 July 2025, Gary and I returned to the Four Courts. I remember sitting with Gary and Clíona in the consultation room before we entered the second-highest tier in the Irish court system.

My palms were sweating as I went over my testimony about

the neighbours from hell. 'Jesus, Nikita, you're trembling all over,' Susan from my legal team said as she hugged me. I was terrified at the prospect of entering the witness box again, this time before a three-judge court, comprising Ms Justice Isobel Kennedy and Mr Justices Brian O'Moore and Michael MacGrath. But then Dave arrived with Diane, and everything changed.

'It's confirmed – the witnesses didn't live on your road on that date,' Dave said.

I was quaking so hard that the words took a moment to land. 'What? You know this for sure?'

A kind person, someone with a conscience, had contacted my solicitors after the pair emerged as new witnesses. They said the couple had not been living there at the time McGregor assaulted me in December 2018. The informant had all the emails to prove it. The pair had been nowhere near my house on the night of 9 December and the morning of 10 December.

'I told you!' I exclaimed, relief and rage mixing inside me in equal measure. I'd been fretting about nothing for months. Dave had withheld the information from me in case another curveball arose. He wanted me fully prepped and ready to go into the courtroom fighting.

I felt so much lighter as I headed for the courtroom in an old building on Inns Quay.

Let them sit in that chair, I thought. *Let their lies be exposed.*

Politicians and other survivors were among a large group of supporters who stood outside the Court of Appeal that morning. They stood behind a banner reading, *We stand with Nikita Hand.* It raised my spirits to have that support inside and outside the court.

But once I sat in the courtroom, the familiar uneasiness returned. My head swung toward the door every time it opened, but there was no sign of McGregor or Lawrence by the time the court rose for the three-judge panel.

Then McGregor's new barrister, Mark Mulholland KC (King's Counsel), dropped a bombshell when he asked the Appeal Court justices for permission to withdraw the application to introduce the witnesses' sworn affidavits. I looked at Gary and Clíona in shock and glanced down the bench at my legal team, who seemed equally aghast. We wanted the neighbours in the witness box, but the withdrawal meant that they wouldn't be called to give oral evidence in the appeal.

The Court of Appeal allowed the withdrawal but noted the circumstances as unusual and 'mysterious'. My senior counsel, John Gordon, immediately rose to object, saying I'd been 'put through the wringer again'. He said that the so-called new evidence had been widely circulated in the media, and the allegations had been made to undermine my reputation.

He wanted to cross-examine the two witnesses and McGregor's solicitor, Michael Staines, saying they had made sworn affidavits calling me and Ste liars. He wanted the matter referred for consideration of possible perjury, including possible induced perjury by McGregor.

I'm not sure why McGregor's legal team withdrew the witnesses at the last moment. Both Samantha O'Reilly and Steven Cummins had shown up near the Four Courts that morning. The media had photographed them walking toward Staines's office, a few minutes away. One of McGregor's flash cars had also been spotted near his solicitor's office that morning. They'd been ready; then suddenly they weren't called. We never learnt exactly why.

However, the case continued that day on two other grounds of appeal. McGregor's legal team complained that the original trial heard he had said 'no comment' around 100 times when gardaí questioned him. They claimed this information was prejudicial evidence that should not have been introduced because McGregor had a right to silence. But my senior counsel, Ray Boland, said they were within their rights to raise the issue because McGregor had put himself forward as someone who wanted to cooperate fully with gardaí.

McGregor's legal team also argued that the issue paper, the questions given to the jury before they went away to deliberate, confused the jurors. They tried to claim the note was misleading because it asked only whether McGregor had 'assaulted' me and not whether he had 'sexually assaulted' me.

My team said the challenge to the issue paper was 'nonsense'. They said there was no ambiguity. My senior counsel said it could not have been clearer in the judge's charge that the jurors were dealing with assault by rape. He added that there was significant physical assault as well, involving strangulation on three occasions.

The following day, the court appeal continued with McGregor's lawyers appealing Lawrence's legal costs. They argued the High Court's decision that Lawrence was not entitled to his costs against me was unfair because the jury had found that he did not rape me.

McGregor's legal team made their submissions, mine made their arguments, and then began another nail-biting wait for the Court of Appeal's decision. It took four long weeks.

On the day of the decision, Thursday, 31 July 2025, Gary couldn't get the time off work, so Janice and I took a taxi to the Four Courts. Media waited outside and inside, their laptops ready to go. By the time the court registrar intoned the familiar 'All rise', my heart was hammering. Clíona, Susan and the rest of my legal team were around me.

The three judges waded through what seemed like hours of paperwork and judgments. I couldn't absorb any of it, but Diane's smiling glances at me were reassuring. I knew it was going in our favour. In the end, the judges dismissed the appeal on all grounds, upholding the High Court jury's decision. They also referred papers to the DPP after my legal team alleged that McGregor's two witnesses had perjured themselves and that he had induced them to do so.

The Appeal Court ruled that Lawrence's evidence that he saw consensual sex between McGregor and me had been rejected by the jury, which found he raped me. The judges found aspects of Lawrence's evidence were at odds with the jury's verdict and could only be regarded as 'untruthful'.

The Appeal Court also ruled that it would not award Lawrence his costs because McGregor had paid his legal fees, and any award of costs to Lawrence would either mean I would make a payment to someone who gave inaccurate evidence against me and ultimately to McGregor, the man who had raped me.

My legal team had won a clean sweep and upheld everything the judge and jury had ruled in the High Court. Still, I shook as I faced the media again, crying with relief and shock as I read a hastily written statement.

> *I want to begin by thanking my legal team, the Rape Crisis Centre and the three judges who delivered the decision today. I'm also deeply grateful to everyone who supported me and those who believed in me and stood by my side throughout this long and painful journey.*
>
> *This appeal has retraumatised me over and over again, being forced to relive it. What happened has had a huge impact on me.*

But I also wanted to address other women out there who had or would suffer similar to me and might waver about pursuing their abusers. The sight of me crying, shaking and clearly distressed was not encouraging, but I wanted them to know that speaking out is a vital part of the healing process.

> *To every survivor out there, I know how hard it is, but please, don't be silent. You deserve to be heard. You also deserve justice. Today, I can finally move on and try to heal. Thank you.'*

In the days following, I exhaled for the first time in ages. McGregor had lost the High Court case and the Court of Appeals case. My legal team filed a new civil claim against McGregor and his two would-be witnesses, alleging 'malicious abuse' of the court process.

Two months later, gardaí arrested Samantha O'Reilly and Steven Cummins as part of a perjury investigation, while McGregor was busy seeking a nomination to run for the Irish presidency. At the time of writing, the DPP was still determining if there was enough evidence for a criminal prosecution.

Looking back, I began to see the shape of the rollercoaster I'd been on. The vast pressure of the trial and then the appeal had been too much and had broken something in me. But as I continued with therapy week after week, slowly, steadily, I began improving.

By September 2025, about nine months after the original trial, the ground under me began to feel firm again, and I realised I was gradually getting back to feeling myself.

That month, after more than a year of living with Gary's cousin Janice, I finally found a place for rent. I had been so grateful to Janice for taking Gary and me in after the home invasion, but I had never intended to stay so long.

I didn't expect it to make such a difference, but my spirits rose once I settled in my bright, new, two-bedroom apartment. The blow-up bed disappeared and Freya now had her own room. Feeling a new sense of permanence and safety in a secure environment helped with my inner transformation.

After the High Court trial victory, people had reached out, wanting to make documentaries or write books to tell my story. They usually contacted Dave, who forwarded the requests. I always wanted to tell my story, but physically I hadn't been able to. It took many months before I felt strong enough even to consider it, and it was many months more before I could sit down and begin the painful work of reliving everything – putting it into words and making sense of what had happened to me. Yet, once I started writing a book, I discovered that process helped enormously too.

The darkness that had consumed me for years began to lift. I had stopped consuming alcohol the way I once had. The suicidal thoughts had disappeared. The girl in the mirror started to look familiar again – recognisable, at least.

When Dave called in September 2025 with news that McGregor had applied for leave to appeal to the Supreme Court, I was a different person: no panic attacks, no tears, no tremors, no retreat. My response was calm, measured, nothing like the girl who used to pace a room in terror at every development.

Instead, I shrugged. Another appeal was inevitable. McGregor had deep pockets, and he would do anything to overturn the verdict. He had already felt the financial repercussions of losing the civil case.

'The Supreme Court? Yeah, no problem, Dave. We'll stay positive.'

We soon learnt that McGregor had parted ways with his defence firm, Michael Staines. Solicitor Ciarán Mulholland announced that his firm, Mulholland Law, was now acting for McGregor and his pal James Lawrence.

The legal firm also confirmed that it had lodged High Court proceedings on behalf of Lawrence, seeking redress for what it described as a 'malicious prosecution' against him, claiming the case I brought against him was 'frivolous' and 'unnecessary'. They said my case exposed Lawrence to costs, media scrutiny and reputational harm.

At first, I didn't know what McGregor's Supreme Court appeal meant, apart from the fact that it would cost a lot of money. I soon learnt that there is no automatic right of appeal to the Supreme Court; the court had to decide whether to hear the appeal. It only agrees to an appeal if it involves a matter of general public importance or if satisfied that it's in the interests of justice to hear the appeal.

McGregor's application focused again on his constitutional right to silence, which his legal team said was unfairly raised in the lower courts. They argued that the High Court jury should not have been allowed to hear that McGregor answered 'no comment' more than a hundred times when he was interviewed by gardaí.

His legal team also wanted to appeal because the High Court and Appeal Court refused to award James Lawrence's costs despite the finding that he had not raped me.

Once again, Lawrence's bid for legal fees was the only issue that gnawed at me. The Court of Appeal had been adamant that he didn't deserve his fees. But if the Supreme Court disagreed, the money I was awarded would be gone, and I could even end up owing more. It would mean I would not have a fresh start after this. I'd be left with debt and exhaustion and the knowledge that I fought for years and had to pay even more for what McGregor did to me.

I did my best to put McGregor's Supreme Court application behind me, but it inevitably followed me around like a small, dark cloud on the distant horizon. Late at night, when Gary was asleep beside me, and the apartment was quiet, the fear crept in. *What if I lose everything? What if it was all for nothing?* I kept trying to push the thoughts away and remind myself that it wasn't for nothing. I won. The jury believed me. The world knew what Conor McGregor did. And that would be enough if the decision didn't go my way.

But whenever Dave or Diane's number appeared on my phone screen, my heart would seize. I was afraid of bad news. Afraid that it would mean I would end up in terrible debt. My mental health was getting stronger by the day, but McGregor's last gasp, his Supreme Court appeal, lurked in a shadowy corner of my mind.

39.

Baby Dream

September–October 2025

I sat down to have a conversation with Gary one evening. It was a talk that had been building for a while. Every month had been the same. Maybe this month, we'd think, and then it wasn't. The hope hurt us more than the disappointment.

We had kept trying for a baby throughout, the way people do when they can't admit defeat. The stress hadn't helped. My periods had stopped entirely for two months around the time of the trial; my body had shut down under the pressure of the process.

But after three years of trying and two miscarriages, I realised it was time to focus on other things.

'I don't want to do this anymore,' I said. 'It's not happening, and it's too upsetting for both of us.'

Gary agreed to let go of the baby dream for the time being. I would focus on counselling, the slow work of healing and on writing my book. *If it happens, it happens,* we said. We might try again at another stage when we felt stronger.

An entire year and a half had passed since I'd last gone out anywhere apart from quiet dinners with Gary. Around that time, a few girlfriends invited me to an event. To be honest, the invitation felt more like a challenge than an enjoyable night out. But the other women wouldn't take no for an answer. *You need to get yourself out. It'll be good for you. Get your mind off things.*

I hesitated, holding the phone, looking around my living room and safe space. 'We'll collect you,' they promised. 'And we'll drop you home. You'll be safe with us.' I wanted to feel like a normal person again. So I said yes.

The taxi arrived for me on a Thursday evening. I had a few glasses of Prosecco at the event. For a few hours, I relaxed and forgot to monitor everyone around me. I laughed and felt a sense of release. I was out without Gary, and it was fine. I really was improving. It felt like I could live a normal life again.

My eyes sprang open the following Sunday morning, 12 October. I had just experienced the most vivid dream I've ever had in my life. It was a vision full of light and happiness, nothing like the terrifying nightmares of being hunted down dark roads. In it, I had a prominent baby bump. It had been so real that I could still feel my hand resting on the curve of my belly. Even the weight of it felt real, perfectly real. The baby had fluttered beneath my palm, and joy flooded through me.

In the dream, I'd been filled with the kind of happiness that I'd forgotten. The type of joy I'd taken for granted before the assault. Gary had been with me, and we were so content and just … happy.

'Gary.' I shook his shoulder in the morning light. 'Gary!'

He squinted at me. 'What, love?'

'I had this dream, and it was so strong. I think I'm pregnant.'

He snorted. 'Go back to sleep.'

'I'm not messing, Gary. I had this mad dream. I had a bump. It was just so real.'

The words came faster now. 'Honestly, I need to get a pregnancy test.'

I knew he thought I was mad.

'I'm telling you, this one was so real.'

The chemist around the corner was open. I bought the test even though I knew Gary's eyes were rolling in his head. When we got home, I didn't pause. I went straight to the bathroom, peed on the stick, and before I could even set it on the counter, the blue line appeared.

Not a faint line, the way it was the last two times, before I had the miscarriages. Not hesitant or uncertain. This line was bold, undeniable, instant. The kind of line that left no room for doubt. I blinked in shock. I wasn't mad.

I dashed from the bathroom with the test in my hand, beaming.

He looked up from the couch. 'What? What are you saying?'

'I was right! I was right! We're pregnant!' I cried.

His eyes were questioning, full of disbelief. I had to thrust the test toward him before his expression changed.

'I fucking told you that dream was true!'

He stood up, staring at the test and then gazing at my face. Then he pulled me to him. We stood hugging each other in the middle of the living room; me sobbing first, but Gary's tears following. I grabbed my phone and recorded a video through my tears, my voice shaking as I tried to explain what had just happened. I needed evidence of this moment. I kept thinking I might wake up again and find out I had been having another dream.

When I rang my mam, I tried to sound calm.

'Mam, I have something to tell you.'

'What's wrong?' That's my mam's default response. She was bracing herself for the worst.

'Nothing's wrong. Are you ready to be a grandmother again?'

Silence. Then, her cry of delight joined mine. I told her about the dream, about the test, about the line that appeared before I'd even set the stick down.

'That wasn't a dream, it was a premonition,' she said.

Standing in my living room with the positive test in my hand and Gary's arms around me, I thought of our conversation two weeks earlier. We'd given up. I'd been ready to focus on healing instead of hoping. And now the dream was happening for real.

It seemed like everything was falling into place. I'd won the court case and the appeal. We were moving on with our lives, and now we were having a baby.

McGregor's appeal to the Supreme Court hung over us, but all I had to do after that morning was to think of the baby in my belly, and my perspective shifted. I found a strength I thought I'd lost. Whatever the Supreme Court ruled, life would still move forward. And I knew I could survive financial ruin, because I had survived far worse.

40.

Freedom Day

Thursday, 4 December 2025

The Christmas shopping sat in bags inside the front door. Janice and I had spent the entire day wandering through shops, looking for gifts and lingering over dessert in our favourite café.

We had the kind of day that makes you forget, for a few hours at least, that you're waiting for something. Waiting weeks longer than expected. A panel of three Supreme Court judges had met on 12 November 2025 to review McGregor's application. I had expected their decision by the end of that week or the week after. But the days rolled on, and my apprehension increased.

I was on a video call with my cousin, halfway through telling her about our day's shopping, when another call came through – my solicitor, Diane.

My fingers fumbled with the phone in fright. I told my cousin I had to answer this call. This could be it, or it could be nothing.

'Hello?' I said, my voice filled with dread, my heart beating wildly. 'Is everything okay?'

'YOU WON!' she screamed.

'What?'

I didn't dare believe it. There had to be more.

But Diane kept yelling: 'You won! You won!'

I heard myself screaming then too – high-pitched cries that must have echoed through the walls to my neighbours' flats. I can't imagine what they thought was happening.

We both tried to talk through the crying, words tumbling over each other, neither of us making sense.

'I'm so happy for you,' she kept saying. 'After everything. After all that fighting, you've finally won. It's over!'

It's over. The words couldn't sink in. The Supreme Court had decided that McGregor had a fair hearing and refused him any further appeal against the High Court jury's findings. He had sexually assaulted me. He had raped me – end of.

The Supreme Court also rejected Lawrence's bid to appeal the decision not to award him his costs. They found the jury rejected both McGregor's and Lawrence's evidence in the face of my allegation of rape.

My hands shook as I ended the call with Diane. Messages started flooding in before I'd caught my breath: texts, DMs, emails.

The first person I rang was Gary. He was still at work when I reached him. Tears were choking me, so I could only manage two words: 'I won!' The silence on the other end stretched long enough that for a second I thought the connection had dropped. Then his voice came through, thick with emotion: 'Oh. My. God.'

The relief expressed in those three words struck me. I'd watched this case weigh on him for five years, watched the stress create lines around his eyes as he tried to look after me and struggle with his own trauma, especially since the home invasion.

I heard only happiness and determination when he spoke again.

'We can start our lives now.'

Gary was right. We both felt it that day; we couldn't stop smiling. For the first time, we could face Christmas with no more court dates hanging over our futures.

Even when I'd won the High Court civil trial in November 2024, the win had felt conditional because we expected McGregor to appeal. With his deep pockets, he was determined to take this to the highest court in the land.

But when that panel of three Supreme Court judges denied McGregor's application for a further appeal, he had nowhere left to go. His money became useless then. He had no more legal manoeuvres, no more appeals to file, no more ways to come at me and attack again. He also had to pay all my legal costs, estimated at least €1.5 million on top of my damages award.

He now had to live with the fact that I had stood up to him and won in court. He also had to live with the verdict that he was civilly liable for sexually assaulting me. The law had spoken, justice had been served and it had carved my truth into stone.

For months, I had been trying hard not to let the pressure of the Supreme Court appeal affect me. After two miscarriages, Gary and I worried about the effect of this added stress on the pregnancy. We couldn't get carried away with joy or let everyone know too soon.

But that day, when the Supreme Court announced its decision, it felt like nothing could stand in the way of our happiness anymore. Gary had only ever known me in the shadow of this thing. Now, the shackles were off at last, and I felt lighter than I'd felt in years. We both did. We exhaled and couldn't contain our joy anymore: we broke our baby news to everyone on social media the next day.

Epilogue

The television flickered in the dimness of the bedroom. I lay up against Gary, his presence warm and comforting. We were watching a film – it was something light and entertaining. Nothing triggering. But the tightness began in my chest without warning. I felt that familiar fist closing around my lungs.

My mouth went dry. I tried to breathe slowly, to tell myself it would pass if I just relaxed and focused on the movie. But the panic had its own momentum and its own will. It rose through me regardless.

I glanced up at Gary. His face was peaceful in the television's glow. I didn't want to pull him into this, didn't want to make him afraid. Not again.

But the fear was climbing now, crawling up my throat.

'I'm feeling a panic attack coming on,' I managed.

His hand found my back immediately.

'It's okay, babe. You're grand.'

I shook my head.

'No, Gary, it's coming.'

Gary moved quickly, disappearing to the kitchen and returning with a lemon – its sharp scent intended to shock my brain back into the present.

I held it to my nose, breathing in the citrus while Gary rubbed circles on my back. Thirty minutes. It only lasted thirty minutes this time. I've endured panic attacks that stretched for hours, and so many that they required medical intervention to break their grip. This one released me quickly, but even a short one leaves its mark.

I know now that trauma doesn't end when the verdict is read. Justice – if you're fortunate enough to get it – doesn't erase what was done. The court case finished, but I didn't cross some invisible threshold into wellness. I didn't wake up the next morning 'fixed'.

Trauma isn't something that medication can eliminate or surgery can remove. Trauma is a scar, a permanent one that I am learning to live with.

The panic attacks still come – when I'm lying in bed, sitting in the apartment, attempting to do the ordinary work of living. I still wake Gary screaming, lost in another nightmare. I ring my mother in tears, gasping for air, ambushed again by the grip of pure fear.

Some days, I cannot bring myself to leave my home, cannot summon the courage to walk to the shops. The problem with trauma is that it never announces itself. It's the enemy within, which never waits for convenient moments.

The fear of being attacked has never left. What if men are watching, lurking outside, preparing to break into my home again? These thoughts still arise and roll around in my mind. Each of these thoughts is a trap, a prison built from trauma. I will never be rid of them.

But I am healing. I am in a better place than I was. I'm still in therapy, still living with what McGregor did. I'm still living with what Samantha O'Reilly said, with Lawrence's lies. I'm still living with the brutality of the courtroom itself. I was torn apart in court because of the violence that a man inflicted on me.

Because here is what no one prepares you for: the court system is not designed to protect victims of rape and sexual assault. It's designed to protect the accused.

First, we wade through all our own guilt, regret and self-blame. From a young age, girls are taught a list of 'don'ts': don't walk alone, don't wear that, don't drink too much. If we break the rules, we internalise the blame that society places on us.

For a time, I wasn't sure if I even deserved to be believed; that by being messy, reckless and foolish, I didn't have the right to speak out. I felt ashamed for a long time.

When it came to the investigation, I handed over my phone, my clothes and my dignity. I stood stripped bare. My family gave up its devices. McGregor never surrendered his phone, his clothes, his underwear. Neither did Lawrence. Every obligation and indignity fell upon me.

The trial system is traumatic in its own right. I was a victim of sexual assault, and then I became a victim of the trial itself – another experience from which I had to heal, another trauma to overcome.

In court, I felt like the accused. Like I was the predator, the one who'd committed the crime. The court shone a light on my life and my lifestyle. If the DPP had gone ahead with a criminal case, the defence would have accessed my therapy notes, shared my most private innermost thoughts with the man who harmed me and then had them picked apart in a public court by a barrister. (As of 2026, significant legislative changes are due to end this at last.)

As the victim, I felt methodically ripped apart. I was made out to be a liar, a loose woman, a bad mother, a habitual drinker, a drug taker and a homewrecker in the courtroom. The inference was always there below the surface: I was 'asking for it'.

But now I know that nothing I did permitted McGregor to do what he did. Nothing I drank or swallowed made me less entitled to say 'no'. Nothing I wore gave him permission. Making poor choices, like going to that hotel room, didn't give him permission. Making mistakes did not give him the right to do what he did. It has taken me a long time to say this with conviction, but nothing I did made it my fault. Nothing cancelled my right to say 'no'. 'No' is a complete sentence. 'No' is inviolable.

McGregor stripped me of all choice in that room. He was bigger and stronger and decided my wishes didn't matter. He decided he didn't need or want my consent. My body was merely an object for him to abuse as he desired. He committed a sexual assault.

A High Court jury agreed and said what happened to me was real, and McGregor's behaviour was wrong. I may have made poor choices, but they were my choices to make. And that is one of the key messages I want other survivors to hear:

There is no such thing as a perfect victim. No matter how much you drank that night, what you wore, where you went – none of it matters. None of it means you deserved what happened. Don't let anyone convince you otherwise. Never let fear of the world's judgment silence you.

You can start small if you can't bear to utter the words aloud. Tell someone: a friend, family or an organisation like the Dublin Rape Crisis Centre. You will be believed. Help is waiting for you when you reach out. Don't be afraid of people with power, money, fame or influence. Silence only gives predators more power. Every moment we stay quiet, we hand them more strength. My story is proof of that. No matter the circumstances, no matter how imperfect your case might seem, you can get justice.

I understand why many women would choose not to pursue

their assailant. And I would blame no one for choosing to settle or drop charges rather than battle through the justice system. I have experienced the torture of six years living in legal limbo, the absolute hell of it. If I had a crystal ball at the beginning that had shown me what was coming, would I have continued? Probably not.

But if I had never stood up to McGregor, my mental health would have suffered too. His face would have been there, unavoidable, on the news and social media, his name everywhere, and I'd have had to live looking at him, knowing I'd given up. I would have had to live knowing that I let him get away with an assault that nearly destroyed my life. If I had walked away and tried to forget, that would have destroyed me in a different way. Slower perhaps, but just as completely. I believe I would have lived to regret it every day of my life afterwards.

I remembered Detective Ger White's words, way back, when we were still waiting to hear if the DPP would prosecute. 'Win or lose,' he'd said, 'going through the system is healing in itself.'

I hadn't understood it then. Now I do. I have no regrets about having done it or about standing up to McGregor.

I was not the perfect victim. Not sober. Not chaste. But I was truthful. The law listened. And I was believed. After the Supreme Court's decision, I could finally put my hands up and say I was proud of myself.

Every day I wake up knowing a jury of my peers believed

me. I wake up as a person who survived what McGregor did to me and fought a lengthy legal process to prove that I mattered. McGregor wakes up knowing a jury of ordinary and extraordinary Irish men and women found that he 'brutally raped and battered' me.

He also wakes up knowing he's a virtual pariah now in terms of sponsorship and marketing. His once celebrated 'bad boy' persona has now shifted into something that appears more sinister. He's become another example of the toxic 'manosphere'. Through his own choices, he has destroyed his legacy as a sports icon and has become legally labelled as a sex assailant.

Sometimes, however, it becomes painfully clear that we still have so much further to go. When Conor McGregor sat down with Jimmy Fallon on NBC's *The Tonight Show Starring Jimmy Fallon* in June 2026, it was as though nothing had happened. They talked about his upcoming fight, his family, his career highlights – a light, buddy-style chat with not a single hard question about the brutal reality of what was laid out in an Irish courtroom.

To see a man found liable for rape receive this level of endorsement on any platform – let alone the major US broadcaster NBC – was deeply upsetting (in an interview that ultimately ran far longer than the fight it was intended to promote. Just two weeks later, McGregor was brought to his knees in the Octagon in 69 seconds). In the wake of the #MeToo movement, after so much hard-won progress for women, moments like the Jimmy Fallon interview reveal how quickly accountability can be set aside when celebrity is in the room. A verdict can't change the past, but it should change what happens next – and NBC and Jimmy Fallon made it clear that we still have a long way to go.

For me, being heard and believed revived parts of me I'd thought I'd lost forever. The burden of shame shifted back to the perpetrator. I was a casualty of someone else's choices and all the shame and liability rest where they should – on Conor McGregor. I have a restored sense of pride, dignity and trust in myself and in the fact that I did the right thing.

And I know I did the right thing – for my daughters and for every other victim out there. The weekend after the verdict, calls to the Dublin Rape Crisis Centre helpline nearly doubled. That told me everything I needed to know about the importance of the case and what it meant to other victims.

The Dublin Rape Crisis Centre has been my lifeline through it all, yet they recently organised an event to thank me. They tell me the calls keep coming, especially from first-time callers who have never reached out before. The callers tell them it was my victim impact statement and my story that gave them the courage to dial. Whenever I think about that, my eyes fill. It makes the battle even more worthwhile.

Since the Supreme Court's decision, McGregor has been gone from my life. Truly gone. He can't impose any legal restrictions on me. His shadow can no longer follow me. Whatever I choose to do with my story from this point forward is on my terms.

I still have a few legal battles ahead – other cases that remain unresolved. I'll also face other battles in life, like all of us do. I need to accept that some days will be good, and some will be dark, and sometimes the demons will be there, waiting in the shadows.

But my future is filled with optimism and joy. Gary and I had our baby girl, Alba, on 21 May 2026. I now have two amazing daughters and the most incredible life partner I could ever have dreamed of. Few relationships could have withstood the stress that this battle put Gary and me through. Six years together now, and the happiness feels solid and real. I wake up grateful for him, for what we've built, for the way he loves our daughters and me. From the beginning, Gary has been my rock – strong, enduring and caring. He was strong enough to carry both of us when my strength failed.

But I know my nanny's iron strength runs through the core of me now. I know I'm stronger than I ever thought possible. I survived. The system didn't break me, and that man couldn't intimidate me.

Many times, I doubted I could ever feel normal again. But here I am, just after putting the baby down to sleep. I hear Gary moving around in the kitchen, and see Freya, head in her phone on the couch. I'm surrounded by the ordinary sights and sounds of normal life I once took for granted. The kind that now feels like living happily ever after.

Acknowledgements

FREYA – To my daughter, who has given me the strength to keep going through the most difficult years. When the days were dark, you always managed to put a smile on my face and make the struggle worthwhile. Thanks too for your encouragement and pride when I told you about my book, for believing in me and for being such a bright light in my life.

ALBA – To my baby girl. Finding out I was pregnant when I was writing this book brought me so much joy and happiness and an even greater reason to tell my story. You came into our lives when we needed you the most. You're our breath of fresh air and have made our family unit complete.

GARY – To my partner, thank you for believing in me and always reassuring me. For holding my hand when times were hard, for being my rock and safe space. I couldn't have done any of this without you. You're my real-life superhero forever.

MAM – Thank you for believing I could do this even when I doubted myself and for being proud of me when I told you I was writing a book. Most of all, thank you for urging me to speak up when I felt I had no voice and for being there for me when I needed you the most. Your strength always amazes me.
NANNY – You may no longer be in this world, but you're still present in my life. I've felt your strength and resilience pulsing through me during some of my worst days, and I know you're watching over me, caring for me all along the way.

JANICE – You've been there for Gary, Freya and me whenever we needed you. You took us in without hesitation, and I will never forget your kindness, generosity and hospitality. Thank you also for all your continued support throughout the writing of this book.

FRIENDS AND FAMILY – Thank you to all my friends and my large, wonderful family. So many of you have been incredible throughout this journey, providing endless encouragement and support. I want to add a special thanks to Gary's family for all your support and care. It has meant so much to me.

COLEMAN LEGAL LLP – To Dave, Diane, Susan, Paddy, Geraldine, Maria and my three barristers, John Gordon SC, Ray Boland SC and Siún Leonowicz BL. You believed in me from day one, applying all your expertise and dedication to my case. You stood by my side, offering empathy and unwavering support throughout the biggest challenge of my life. From the bottom of my heart, thank you.

DETECTIVES PETER WOODS AND GER WHITE – Thank you too for all your hard work and dedication to my case. You both made me feel believed and always treated me with such kindness, care and dignity. I appreciate it all.

SATU ROTUNDA HOSPITAL – Thank you to the staff at SATU for being so caring, diligent and patient. You are truly amazing at what you do. A special thank you to Dr Daniel Kane. I will be forever grateful for your professionalism, but I'll never forget your kindness.

DUBLIN FIRE BRIGADE PARAMEDICS – To Neal Dempsey and Eithne Scully, my special appreciation for your care and amazing professionalism. Thank you for the quiet compassion you showed to my mam and me. You both made me feel safe and believed.

DR FRANK CLARKE – Thank you for being an amazing GP all through my teenage years and into adult life. I'm lucky to have a family doctor with expertise, a willingness to truly listen and genuine compassion. I've always felt heard and supported by you at the most difficult times in my life. I will forever be thankful to you and all the staff at Walkinstown Medical Centre.

DUBLIN RAPE CRISIS CENTRE – To all at the centre, thank you so much. You are all amazing people, and I always felt believed and protected.

SARAH MCDERMOTT, DUBLIN RAPE CRISIS CENTRE – Special thanks to my therapist, Sarah McDermott, for your support, patience and guidance. You've helped lead me back into the light, and I can never thank you enough.

CLÍONA WOODS, DUBLIN RAPE CRISIS CENTRE – Thank you for gripping my hand every day in court and for your unwavering support every day. Without Gary and you, I wouldn't have been able to get through it. You turned up for me day after day with a smile on your face, full of positivity. You kept me going even when the world's weight felt on my shoulders. I'll never forget you.

HACHETTE IRELAND – to Ciara Considine, my publisher and editor. Thank you for trusting me and my story, and for helping turn the worst thing to happen to me into something so positive. You offered me such an amazing opportunity, and you were always there for me throughout. Your words of encouragement always kept me going. I can't thank you enough. To Elaine Egan, Publicity Director, and all at Hachette who have been so supportive from the start: Charlie King, Ciara Doorley, Jim Binchy, Siobhan Tierney, Joanna Smyth, Stephen Riordan, Shauna O'Regan and Chloe O'Brien – thank you all for your dedication and commitment in publishing my book. It was amazing to work with such a lovely team of people.

Many thanks to photographer Emily Quinn and make-up artist Ailbhe Lynch for a memorable and lovely time shooting my book cover.

KATHRYN ROGERS – my co-writer. Working with you was such an honour. Your understanding helped on the days when I felt overwhelmed and your patience and kind nature made it all easier. Working with you and writing this book has healed me in more ways than I thought possible. It's a journey I'll never forget. Thank you for being part of it.
SURVIVORS – To all of you who reached out to me to share your journeys and stories and offer encouragement, thank you. I'm grateful for all the friends I've met on this journey. Thank you for standing beside and behind me. You made me feel less alone when I needed you the most.
KIND STRANGERS – Thanks to all the men and women who have reached out to me with beautiful cards, letters, small gifts and messages of empathy and support. Every unexpected note, shared story and word of encouragement has been a lifeline. You will never know how much your unexpected kindness helped lift my spirits on the worst of days.
THE MEMBERS OF THE IRISH JUDICIARY – I wish to express my deepest gratitude to the judges across the High Court, the Court of Appeal and the Supreme Court who presided over this case. I appreciate your consistent commitment to justice, rigorous application of the law, perception and wisdom, and especially your courtesy and kindness to a terrified witness and plaintiff.
WITNESSES AND JURY – Before I close, I want to express my deepest gratitude for your time and courage in the face of a high-profile, stressful case. Thank you all for your dedication and commitment to a fair and just outcome.

Resources and Support Services

If you have experienced rape, sexual assault, sexual abuse, sexual harassment or any form of sexual violence, support is available. You do not have to cope alone. The organisations below offer confidential information, emotional support, counselling, advocacy and practical assistance, whether the violence happened recently or many years ago.

IRELAND

National 24-Hour Helpline (Dublin Rape Crisis Centre)

Provides a free, confidential listening and support service for victims and survivors of sexual violence, as well as family members, friends and supporters. Interpretation is available in more than 240 languages.

- Freephone: 1800 778 888 (24 hours a day, 365 days a year)
- Website: www.drcc.ie
- Email: helpline@rcc.ie

Rape Crisis Ireland

Coordinates and supports rape crisis services across Ireland and provides information about reporting, recovery, court processes, local support services and survivors' rights.

- Website: www.rapecrisisireland.ie
- Information portal: www.rapecrisishelp.ie

Rape Crisis Centres throughout Ireland provide counselling, accompaniment, advocacy and support services. Regional centres include:

- Sexual Violence Centre Cork – 1800 496 496
- Galway Rape Crisis Centre – 1800 355 355
- Kerry Rape and Sexual Abuse Centre – 1800 633 333
- Mayo Rape Crisis Centre – 1800 234 900
- Rape Crisis Centre North East – 1800 212 122
- Rape Crisis Centre Midwest – 1800 311 511
- Sligo Rape Crisis Centre – 1800 750 780
- Donegal Sexual Abuse and Rape Crisis Centre – 1800 448 844
- Carlow & South Leinster Rape Crisis Centre – 1800 727 737

Women's Aid

Offers support to women experiencing domestic, sexual or coercive abuse, including information, advocacy and court support services.

- Freephone: 1800 341 900 (24-hour service)
- Website: www.womensaid.ie

Sexual Assault Treatment Units (SATUs)

SATUs provide medical care, forensic examinations, emergency contraception, STI prevention and referrals to counselling and support services. Attendance is free, confidential and does not require a report to An Garda Síochána.

- Website: www2.hse.ie/services/satu

One in Four

Supports adults who have experienced childhood sexual abuse through counselling, advocacy and other specialist services.

- Telephone: 01 662 4070
- Website: www.oneinfour.ie

Crime Victims Helpline

Provides emotional support, information on victims' rights and referrals to specialist services nationwide.

- Freephone: 116 006
- Text: 085 133 7711
- Website: www.crimevictimshelpline.ie

UNITED KINGDOM

Rape Crisis England & Wales

Provides confidential emotional support, information and access to local rape crisis services.

- 24/7 Support Line: 0808 500 2222
- Website: www.rapecrisis.org.uk
- Online chat available via the website.

NHS Sexual Assault Referral Centres (SARCs)

SARCs offer crisis support, medical care, forensic examinations and referrals to counselling and advocacy services for anyone affected by sexual violence.

- Information: www.nhs.uk

IN AN EMERGENCY

If you are in immediate danger or require urgent medical assistance:

- Ireland: Call 999 or 112
- United Kingdom: Call 999

Remember: what happened was not your fault. Support is available, and help can be accessed whether the experience occurred recently or many years ago.